W9-DFZ-519

SCHAUMBURG TOWNSHIP DISTRICT LIBRARY

3 1257 02420 1450

WITHDRAWN

Schaumburg Township District Library
130 South Roselle Road
Schaumburg, Illinois 60193

Schaumburg Township
District Library
schaumburglibrary.org
Renewals: (847) 923-3158

DEATH
GRIP

DEATH
GRIP

A CLIMBER'S
ESCAPE FROM
BENZO MADNESS

MATT SAMET

Schaumburg Township District Library
130 South Roselle Road
Schaumburg, IL 60193

ST. MARTIN'S PRESS ≈ NEW YORK

2113
dmg.

921
SAMET, M

3 1257 02420 1450

The author is neither a physician nor a medical professional. Readers should not view the information presented in this book as medical advice or as a substitute for medical care.

DEATH GRIP. Copyright © 2013 by Matt Samet. All rights reserved. Printed in the United States of America. For information, address St. Martin's Press, 175 Fifth Avenue, New York, N.Y. 10010.

www.stmartins.com

Design by Steven Seighman

Library of Congress Cataloging-in-Publication Data

Samet, Matt.
   Death grip : a climber's escape from benzo madness / Matt Samet.
      p. cm.
   ISBN 978-1-250-00423-9 (hardcover)
   ISBN 978-1-250-02236-3 (e-book)
   1. Samet, Matt.   2. Mountaineers—United States—
Biography.   3. Mountaineers—United States—Psychology.
4. Mountaineers—United States—Mental health.   5. Benzodiazepine
abuse—United States.   I. Title.
   GV199.92.S295A3 2013
   796.522092—dc23

                                                    2012037798

First Edition: February 2013

10 9 8 7 6 5 4 3 2 1

AUTHOR'S NOTE

This book is a memoir and is based on real events. The names and characteristics of certain people have been changed.

To Kristin and Ivan, for coming into my life with beauty and love. To my parents and friends, who stood by me even when there was no "me." To Dr. Heather Ashton, for shining the light of science onto a confounding darkness. To Alex, Neal, Lydia, and George, for giving an unproven writer a chance to tell his story. And to the late Alison Kellagher, who showed me that there was hope.

ACKNOWLEDGMENTS

I would like to thank the following people, without whom this book would not be possible. First off, my wife, Kristin, for helping me find my way to life as a full-time writer. To Alex Heard at *Outside*, who picked my cold query off the slush pile and believed in it enough to bring to fruition the article that inspired this book. To Tracy Ross, for taking the time to advise me on the book business. To Neal Baer, and my agent, Lydia Wills, who gave me an ear, a sounding board, and most of all a chance to craft the proposal that became this memoir. And to George Witte for his wisdom and expertise shaping the manuscript, and to Terra Layton, Sam B., and all the good people at St. Martin's Press who've helped finalize the printed product.

First and foremost this is a book about benzodiazepine addiction, and I owe no small debt to Dr. Heather Ashton, the world's leading expert on the subject, who has not only provided a vast, thorough, sane, and compassionate body of research on these pills, but also advised me on certain scientific aspects of this memoir. Without Dr. Ashton and the work of other dedicated scholars and benzo experts, there would be a continuing black hole of mistruth and despair where instead you find knowledge and hope. Other people whose work, writings, and research have informed and inspired this book include Marcia Angell, M.D.; Peter Breggin, M.D.; Geraldine Burns; Daniel Carlat, M.D.; Terri Cheney; David Cohen, Ph.D.; Beatrice Faust; Paul Foxman; Joan Gadsby; Barbara Gordon; Leah Harris; David Healy, M.D.; Jack Hobson-Dupont; Kay Redfield Jamison, Ph.D.; the late Alison Kellagher (we miss you, Alison); Irving Kirsch, Ph.D.; E. Robert Mercer; Ray Nimmo; Reg Peart, Ph.D.; Sylvia Plath; Di Porritt; Richard Restak, M.D.; Di Russell; Andrew Solomon; William Styron; Andrea Tone; Ben Wallace-Wells; and Robert Whitaker. We must admire any writer who stares head-on into madness, confusion, and darkness, and then gets on with the desperate business of documenting it.

I'd also like to acknowledge the friends and family who stood by me through my ordeal. Some days it was all I could do to shuffle around the block, pull a few weeds from the garden, or come to the cliffs and climb half a pitch, but you all got me out the door and into the world without judgment. And finally, to my dog, Clyde, you big, crazy Plott hound: If I didn't take you for a walk every day, even on my worst days, you'd let me know. And it was and continues to be those walks that have helped restore physical and spiritual integrity.

DEATH GRIP

PROLOGUE

S*uffercation*, a three-by-four-foot oil on wood painting, hangs in our home in Gunbarrel, Colorado, a suburb of the climber's mecca of Boulder. I've lived in Boulder, minus a few stints in Italy and on Colorado's West Slope, since 1991. Red, black, blue, mustard, livid, and impossible to miss, the painting anchors a windowless wall. Were a window there, it would open south toward the steeply pitched Boulder Mountains. Cloaked in Ponderosa and beetling with the planed, pyramidal sandstone Flatirons formations, it's here that I've climbed twenty-three of my twenty-seven years on rock. The Flatirons are a second home, a place where I've faced down brute, cold fear, but also where I've had great moments of peace: repair from the black waves of depression, anxiety, and addiction that nearly killed me.

The painting, by the talented climbing artist Jeremy Collins, was a parting gift in 2005 from the staff at *Rock and Ice*, a climbing magazine. I'd been editor there for a year until I had to resign, tumbled through the barrel by a mounting wave of bizarre, inexplicable panic attacks that made it impossible to focus or sit at my desk. They were the result, I would come to realize far too late, of addiction to and then withdrawal from the minor tranquilizer

Klonopin (clonazepam*), complicated by a tangled, on-and-off love affair with marijuana, wine, and the narcotic painkiller Vicodin. Klonopin is a high-potency, fast-acting benzodiazepine, a family of drugs most commonly prescribed for anxiety, insomnia, and seizure disorders that also includes the notorious Valium, which was from 1968 until 1981 the West's most-prescribed medicine.[1] Jer created the original artwork in 2003 to accompany a column I'd written on life as a climber with a panic disorder—recurrent panic attacks—and how I and others similarly afflicted balanced vertical pursuits with the omnipresent specter of anxiety.

And how I sometimes—well, by that point, daily, a fact omitted in the article—took benzos, unaware that the pills were perpetuating the problem.

Jer's painting is astonishing, shocking even: A black figure in profile circles his arms over his head, a mosaic of diffuse white, yellow, and blue geometric figures filling in the arms, with yellow ribs and a gray spine subtly scribing the torso. In a semicircle around the head run the words "suffercation," "death," "doubt," "fear," and "paranoia" in white block letters, best seen up close. At this distance, nose hard to Jer's considered oil strokes, you'll also see that the figure's "brain" is a slate-blue homunculus turned sideways. The crown of his head orients toward the main figure's eye socket. Arms slung about his knees and his eyes lidded shut, the homunculus seems like a weary refugee; his same slate-blue skin tone beams in a ray from the main figure's head.

The homunculus is either shooting dark energy into the cosmos or absorbing blue gamma rays of ruination—or both. It's difficult to say. The blue almost matches the blue-green of those tiny Klonopin that nearly killed me, that pitched me into seas of panicking anguish, shuffling along cold, linoleum psych-ward hallways, spiraling down through gyres of the blackest depression pullulating

---

* Although I often took the generic form of the drug, clonazepam, I refer to it by its brand name in this book to reflect the vernacular usage among psychiatrists and patients.

with garish little pills until I could no longer see the surface. Until, strung out on five or six psych meds a day, I wanted nothing other than to die.

Until I was no longer myself, no longer a climber, but just a rotting bouquet of vague, untreatable disorders and syndromes, imprisoned in a chemical straitjacket.

At my sickest, I wanted to exile the painting from me: to give it away, despite its beauty. Instead I stored it wherever I happened to live, until I felt well enough—the meds clearing from my system—to display it again. In time I could walk by "Suffercation" without suffercating, without wincing from its incisive embodiment of the deepest fear state. In time I could stand before it and simply appreciate the painting on its artistic merits.

So there it hangs, where I could have that window. A reminder of the many things lost during the years on drugs, but also of the innumerable gifts since gained. A reminder of the suffercation endured, a fear beyond any I've felt on a cliff or mountain, even when I faced unroped falls of thousands of feet, the rock giving way about (or onto) me, or encroaching lightning flashing blue-white off the stone. A memento, no longer fearsome seven years after I took my last psychiatric medicine, of the wasteland I journeyed through to escape the last milligram.

PART ONE

ANXIETY RISING

CHAPTER 1

I t's best to begin at the end: the last withdrawal, the final sucker punch to the kidneys. I was sick, you see; so, so sick. I'd been driven to madness by withdrawal from legally prescribed psychotropic agents, all while being told that the insanity was my own. The scary thing is, my story is not an anomaly.

One clear, sterile autumn morning—September 2006, to be exact—a hand not my own but that belonged to me smashed a beer bottle against a rock in Rifle Mountain Park, in Western Colorado. It hunted a shard of glass. The hand, once rough with climber callus and ropy with vein, had withered sickbed soft and pallid. Now it had designs—a theatrical slashing at the wrists—on its paranoid and bloated host. The hand couldn't have picked a more apt arena, for it was here in limestone-lined Rifle Canyon that I'd peaked as a rock climber, where I'd starved down to my lowest "fighting" (well, climbing) weight and pushed my body the utmost. It was in fact along the ceiling of the gloomy gray amphitheater above, an upside-down bowl we'd named "the Arsenal," that I'd once done some of its hardest routes in running shoes, foreswearing the special sticky-rubber rock boots that climbers use for precision footwork.

Rifle Canyon is known as an international destination for "free climbers," who ascend via their fingers and toes, the rope there only to safeguard a fall. The canyon is a lush riparian defile—at the narrowest bend, you could toss a tennis ball across, the cliff walls leaning in so close that there's barely room for the river, a footpath, and a graded dirt road. Rifle can be a bright place when the sun's slanting in, but in the steepest caves that house the most difficult climbs it's usually blanketed in shadow. Like tethered newts wearing seat harnesses, climbing shoes, and waist-bags of gymnast's chalk to dry their hands, rock jocks slither toward the light only to lower off and do it again. Their goal might be a 5.13 or a 5.14, technical grades given to climbs well past vertical in which the holds shrink to the width of doorjambs and grow ever farther apart, sometimes so distant you have to leap in key, or "crux," sections. These tiny holds, in the climber's isometric battle against gravity, re-form your mitts into workman's hands. Over time, your digits might curl with arthritis and gnarled, swollen knuckles. In clinging for dear life, you restructure your very anatomy.

When I first visited Rifle in 1991, I was an emaciated, self-obsessed nineteen-year-old would-be rock star. I was young and brash, coming up through the difficulty grades, and I wanted to be the best. It never occurred to me that fifteen years later I'd be genuflecting desperately in the same roadbed. It didn't occur to me that I'd be in the throes of protracted benzodiazepine withdrawal, a syndrome that, in the words of one survivor, "brought the strongest man in the world to his knees." I had no idea that the sport that had cured an agoraphobia born on the streets of my hometown, Albuquerque, New Mexico, would turn on me, growling, like a beloved dog gone rabid. It never occurred to me that self-starvation in the name of performance rock climbing would lead to panic attacks, which would in turn help sow tranquilizer and drug addiction, which would in turn lead to a ferocious withdrawal and post-withdrawal syndrome complicated by misdiagnoses, overmedication, hospitalization, and an attendant leper's bell of bizarre, nutso behavior. I couldn't have known that "psychopharmacology," a profit-mongering psychiatric pseudo-science predicated on bombarding emotional anomalies with chemicals, would almost kill me. I could never have known driving into Rifle that first time, a September night in 1991, and seeing the undercut walls arc toward the full moon like silver parabolas, that I would find myself kneeling atop the hardpack, not wanting to live anymore but still not convinced that death was the answer. I could not have known that the one friend with me that day—Andrew, a fellow magazine editor and Rifle junkie—would have to run across the road and prevent me from opening my veins.

As a teenager I'd seen some poor, deranged sod do this down in Albuquerque. He'd opened his wrists in Summit Park, a shady square of grass near my mother's home by the University of New Mexico. Three friends and I were skateboarding around a concrete loop that encircled the park's central playground, and I'd noticed the man, raccoon-eyed and wild-haired, slumped against a cottonwood eating watermelon. We looped around again, paddling under a hot dappling of July sun, avoiding alluvia of gravel. We passed the man a second time, but now I noticed something off about his "watermelon." I looked closer, saw how the watermelon was in fact the man's two forearms wet with blood. He held them and a gleaming blade before him, alternately slashing at each like a fisherman cleaning carp.

"Hey, man," one of us said, as our little band stopped by his tree. "You need some help?"

The man stared at us blankly, said nothing, and then stood up unsteadily and ran off into the neighborhood. The cops came and we helped them search, following the man's gore trail along the sidewalk until we found him cowering behind a hedgerow. I remember wondering what would drive someone to such a ghastly and public act—how could life become so unbearable? Only thirteen then, the worst of the anxiety storm still before me, I vowed never to be "that guy"—to force some unsuspecting other to witness my self-murder.

As I now did to Andrew.

I'd pulled the bottle from a crease off the shoulder, where we'd screeched to a halt in a pullout along Rifle Creek only thirty seconds earlier. (Much of this is reconstructed from Andrew's memory, for the obvious reason that my own was compromised.) We were: me; my brindled, Bengali-striped, eighty-pound Plott hound, Clyde; and Andrew. We'd driven out from our homes in the mountain hamlet of Carbondale, an hour away, in my silver VW Golf, a climber car in stage 4 disrepair. I'd first met Andrew in 2005 when he was an intern at *Rock and Ice*, where he stayed on as associate editor. Andrew is tall, thin, dark-skinned, half-Arab, with a strong wit and iron fingers to match. I shouldn't have come with him to Rifle that day. I should have been home in bed, rigid atop the sheets, vibrating, staring at the ceiling, sweating, "resting," waiting for the seconds to congeal into minutes to congeal into hours until I could steal a few hours of nightmare-haunted sleep. But a coworker at *Climbing*, *Rock and Ice*'s main competitor but a block away in Carbondale and where I now—somehow, barely—held an editorial job, had shanghaied me into replacing old protection bolts during a *Climbing*-sponsored event. And so I'd come out, fearing all the while that being back in my old stomping grounds thusly compromised might trigger an epic blowout.

And now I ate my "watermelon" and forced Andrew to watch.

I'd called Andrew and asked him to come in part because I thought having a friend there might anchor me. The last time I'd visited Rifle, that spring of 2006, I'd been in the grips of a similarly stark terror. Only four months out from my last dose of benzodiazepine after seven continuous years on the drugs, I was so dizzy, fearful, and winded (among dozens of other troubling symptoms) that I'd not made it more than halfway up the warm-up, a climb I'd done hundreds of times before. I was so weak I could barely shuffle *down* the canyon road without wheezing, as a friend, Derek, and I walked from one wall to the next. It had been a horror, a disaster, a demoralizing failure. The climb whose protection bolts I was supposed to update this day was called *Sprayathon*, a severely overhanging 5.13c. (Fifth-class, or roped, technical rock climbing, is subdivided by the Yosemite Decimal System, originally designed to be a close-ended scale from 5.0 to 5.9 but that now goes to the mathematically improbable 5.15. At 5.10 and above, the YDS further subdivides into the letter grades "a" through "d"—5.10a, 5.10b, 5.10c, 5.10d, 5.11a, etc.) Andrew would go first and get the rope up, and then I would use mechanical ascenders called Jumars to reach the old bolts and, with a cordless hammer drill, replace them. The reality, however, was that I had to *crawl* up the stairs to reach my bedroom, rented from friends back in Carbondale. If stairs were too much, hoisting my fat carcass up a taut, free-hanging 10-millimeter rope was going to be impossible. At my physical peak in the nineties and early aughts, I could run laps on *Sprayathon*, and even used it as a warm-up when I was trying a 5.14, *Zulu*, down the road. *Sprayathon* had always been a handy benchmark of personal fitness, and for a time I'd been one of the stronger climbers in the canyon.

Now, however, I couldn't get up *Sprayathon* on Jumars, and I'd tried to tell that to my coworker at *Climbing*. But like most everyone around me he just could not or would not believe me.

"Don't worry about it, Matt," he'd told me. "I know how hard you climb."

I didn't bother mentioning that he'd described another person: the Matt before benzodiazepine withdrawal.

By all outward appearances, I looked normal . . . enough. Overweight from inactivity, sure, with a comically "pregnant" stress belly; and downtrodden, my eyes perpetually glued to the floor. But not nearly as sick as I felt. It would have been better had I had a compound fracture: splintered bone poking through the skin. A *tangible*, *relatable* malady that elicited sympathy and didn't require so much by way of explanation that I eventually gave up and just told people, "Well, I have chronic fatigue."

I'd barely climbed over the last year, and not at all in the month prior. I'd done a disappearing act that began in summer 2005 as I struggled to taper off benzos. Since then, I'd been hospitalized thrice, labeled "bipolar" and "majorly depressed," chemically lobotomized by antipsychotic major tranquilizers and epilepsy-drug mood stabilizers, held in locked wards, recommended electroshock, and then ultimately tapered off the benzos at a big East Coast hospital, the Johns Hopkins Institute, only to be "snowed under" by further meds and released into the world sicker than ever. The root problem had for years been benzo addiction—tolerance and then withdrawal—but the doctors and therapists, the so-called experts, refused to acknowledge this. Instead, I'd been told repeatedly that my anguish was endogenous, the result of a permanent, life-long panic disorder, and that I would always need to be medicated. And I'd been blamed as an addict—for recreational abuse of marijuana, painkillers, alcohol, and benzos. This addiction, I'd been led to believe, might even have given me a sort of incurable "super-anxiety."

It was only after my final hospitalization, at Hopkins, that I realized through my own research, meeting a benzo survivor in Boulder who would become a good friend and advisor, and connecting with online support groups that I needed to be rid of psychiatric medicine or I would never get better.

Which had brought me to this impasse: only one week free from *all* chemicals for the first time in years, I'd rekindled the most acute benzo-withdrawal symptoms and unstoppered the toxic backlog that infused my brain and nervous system, leaving me enraged, delusional, hallucinating, rudderless, and floppy-infant weak, awash in a confused depression, prone to internal psychotic meanderings, and filled with self-animus so paranoid and acid that I kept hearing sirens ("They're coming for me") when I lay my head on the pillow each night. I brimmed with burning, unremitting muscular pain from head to toe and an impulse to self-annihilate so strong that I had to start each morning by looking in the mirror and saying, "I promise not to kill you today," keeping knives and ropes and other potential implements of death as far from my person as possible.

I had never been so terrified. The final medicine I'd stopped had been a powerful tricyclic antidepressant, nortriptyline. Nortriptyline is a chemical descendant of Thorazine, the notorious antipsychotic originally applied as a surgical antihistamine, to prevent a sudden drop in blood pressure called surgical shock.[1] You'd not be reading this book if it weren't for Thorazine, for it was this drug that in 1954 launched the modern era of psychopharmacology—

psychiatry's medication of mental illness through chemical agents touted as "specific antidotes to mental disorders," e.g., antipsychotics, antidepressants, and antianxiety pills.[2] Until then psychiatrists had had their Freudian therapy, straitjackets, ice-water baths, padded rooms, ice-pick lobotomies, insulin comas, electroshock, and even tooth- and organ-removal,[3] but with Thorazine they latched onto something more legitimizing: a pill, a specific pharmaceutical "cure" much like the penicillin discovered decades earlier that revolutionized modern medicine. As my "cure," nortriptyline, wore off, I began to feel that a dark shadow stood in the corner of my room each night, silently observing, sucking away sleep, encouraging my death. All the fine hairs on my body would stand up with gooseflesh as I willed it to disappear.

It was as if, as William Styron wrote in his masterpiece memoir of depression, *Darkness Visible*, "many of the artifacts of my house had become potential devices for my own destruction: the attic rafters (and an outside maple or two) a means to hang myself, the garage a place to inhale carbon monoxide, the bathtub a vessel to receive the flow from my opened arteries."[4] I'd visited Bureau of Land Management open space in the foothills west of Carbondale the previous weekend with my two roommates, waiting at their truck with Clyde while they finished a trail run, shivering with despair. I had the hound on a twenty-foot length of climbing rope, and headed into a fairy ring of oaks near the parking lot to hang myself. I needed to do it quickly, before my friends returned. I had the noose tied, Clyde's leash-rope over a stout limb biting into my neck as I leaned into it and began to see stars. Then I realized that without his leash Clyde would run off. We were in rocky, scrubby, ridgy terrain home to bears and mountain lions, and cattle ranchers who shoot nuisance dogs. Clyde whined beneath the trees as he tracked my every move, his big brown eyes liquid with confusion. He deserved better than this. I undid the noose and headed back to the truck in tears, rubbing Clyde behind his lop ears, sobbing as I gushed apologies: the horror of doing this to him, an abandoned puppy whom I'd adopted from the shelter. The horror of being left alone that way. Yet, I wanted to die; I fixated on this one idea as a solution to end my pain.

The next day I took four carloads of belongings to a thrift store in nearby Glenwood Springs, giving my possessions away so that my friends and parents didn't have to dispose of them later. I considered hanging myself from a bridge over the Crystal River near our home, but dismissed the idea because, on the level of pure vanity, I didn't want my fat, bloated corpse swinging there for everyone to see. Neither did I want my bad juju haunting this singular spot over the river's unsullied wavelets, the twin-summited Mount Sopris framing the southern horizon beyond—a summit I'd not stood on in two years.

Andrew had stepped into the car that morning not knowing any of this.

The first stirrings had begun when I picked him up where he lived, at the efficiency apartment I'd once rented in Carbondale. It was a bright, woody, ell-shaped add-on that my friend Lee, a climbing buddy I'd known since New Mexico, had originally built for his aging mother. Inside, I'd seen my old desk jammed under a window in the northwest corner beneath the windows. I'd left the desk for Andrew when I moved back to Boulder in 2005. (I've lived in Boulder most of my adult life, and hold two degrees from its university.) From 2003 until leaving Carbondale, I'd entertained grand notions of writing a novel at that desk. The truth, however, was that I'd come home from work, chew Vicodin ordered off the Internet (opiates had inspired the great poets, had they not?), sit at the computer trolling climbing forums and doing zero writing, and then pop one of my various daily benzo doses, guzzle red wine, and play Halo 2 until I nodded into narcotized sleep, too pasted to fold out my futon. Spike, my black Maine coon cat, would crawl atop my belly and we'd both awaken with the night terrors and screaming fits I had around 2:00 A.M. as the benzos wore off, as I leapt up choking and bellowing, wondering who'd left the lights on. The desk, so cheap, so nondescript with its flimsy black metal and crappy wood laminate, reified those wasted hours. It brought home how little I'd cared for myself.

And so, I'd fixated on the desk. And begun to resent Andrew for having it: that sonofabitch—he had "my" desk. Never mind that I had a perfectly serviceable look-alike from Target, the writing station at which I now sit. Andrew's desk had a sliding keyboard rack—I needed it! Everyone needed it! Shit, famine babies in Africa needed it! My mind was so fragile, so Byzantine in its psycho logic; no other path threaded the rat maze. I'd have to go buy another desk *exactly* like this one if I were to fix the world again. But I was too brittle even to conceptualize driving, solo, the fifteen miles to the Glenwood Springs Walmart to buy a replacement. I could barely go to Carbondale's grocery store without breaking down, sweating and shaking and sprinting for the exit. No way then could I venture into Walmart's vast, booming warehouse space under those white fluorescents, which worsened the ongoing "nothing is real" symptom of derealization, flattening the world into two dimensions. And my voice was a hyperventilated wheeze: How even to inquire where the office furniture was? And how to comprehend a two-page assembly printout well enough to put a desk together? At that point, I could barely get through the jokes page in *Maxim*.

When, a few days earlier, I'd told my mother how poorly I felt post-nortriptyline, she'd e-mailed back that "it was too early after benzos to stop the final medicine," meaning she felt that I was still too fragile. (I still deal with a protracted post-benzo-withdrawal syndrome that ameliorates in barely perceptible increments; more on that later.) By way of a response, I'd plunged my right fist through my iMac, shattering the screen with one punch. I was at my office at *Climbing*, fumbling through the days, shying away from coworkers, doing line-editing work while lying flat on the floor because a therapist had told me it was impossible to hyperventilate in this position. (She was wrong.) I wanted nothing more than to be free of all medications—*now*—and my mother's response had enraged me beyond all logic. My boss and I, to explain the spiderwebbed computer screen to our IT department, had to dissemble my knocking over the computer while reaching for a mug of coffee. I remember the texture, a garish slab of high-September sun invading my office's east-facing windowpanes and how easily my hand breached the glass; the lack of pain; how easy it was to destroy.

Now in the car with Andrew, desk-obsessed and nauseous with anxiety, I'd felt the ride out go from bad to worse. I was barely able to hold up my end of the conversation as Andrew made small talk, the kind so easily shared among climbers—which Rifle routes he was trying, upcoming road trips. I'd grown ever tetchier, ever more envious of his perfect health and his goddamned desk, the nauseating, withdrawal-induced current that arced along my spine, thrumming in a rising crescendo. Strong sun beamed in unfiltered by clouds, sluicing across the Flat Tops to fluoresce their autumnal quilt of aspen yellow and scrub-oak purple, filling eyes insomnia-raw with photonic sand, amping my rage. Clyde, a year and a half old and brimming with puppyish angst, *woo-woo-woo'ed* from the backseat, writhing about and trying to nose through the gap.

As Andrew recalls, I'd been "on edge" the whole morning, my voice angry when I shooed the dog back as we wound our way up Colorado Road 217, an idyllic byway that enters the canyon past a state fish hatchery. Each time, Andrew said, that I told Clyde to "get back" my voice had a harder edge. Like me, Clyde is a New Mexican (from Taos), and as a rescue dog, has his own anxieties. He must have been cut loose by a highway, because he flips out on certain roads or when we pull over in a strange place. Clyde had been with me through the horror of the previous year, and it was his photo—not my then-girlfriend's—that I displayed most prominently in my hospital room at Johns Hopkins.

Andrew and I stopped to pay our day-use fee just inside the canyon mouth, where an information table for the day's event had been set up at a kiosk. There a coworker manning the table said simply, "Samet . . . !" It was too much to hear my cursed name. Other climbers milled about; they all hated me. They all hated "Samet": of this I was certain. I'd been off course—or as climbers say, "off route"—for years, an elitist prick at the rocks, penning snarky columns in the magazines and at times being too harsh, in print, on fellow climbers, but without the self-deprecation you need to pull it off. And *everyone* knew this; the whole world knew it and stood united in monolithic opprobrium. So what was I doing here, displaying myself like some three-legged freak so my enemies could mock me? I could picture it now: I would Jumar but a few feet up *Sprayathon*, dangling there too exhausted to continue, and someone would drive by and see me twisting in the breeze like a piñata.

"Hey, isn't that Matt Samet?" they might ask their friends. "I hear he used to be some sorta hot-shit climber. Wow, look at him now . . . he's so fat he can't even get up the Arsenal using Jumars. What a jackoff."

You see, these are not normal thoughts. But I no longer controlled my mind, and Andrew was beginning to sense this. I had the final eruption after we pulled away from the kiosk.

"I remember this," he later told me. "You pounded on the steering wheel really violently, five, ten times—while still driving forward. It was just complete, pure rage. Then you ripped off both turning/wiping levers." I can remember howling a single word—"Fuck!"—repeatedly as I snapped the levers from the steering column.

What a cloddish word: "Fuck." Still, I could do no better. When a pumped (tired) climber snaps, frustrated, to the end of his rope after falling off some Rifle crux, that's usually the first thing you'll hear: *"Fuckkk!"* Our juvenile, fuck-filled tantrums had been so frequent the first two years in the canyon that local picknickers and fishermen had complained to the city about the influx of "foul-mouthed rock rats." We came from Boulder in import sedans, using loud power drills to install the expansion bolts that protect the climbs, taking up the parking spots, hurling F-bombs. Imagine that: a bunch of skinny college-town weirdos in pink tank tops and garish spandex tights, hanging off the walls and screaming "Fuck!" like petulant middle-schoolers. Until climbers showed up, the canyon had been a quiet, cool summer repair for the busted shale-mining town of Rifle. By the mid-1990s, it had become *the* place to sport-climb in North America, and I'd been on the scene since the beginning, starving and striving and screaming with the best of them.

Andrew recalls what happened next: "You swerved to the right, and I felt like you were trying to drive us into the river." (I don't recall intending to do so; anyway, the river is barely three-feet deep come autumn.) I jumped out, Clyde yowling from the back, his nose greasing the glass. I began to mill around in the pullout. Andrew leapt out to console me, and I growled at him to "get the fuck away from me."

Apparently I said this a few times, with enough ferocity that Andrew did precisely that.

Andrew then crossed the road, going over by the base of the Arsenal to give me space. I paced about agitated, gaining fury, beating my car with feet and fists. I pounced on the Golf's rear bumper, kicked at the back windscreen, punched at the safety glass, hoping it might swallow my arms and bleed them out. The glass barely flexed; the rage needed another outlet. Two friends drove by, perhaps only half-seeing what was transpiring or lacking a ready context for it. They gave a little wave and continued up canyon. Andrew waved back like everything was okay, hoping it soon would be. It was then that I found that bottle, an empty Corona down in the reeds.

I broke the glass on a gray chunk of limestone, took up the largest shard, staggered back up on the road, knelt in the dirt, and began cutting at my wrists. I was like a kettle at high boil: The steam has to gush out or the whole thing will blow. Andrew screamed, "*No!*," and ran over. He bear-hugged me from behind. Andrew enclosed my hands in his own, trying to prize away the glass.

"I can't do this. I can't do this. I can't be here," I kept saying.

Then: "Where were you?!" I yelled at him. "Where were you where were you where were you?!"

It was a disingenuous accusation, leveled at Andrew in particular simply because he happened to be there. His bad luck: He would have to serve as proxy for those friends and family members who'd failed to believe the profundity of my struggle, who'd let me wander into the wilderness sick and crazed to die alone.

"I'm right here," he said. "I'm here now. I'm here right now. Stop it, Matt! You need to stop! I'm here now, I'm here for you." And he was.

I craned around wildly, catching glints of the Arsenal from behind its roadside screen of slender elms. The trees had turned yellow-gold with autumn's apogee—not that I cared, about the damned, beautiful trees or the climbs behind them. Nine years earlier, I would routinely climb these routes in running, not rock, shoes. I'd been such a prickish, competitive lout that I made a point of doing so when I saw someone failing on one of the climbs. One day in 1997, sporting an early-spring wine gut, wearing garish yellow MC Hammer pants and a monster-truck cap, and half-covered in mud (I'd fallen into the creek), I'd walked up without fanfare and done the very overhanging 5.12+ *Vitamin H* in blown-out New Balance running shoes before one such suitor. This was the kind of Dadaesque stuff we'd do. Another buddy, Charley, had done the same climb naked with a watermelon hanging off his harness. And another friend, Steve, had climbed out an eighty-foot overhang called *Pump-O-Rama*, in the Arsenal's guts, wearing a tutu and high heels. Now I pushed two hundred pounds, a sad, crazed, hobbled, fatty. Karma is a cruel mistress.

I shook Andrew off and flung the bloodied glass into the reeds. My left wrist seeped sorry serums, dewing there in gashes and clots. I'd done some damage, but not enough even to leave scars. I'd been cutting, recalls Andrew, like I was "trying to saw through a rope with a dull knife." And as any climber knows, you never cut the rope.

Another "*Fuck!*" Then as suddenly as it began, it was over; the fire left my body.

Andrew drove us back to Carbondale. I was too depleted, too unreliable to drive. We drove slowly, unable to use the turn signals, the wiper blades locked at 3 o'clock on the windshield then occasionally going into spasm before freezing back in place. We said little, Andrew worried that one wrong word—hell, even a frisson of the wiper blades—might trigger another episode. We came to Glenwood Springs and drove over the Colorado River, heading up-valley toward Carbondale and Aspen, the dark green waters slow and languid below. Then Andrew informed me that he was taking me to the hospital.

"No, you aren't," I spat. "If you drive toward the hospital, I will jump out of this fucking car."

I meant it; to prove my point, I opened the door as we poked along in traffic. I knew I was being unfair: I'd saddled Andrew with a tremendous burden, and his response was of course the most logical one—if a friend is suicidal, you take him to the hospital. But I also knew what would happen there, because I'd been through it a year earlier: They'd refer me to a psych ward, lock me up on a seventy-two-hour hold, and pump me full of pills. Even though I knew the position I'd put Andrew in, I refused to let him deliver me back to my tormentors. Death would be preferable. I would not swallow another pill.

"I'm sorry, man. I really am," I said without affect. My voice oscillated between a flat trauma monotone and an anemic whisper—Styron's "ancient wheeze" of depression. "But I can't let you do that. I'm this way *because* of the psychiatrists, and if I go back this will never end. They will put me back on meds and zero out the clock again. I just can't let you take me there. It would be the end of me."

Andrew looked at me, a fellow climber, and I could see that he believed me. The Matt he'd known for the previous two years lay somewhere beneath the pain. And the *real* Matt would never act this way; Andrew had spent enough time with me on rock to know this. On dangerous or "death" leads there is a shared faith between partners; the belayer (the climber securing the rope) needs to believe just as much as the climber that the outcome will be favorable. If it is otherwise, the belayer's fear permeates the leader, and the endeavor—and the partnership—will crumble. Two springs earlier, Andrew and I had climbed a death route in Eldorado Canyon, outside Boulder, called *High Anxiety*, a fussy, difficult-to-protect 5.11 up red-brown dihedrals (open-book–shaped corners).

As I stemmed, opposing my feet on two walls at the crux, placing RP nuts a quarter of the size of a pinkie nail for protection, Andrew held the rope expertly, only occasionally voicing encouragement. If I fell in the wrong spot, I'd break my legs . . . or worse. I could feel his *belief* in me vibrating along the cord, just as he believed me now even if this day would so punish Andrew that he couldn't climb for a week, his back muscles locked with residual stress.

"Okay, Matt," he said. "But we need to find a way to keep you safe."

"I know, man. I know . . ." And we did.

Andrew and I reached a compromise: I would call my father, and my family and I would sort out the situation. I shut the car door. This day, at least, there would be no more hospitals, no more psychiatrists. Back in Carbondale, Andrew dropped me off at home and then called other friends to come over for lunch so we could debrief. Four of us sat at the table eating bread and slurping yam soup while I assured them I would not harm myself again.

"Well, you're a pretty clever guy, Matt," one friend, Jeff, said. "I'd hate for us to leave here and then you go and try something like this again."

"I won't, Jeff," I said. "I promise." I could see in his half smile that he didn't quite believe me. I explained the situation as best I could, emphasizing that I could not return to the doctors. I laid out the specifics to strengthen my case. Barely anyone around me knew what was going on. It was too complex, too convoluted, to be elevator chat, so I mostly kept mum about my situation; besides, I needed *time* more than I needed friends' well-meaning platitudes in order to heal.

I'd taken my final dose of nortriptyline only a week earlier, a twenty-five-milligram capsule washed down after dinner. Psychiatrists at Johns Hopkins had prescribed the pill to treat major depression, though it had served mainly to mask anxiety caused by the cessation of benzos nine months earlier. That last nortriptyline brought to a close a checkered fourteen-year history with crazy pills: Had I been lucid enough to do the math, I would have realized I'd been on thirteen psychiatric medicines in as many months. Now I'd entered a rawer, more fragile epoch, the underlying benzo withdrawal kicked into hyperdrive by this final chemical insult. The worst, ongoing benzo symptom had been hyperventilation, which left me wheezing, irritable, and in physical distress. The overabundance of CO_2 set my muscles on fire, and only increased the constant, black, gut-piercing terror. I couldn't walk up hills, and could spit out only three or four words at a time, punctuated by flurries of weird, shallow, triplicate yawns that worsened as my nortriptyline dose declined. I slept with my mouth duct-taped shut and nostrils opened with breathing strips to promote diaphragmatic breathing, in the hopes that my body might find equilibrium. It didn't, and would not for some time. I was not safe out in the world, but neither did I have real refuge—especially not in my bedroom, alone with my ex-junkie's guilt and self-hatred. I needed time, distraction, and somewhere to lie low, but it wasn't happening. No one would let me. I'd tried to tell a few friends, family, and coworkers of my plight even as some urged me to "get help," "go back on the meds," and exploit my "support network." But the support network—of therapists, doctors, and hospitals—had, through chemical paternalism, helped orchestrate this undoing. In fact, the only people who'd verified the reality of my experience were people who'd been through it themselves, ex-patients and survivors of benzodiazepines. It hadn't been the doctors. It was as if I had vertigo after an hour strapped to a merry-go-round, but everyone I lurched toward for help asked, "How can you have vertigo? I don't see any merry-go-round."

There is no merry-go-round.

Imagine that you have been poisoned for years but have eventually come to realize the mechanism. And you know that, given time and a safe harbor, your system will normalize. But no one believes you because the poison is medically legitimized. In fact, the withdrawal symptoms themselves mimic the very conditions—anxiety, depression—for which the medicines were originally prescribed. They mimic conditions you've tussled with your whole life, only amplified so profoundly—a banshee howl piped through a bullhorn—that you can no longer function. Which is sure proof that you mustn't stop your medicines, because your original condition is *worse than ever.* In fact, you may need new pills, and at ever higher doses.

It is a tough cycle to break.

Mind you, I don't have these fits anymore. Writing this seven-plus years later, it would not occur to me to behave this way. I go about my days assuming sanity, climbing again, taking long walks with Clyde and my wife, Kristin, and our little boy, Ivan. Working, writing, being a husband and father. The madness is as remote, as hypothetical, as the ice rings of Pluto. And it's all because I stopped listening to the doctors and started listening to myself.

I kicked myself in the ass and changed the basic message. I changed it from, "You, Mr. Samet, have a *lifelong* anxiety disorder that must always be treated," and, "We need to approach this benzo withdrawal from a place of strength, with other medicines on board" and, "It's very dangerous to stop your antidepressants. What if you become suicidal?" and, "Meds give you choices," to, "You are a whole, functional human being and not just the sum of your symptoms and diagnostic labels." I changed it to: "You do not need these meds." I changed it to: "The choice to live chemical free is a good and a necessary one." Choices: It's all about making choices. The five times I've been hospitalized—four of those for what I now realize was benzo withdrawal—the psychiatric establishment always offered more "choices." This blue-green pill or this white one, this pink pill or this yellow one. This useless support group or that one. This endless, navel-gazing talk therapy or that one. Their choices have given me rashes, headaches, dry mouth, a deadened libido, dampened creativity, palpitations, head rushes, electrical zaps to the brain, slurred speech, glassy eyes, sleepless nights, rage . . . "Choices." Without such choices, I might have healed years ago.

Writing this, seven years after "the incident," with a drug-free mind and hard-earned lucidity, I will say that the "choice" to trash my car and slash my wrists beneath a beloved cliff, in front of a beloved friend, is not one I will make again. I won't take another med; I'd rather swing from a noose. Try me: I will end it before I let the brain-vultures spiral in again. I will endure every thunderous brainstorm and the filmiest wisp of depressive fog, knowing that this is my lot and that here, in darkness, rests my core, authentic self. I will sit with depression when it comes and listen, to decipher its barbed and cryptic teachings.

Now, listen: I'm *not* some rabid coyote ululating from the badlands. I'm just a guy. I have a graduate degree, grew up on middle-class streets, held jobs, paid taxes, flew in airplanes, went grocery shopping, slept with women, brushed my teeth, tied my shoelaces. And whether you admit it or not, you *do* know someone like me. A friend, perhaps, who has trouble sleeping and ended up on three different pills that came to worsen her insomnia. Aunt Betty who lost her husband to cancer and was given "a little something" for her grief, and soon that something snowballed into a polydrug cocktail and she can no longer leave the house, her face a jelly of twitches and tics. Your nephew, an overly plump "bipolar" five-year-old taking an antipsychotic drug to control "irritable outbursts" and to temper the side effects of the ADHD drug he's been on since age three. Grandpa Tom benzo-anesthetized at the nursing home so he'll be less belligerent, less prone to sclerotic frissons, though now he can only count stucco dots on the wall, his mien gray-washed and slack. A co-worker who ghosts white during meetings and escapes for a high-potency benzo, only to return composed; but now, five years in and three milligrams deep, she has a constant tremor and must carry a pill vial from which she never separates.

Do these characters sound familiar? Are you one? Do you believe that these people have been given "choices"?

Surely the cure outstrips the disease.

Welcome to the Psychiatric Death Machine—hospitals, doctors, the FDA, and their bedfellow Big Pharma—which has created an ever-expanding universe of dependency-fostering, side-effects–laden pills and profitable "mental illnesses." If we are to take certain facts at face value, there has been an explosion in mental illness in America in the past quarter century, an epidemic requiring aggressive pharmaceutical intervention. More than 1.5 million Americans are on disability due to anxiety, depression, or bipolar illness,[5] a 2.5-fold increase between 1987 and 2007.[6] Six million adults are now considered bipolar,[7] with a forty-fold increase in the diagnosis of children and adolescents with bipolar disorder between 1995 and 2003.[8] Between 1996 and 2005, the number of Americans taking an antidepressant more than doubled, from 13 million to 27 million (10 percent of us over the age of six are now on antidepressants),[9] with global sales of antidepressants equaling $19 billion a year.[10] A 2006 estimate cited a whopping 8.6 million Americans who take sleep medication.[11] The atypical antipsychotics Zyprexa, Seroquel, and Risperdal have surpassed cholesterol drugs to become America's top-selling class of pharmaceuticals.[12] And benzodiazepine sales are on the rise, climbing from 69 million prescriptions in 2002 to 83 million in 2007.[13] In total, one in every eight Americans is regularly popping psychotropic pills, with total sales of these drugs in the tens of billions: $40-plus billion in 2008 alone.[14] If you look at it one way, we've all gotten crazier, driven mad by the exigencies of modern life. But if you look at it another, it's that the psychiatry has swollen like a bloodsucking tick, infiltrating the darkest corners of the human soul with empty promises and dangerous nostrums that are only making us sicker.

In my experience, it's the latter.

You see, I'm whispering from outside the concertina wire, but soon it will be a scream. I crab-crawled through the spools one moonless night while the guards dipped their heads for a smoke, one of the few to slip away. I drew on my strength as a climber—my firsthand experiences with fear and mortal peril—to do so. From what I see peering back, too many prisoners yet languish. We should free them. We should bring them back into the world, back into the daylight. We should show them that this insanity need not continue.

CHAPTER 2

Before we go too far, I need to point out the difference between fear and anxiety, because this book deals with both and because they're not quite the same. *Fear* is our gut, animal reaction to a perilous situation—it's a physical response. *Anxiety*, meanwhile, is psychological: It's nameless dread, a mentally concocted fear state. The psychologist Paul Foxman's treatise on anxiety, *Dancing with Fear*, better explains the distinction: "Fear is the instinctive reaction to danger. Anxiety is a learned, irrational reaction to fear—a fear of fear."[1] If a mugger holds a gun to your face and demands your wallet, that's fear; if you wake up in a cold sweat for the month afterward, flashing back to the robbery and feeling helpless, your hands shaking and your heart slamming, that's anxiety. Anxiety can wear many guises, both physical and mental. My 2,600-page *Webster's Third New International Dictionary* defines anxiety as "a state of being anxious or of experiencing a strong or dominating blend of uncertainty, agitation or dread, and brooding fear about some contingency."[2] Part two of the definition gets at the physical manifestations: "an abnormal and overwhelming sense of apprehension or fear often marked by such physical symptoms as tension, tremor, sweating, palpitation, and increased pulse rate."[3]

Climbing exposes you to *both* fear and anxiety, often in spades. This much I learned early on. When I was sixteen, my father and I and his college roommate, Bob, who introduced me to climbing, along with Bob's girlfriend, Marion, climbed the enormous glaciated volcano Mount Rainier, at 14,410 feet Washington State's highest point. The mountain is a singular heap, a mammoth castle of ice visible for hundreds of miles, floating in the sky like a hallucination. An ascent via the standard Disappointment Cleaver route is a two-stage affair: Stage one takes you up broad, gentle, nontechnical snowfields to a stone shelter at Camp Muir, at 10,000 feet. Climbers bivouac here, cook dinner, rehydrate, and prepare for stage two, which involves roped travel on crevassed glaciers, steep fields of frozen snow, and scrambling across loose, black volcanic crags. You leave Muir in the wee hours when the mountain is quietest, before sunrise. As the sun heats the slopes, Rainier comes to life, shedding its skin through rock and ice avalanches. You want to tag the summit and return to Muir before the peak heat of midday. Falling seracs—huge, semidetached blocks of glacial ice— and stones have killed dozens.

Our party of four left Muir at midnight, crossing the Cowlitz Glacier on a well-worn trough in the snow, the headlamps of dozens of guided climbers in pack trains bobbing behind us like fireflies. We soon neared the end of a rising traverse to a col called Cathedral Gap, Bob and Marion on a rope team ahead, my father and me behind. As our friends stepped from the snow onto a protected scree field, my dad and I heard a calamitous clattering: stones peeling off a giant cliff called the Beehive that loomed overhead. They seemed to hurtle unseen from the stars, bright in the night sky above.

"Run, run, run, run, *RUN!*" Bob yelled.

Our headlamp beams playing wildly across the ice, crampons biting—*nitch, nitch, nitch, nitch*—in the snow, my father and I sprinted through the dark, making it to the col just in time. When we recrossed this stretch on the descent, we saw dark rocks as big as televisions scattered in the snow, the kind that can cut you in half. *Fear* had been our motivator that night; *fear* had kicked us into overdrive, keeping us alive. Yet until we returned safely to Camp Muir from Rainier's upper flanks, I'd also felt *anxiety*, a buzzing, all-consuming meta-awareness of our frailty on a mountain as massive and indifferent as Rainier, a knot in my gut over the possibility of more rockfall, an idea I could not, no matter how hard I tried, dismiss. *Anxiety*—the fear that another boulder will hurtle through the darkness.

My first tangible memory of anxiety comes a couple of months after my parents' divorce—the night in February 1982 that my mother went missing. They had had a good marriage, at least while it lasted, with much in common. My parents are both bright, rational, science-minded people. My father skipped ninth grade, going straight from elementary school to the boarding school Christchurch School for Boys and then on to Choate Rosemary Hall—and thence to Harvard. And my mother graduated in the top 5 percent of her class at the University of Rochester School of Nursing, winning its Dorothea Lynde Dix Prize for outstanding performance in psychiatric nursing. Both worked in health care, my mother as a pediatric nurse practitioner, my father in clinical medicine (pulmonology) and as an epidemiologist. (Today my father is still an epidemiologist, specializing in public-health issues including smoking and air quality, while my mother pet-sits and raises honeybees.) And both had grown up in quiet East Coast settings, my father in Newport News, Virginia, my mother in Chevy Chase, Maryland, and northwest Washington, D.C. I was born in Panama, in the Canal Zone, where my father served as an army physician during the Vietnam War draft, working as an anesthesiologist at Gorgas Hospital in the army's Canal Zone company. After his discharge, we'd moved to Albuquerque, stayed two years, moved to Boston for three years so my father could complete a fellowship in clinical epidemiology, and returned to Albuquerque when I was six. I would live there until I was nineteen. It's a tough, eclectic city that shaped me in a tough, eclectic way. I was always a smart kid, or at least bull-headed about getting the highest grades: In elementary and middle school, I always had the highest marks. When you're the child of university people—and an only child, moreover—academic excellence is a given. It all starts at home: Instead of the Atari 2600 that all the other kids owned, I had a Mattel Intellivision with its more cerebral titles. Instead of a Lite-Brite, I had a Speak & Spell. Instead of cable TV, we had literature. Instead of seeing *The Bad News Bears* at the mall, we'd see a Woody Allen revival at the art-house theater. Everything, even play, had to have a purpose. It was simply understood that one lived this way.

Another thing about my parents is that both are exercise fanatics. Even today, when they visit Boulder, each parent pair stays either at a hotel with an Olympic-sized pool or near the rec center, so they can swim laps each morning. Weekends in Albuquerque would find us running around a grassy triangle called Altura Park or on the two-mile loop around the University of New Mexico golf course. Or at the pool. Or in the backyard, lobbing the birdie across a badminton net. Or playing tetherball on a maypole cemented into the grass. Or on our half basketball court, playing one-on-one or horse. (At only five foot six, my dad is a crypto-missile of a basketball player: the Jewish Spud Webb.) In winter we'd head to the gentle east side of the Sandias—the 10,500-foot mountain range framing Albuquerque to the east—or the nearby volcanic swell of the Jemez Mountains and cross-country ski through silent stands of Ponderosa. We loved to hike, and it was in the Sandias that I'd crane up at the range's stark pink Precambrian cliffs and spires as we switchbacked along the La Luz Trail, wondering what it might be like to climb them. I had a child's curiosity about the vertical world, dating back to an incident at the Grand Canyon at age four.

My parents and I had stopped there on a driving tour of the Southwest. Standing by a guardrail, I'd taken one bite of a Red Delicious apple then flung it capriciously into the abyss. Off to the side, two climbers were rappelling off the guardrail, and I asked my parents if I could ask them to retrieve the apple, or if I could go down there with them. The men looked like superheroes, wearing sit harnesses, red helmets, and bedecked with glinting metal carabiners, their stubbled jaws beaded with sweat.

"I don't think so, Matthew," my father said, chuckling. "Your apple is gone."

And it had been the last apple, I was told. There would be no others that day. I bawled, "My apple-buh-buh-buh-my apple-buh-buh-buh-buh-buh-I want my apple back!" as my parents led me to the car, the void pulling at my back. I've heard climbing described as a search for that magical place "where rock meets sky," a metaphor perhaps for how man transposes his eternal quest for meaning, for God, onto the mountains. Each boulder, cliff, wall, and peak has its particular curl of light and unique angulations, its peculiar sliver of sky, all in flux from instant to instant; you can climb the same rock hundreds of times, yet meet the sky a new way with each ascent. You could say then that I climb not only to find the place where rock meets sky, but also where the Grand Canyon meets the apple.

It's as good a reason as any.

All children take naturally to climbing, but I was an especial fanatic: I was often up in a mulberry tree in our backyard, contriving vertical narratives as I threaded my way from limb to limb, seeing how high I could go before the cross branches grew too slender. Whenever we hiked out of the Sandias, I'd beg my parents to let me scramble on the trailhead boulders while they sat on the rear bumper of our red VW Dasher, rubbing sore feet, applying ointment to blisters. Amorphous white granite blobs, the foothills blocks poked up amidst copses of scrub oak, and tracts of cholla and barrel and prickly pear cactus. I would navigate the boulders' gentlest facets in my Keds, scrabbling between black extruded xenolith knobs, my mother watchful below, warning me not to fall into the cactus. Once, at around age eight, I convinced her to drive me up there specifically to do this "bouldering." In the age before rock gyms, places like these were a kid's only introduction.

My parents loved that I loved the mountains. The outdoors and fitness had always been the Samet way.

Like any child, I absorbed their ethos. I had miniature dumbbells and would join my father lifting weights in our rec room. I had a fixed, daily regimen of sit-ups and push-ups that began in third grade and ran through my early twenties; I even did them religiously at music camp, where the other kids made fun of me. In summer I'd wake up early to run around our neighborhood, jogging atop soft, desert-hot asphalt in a withershins square. We didn't own a Walkman, so I'd take the black transistor radio from my parents' bathroom, throw it in a day pack, and trot along with the antenna sticking up through the zipper. I kept the band dialed to FM 94 Rock. I'm sure anyone who saw a goofy kid hustle by in the white-hot morning, Bad Company piping tinnily from his pack, had to laugh at the spectacle. One lap around was a mile and change, but the goal was two. I'd come home drenched in sweat, weigh myself, sneak spoonfuls of ice cream from the carton, and then launch into the "ups" and weights while I watched *The Price Is Right*. On runs with my father, he would push me to go faster, timing us, numbering our laps around Altura Park, my little lungs burning. When we entered a 10K in Santa Fe, I tried so hard that I shat myself at the finish line.

We all three of us pushed ourselves to perform to sport. My father was hardcore into distance running from 1973 through 1976, until all those pavement miles in the era's crude footwear finally sidelined him with plantar fasciitis. In his first marathon, in Framingham, Massachusetts, in 1975, Jon Samet went all-out from the start only to tank at mile sixteen; he finished nonetheless, hobbling across the finish line with severe leg cramps (and possible stress fractures in his feet) and experiencing discomfort walking for months. And my mother went hard *all* the time because she'd become a competitive, ranking marathoner. Kathleen Samet won the woman's division at Albuquerque's Duke City Marathon in 1978 and 1979,[4] and placed second in two Arizona marathons (Tucson and Phoenix) in 1979/80, winning her a listing as a world-class marathoner in *Runner's World* magazine and a seeded place at the 1980 Boston Marathon. That year at Boston—the year Rosie Ruiz snuck into the fray a half-mile from the finish and sprinted to the tape to claim "victory"—my mother placed fifth in 2:41:50, her best race time and her final marathon ever, due to subsequent injury.[5] She would also, through immersion in competitive running, further an eating disorder, a loose thread that helped to unravel my parents' marriage.

My mother is a petite five-four, and during her peak years as a runner (1979–1981) maintained her weight close to an amenorrheic hundred pounds. In photos of her breaking the tape at the Duke City Marathon, she looks like a stick-person, her skin dark brown from the desert sun. She's shown me childhood pictures of her, and while a little pudgy, my mom, the first of five children in an Irish-Catholic family, was never fat. Yet her mother—my grandmother, Patricia—criticized her weight. During my mother's preteen years, Patricia would stand Kathleen in front of a mirror and point out her size, saying, "You'll never have a boyfriend if you don't lose weight." She also controlled my mother's portions at meals, for example, denying her seconds on rolls. It was a point of pride with Patricia that despite having five children, she always weighed an aristocratically svelte 115 pounds—never mind that she stayed thin mostly via cigarettes and by replacing food with the alcohol that eventually caused cirrhosis of her liver, killing her in her sixties. Patricia's husband, Tom, a general practitioner, was little better. The final time I saw him, in Albuquerque when I was fifteen (and five-seven and 145 pounds of muscle), he called me "doughboy" and pinched my stomach. My father was a portly child as well, and still jokes (with some pain) about clothes shopping in the "Husky Boys" section at the department store. He had a doting Jewish mother who ensured that milk and fresh chocolate-chip cookies awaited him each day after elementary school. My father lost the weight at boarding school, but has always been very body conscious. I imagine that he and my mother, in their marriage, reflected these traits off each other even as they passed them on to me.

The fighting—angry murmurings and raised voices behind a closed bedroom door—began in 1980. My parents separated in July 1981, and my mother moved into a two-bedroom apartment a few miles west—Aspen Plaza, a generic triple-decker complex behind a

Safeway. On paper, as part of a shared-custody agreement, I was to spend two days a week with her, but it didn't always work out that way. My mom was often sidelined with bulimarexia, an eating disorder in which you binge-eat without purging, and depression. (Bulimarexics expunge the calories through starvation and exercise, instead of via vomiting and laxatives as bulimics do. My mother used running, biking, and swimming to stay thin.) Learning that she wasn't "feeling well," I'd happily stay put at my father's. I had no great love for Aspen Plaza; it was a nowhere place adjacent to a bay of supermarket loading docks. It was limbo, a place where the security light outside my bedroom changed from white to orange to black then back to white again, an ever-rising sun that made it impossible to sleep. It was purgatory, a place where I'd stay up queasy and plagued by insomnia, knowing something was wrong with my mother one room over but lacking the words for it. It was hell, a place where we'd coated my walls and ceiling in phosphorescent stickers of stars, moons, planets, and comets to create a false firmament that somehow claimed the generic bedroom as "mine." That, like the slick, itchy, Kmart comforter decorated with race cars that covered my bed, and the slippery motel-grade pillow in a cotton case similarly patterned, somehow made of this cell a little boy's room. I'd watch the sticker-stars emerge during those precious fifteen seconds when the light extinguished, only to see them disappear as its glare poured back in. My mother often sent me to the Safeway to pick up binge fodder: tiny jars of Gerber baby food, blocks of cheese, Oreos, ice cream. At night, I'd go to the window and look out at that damnable store, at the high-stacked milk crates and pallets, at the cars in the lot—metal chameleons changing colors with the light. I couldn't wait to leave. Her first Christmas there, my mom gave me roller skates, and I puttered around in the store's vacant front lot as far from her as possible until my dad drove up to collect me and my duffel bag of presents.

We were in the pool the following summer, my mother and I, horsing around on an inflatable raft. Her eating had caused her to put on weight.

"You look like a jellybean, Mom," I said, before I could stop my-self. In lieu of a swimsuit, she wore a yellow one-piece terry-cloth jumpsuit with short pants. "A big yellow jelly bean."

"I do?"

"Yes, you do a bit!"

"Well, that's not a very nice thing to say," she said. "Do you mean that I'm fat?"

"No. You're not fat, Mom, but you have a big, round yellow belly like a jellybean." I laughed at my joke. It seemed harmless enough.

My mother frowned and went to lie in a deck chair, leaving me bobbing on the raft. I'd finally found the words, it seems: I'd named her disease. I'd had enough of the missions to the store, of the giant bowls of ice cream, cookies, and crème de menthe my mother tore into once a week and that had been the focus of my father's run-ning commentary before they split. ("Someone's having an ice-cream pig-out," he'd say. "Get the big spoon.") Of how her love-hate relationship with food took primacy over being a mother; of how she spent so much time training with her runner friends, so many of them likewise afflicted. Of watching her stand before the re-frigerator, spooning baby food into her mouth like a starving rac-coon. Of how, as she and my father separated, the bulimarexia, overtraining, and emotional havoc wreaked by their dissolving union pushed her into ever blacker straits. Of weekends when she was too "sick" for me to visit, even though I didn't want to anyway. Of how powerless I was to fix any of this. Of how my mom came to do more overeating than running and had developed a strange, swollen belly that didn't match her twiggy runner's limbs. And of how this downward spiral drove her thrice, between 1981 and 1982, to attempt suicide.

Had I known just how hard it was for her, and had I known what lay in store for me, I'm sure I would have been much more sympa-thetic.

On the evening of my mother's disappearance, I sat with my fa-ther in the long, boxcar-shaped living room of our home on Arizona Street, in the middle of town near the state fairgrounds. Behind us, a bank of floor-to-ceiling windows bracketed an interior patio giving onto a redbrick porch. At night the glass reflected the room, only blacker, more diffuse, an opaque screen revealing nothing. We kept a three-setting standing lamp beside the couch, and this night it was dimmed to a golden glow that pooled in the glass. Post-separation, my father had grown a beard shot through with white. There was something he wasn't telling me. He would say only that it was important we find my mother. He held my hand as he said this, and I could see that the world had broken in some new and unknowable way.

"Why?" I asked him. "Where has she gone?"

"We don't know, Matthew," he said. "But we're trying to find her."

Two family friends had called with the news that she was missing. She'd not shown up for dinner at their house and wasn't answering her phone or her door. My mother—I would later learn—checked into a Motel 6 that evening and took an overdose of tricyclic antidepressants. The first time she'd tried—Christmas of 1981, just two months earlier—she'd taken an overdose of barbiturates at her apartment, woke up the next morning, called her psychiatrist, and was admitted to a hospital. This second time was much the same, my mother has told me—she knew more or less what a lethal dose was but "skirted it just by a bit." Both times, some part of her wanted to live. Again she called her psychiatrist and had herself admitted—the second of four hospitalizations between December 1981 and early 1983. The third time that my mother contemplated taking her life, she drove out to the national forest above Santa Fe with intentions to wander off and die of exposure, but then thought better of it and returned to Albuquerque—and the hospital. In November 1982, the fourth and final time she was admitted, it was to prevent suicide, as my mom had felt herself becoming extremely depressed again. She finally left the ward against medical advice, breaking with her psychiatrist, who refused to discharge her even though she felt ready to return home.

That period is a fog, but I do recall going to visit my mother in whichever hospital she was in. Once, my father and I visited her at some drab, fenced-in ratbox along the interstate. We visited the ward once or twice, my father and I. The hospital had a basketball court where it backed to the freeway, and he and my mother and I went out and played horse, a bloodless facsimile of the games once played in our backyard. I could barely lift my arms to take the shots. The ward breathed inanition, a close, sicklit space full of society's castoffs. One old woman paced the halls with a pushbroom, sweeping the linoleum, the only action that calmed her sclerotic brain. My dad and I sat on plastic chairs in the hall talking to my mother, but when orderlies took the woman's broom away she began to shriek so loudly you couldn't hear yourself talk. It was time to leave. When my father and I would drive by on the highway and I'd see the net-less basketball hoop sticking up over the fence, I'd think of my poor mother locked up inside and wonder how she was doing.

"When will they let her out, dad?" I'd ask.

"When she gets better," he'd say.

"And when will that be?"

"I don't know. Soon . . ."

My father's answer, with all its open-ended hopelessness, put me on tenterhooks. His answer made me *anxious*.

Three decades along, I can still invoke the texture of the night my mom disappeared, the uncertainty, the knowledge that some calamity was about to happen or already had beyond eye- and ear-shot, its soundless echoes rippling through the darkness. When my parents separated, I'd become prone to night terrors and would often awaken feverish, disoriented, and in tears, padding down to my father's room clenching and unclenching my hands. I'd stand at the foot of his bed moaning until he awoke and took my head in his lap, stroking the soft skin between my eyebrows. The dream-sensation was of the most terrible thing in existence. Me, a me/not-me atom trapped in meat-red organspace at once infinitesimal and infinite, an isolating vastness birthed from my forehead out-ward and saturated with atonal buzzing, heaving ebony flashes, and unboundaried shock. Red-black masses roiling like I was locked, an enzyme-slimed ort, within some titan's spasticated colon; a fear-some parade of impossible addends all amounting to the number

one, which was me, a singularity-weight supermass beyond all cal-
culus. I would try to convey this ancient abomination and found the
words only once, in metaphor: "A dark cloud coming over the mountains, Dad, and bad things falling out of the sky to kill you and me . . ."

"A dark cloud coming over the mountains"—what I felt the night
my mother tried to take her life. "Bad things falling out of the sky
to kill you and me," like the rocks on Mount Rainier.

Anxiety: Heart *bit-bit-bitting* and painfully squeeze-clenching, a
desperate mouse fluttering against a rib cage hull; cotton mouth,
gumming lips around questions I was too timorous to ask; nausea,
the green chili from dinner shooting hot acid back up my throat;
hyperacuity of vision and hearing, the way the lamp bulb seemed to
recede like an imploding sun and how my father's voice growled in
the baritone range, the vibrating of his Adam's Apple as he said, "She
has to be *somewhere*, Matthew." At 1:00 A.M., on my father's orders,
I slunk off to my room to stare at the ceiling above my upper bunk
and hug my arms to my chest. *Anxiety:* I wanted my mother gone
so I wouldn't have to abide this terror. I wanted her to disappear
forever because that seemed the quickest way to end the anxiety.

Surely I was a bad son for thinking these things. The guilt was
tremendous.

Six years later, in 1988, my mom felt recovered enough to share
the suicide note she'd left at Aspen Plaza before her second attempt. Starting in 1983 she'd gotten better, mostly through an
eating-disorder group and a caring therapist but also through cultivating a more balanced relationship to exercise. Most of her note
addressed how much she loved me and how much she didn't want
to do this, but that her anguish left her no choice. As I listened to
her read the missive, even with its loopholes and rationalizations, I
realized I never had wanted her dead; I just wanted an end to *my*
pain and could think of no solution other than to end hers, by ending *her.* That's how anxiety works: When you're in the throes of it,
you'd give almost anything to escape its clutches. Kathleen, my

mother, the woman who gave birth to me, stood by the mirror above the fireplace mantel in the home she shared with a good man, Bo. She would marry Bo the next year when I gave her away at an outdoor ceremony beneath the Sandia Mountains, on a perfect bluebird summer evening. My mother: reading from that yellow legal paper but not allowing me to hold the note, her straight brown hair reflected in the glass. I thanked her. I didn't need to see the words to believe them anyway. A brightness had returned to my mother's eyes and she ate normally now, three meals a day, no bingeing. Her lean runner's legs, worried frown of Irish-Catholic sorrow, freckles and moles from years of backyard tanning: my mother, whom I'd wanted to lose forever.

I love her and I'd wanted her dead. As she'd healed, my anxiety evaporated like autumn mist in a high-desert draw. Nearly a quarter century after she tried to commit suicide, the roles would reverse, my mother sitting beside me at Boulder Community Hospital after I'd gilled my thumbs with a steak knife and, with querulous voice, announced to my girlfriend plans to jettison myself from the cliffs of Boulder's Mount Sanitas. This came as I reached my last milligram of Klonopin during the final 2005 taper. It came after six endless days and nights without sleep. The fear avalanche triggered nearly a quarter-century earlier would sweep me into a gaping, blue-walled crevasse, ice crowding over to seal out the sun.

CHAPTER 3

One bright, hot summer day in the early 1980s, a teenage girl held a younger girl under at Albuquerque's Los Altos Pool, pinning her in a corner and drowning the life out of her. The pool, built in the 1950s and twenty-five meters long, has since been converted to an indoor pool,[1] but at the time it was a Mediterranean-blue rectangle filled with summer hellions and exposed to a harsh glaze of sun. Lifeguards noticed the victim only after she floated to the surface, bobbing facedown amidst throngs of screaming, thrashing death-monkeys. The murderess was remanded to a psychiatrist for pretrial evaluation.

This heinous crime is important only insofar as the murderess also saw the same psychiatrist I first saw, "Dr. Salami" we might call him, a child specialist one building over from my father at UNM's medical center. I read about her in the paper, recognized my doctor's name, and asked him during session about the pretrial evaluation, but he couldn't tell me much. I saw the shrink at least once a week, at my father's insistence. After elementary school, I'd skip latchkey camp at the YMCA to accompany my dad to his basement office in the Tumor Registry, and then hasten through a creepy, echoing concrete underpassage that linked the two buildings. Ducts, water pipes, and spindles of wire ran in great cablings along the walls, hissing, thrumming, seeping clear liquors—alive and tactile like the set pieces in *Alien* or *Eraserhead*. In there alone or hearing foreign footfalls resound through the gloom, from around the hall's single corner, I'd feel nervous electricity in my gut. I'd dare myself not to run, but it was rare that I didn't at least break into a canter. I dreaded the visits, loathed talking about myself and about how my parents' breakup made me feel (quite obviously, rotten), but I ran toward the sessions nevertheless just to flee that hallway. After my behavior mark at school had fallen from a "plus" to a "check minus," my father left me little choice. If I agreed to see the doctor regularly and earned at least a "check plus" two quarters in a row, my dad would buy me the video-game system I'd been lusting after. It was for a $299 Intellivision, then, that ten-year-old me sold my soul to psychiatry. I'd wait in Dr. Salami's antechamber, and then he'd come out with his beetling white eyebrows and lead me to an interior therapy room; the room had one-way glass so parents could observe the sessions, though I'm not sure my father ever came.

I can't recall the specifics of our conversations other than the pageantry of the dialogue, a superficial level I fought hard to maintain. An only child, a lifelong introvert, I like keeping my thoughts for me. With the doctor, I'd playact interactions amongst a family of interracial dolls who cohabitated in a dollhouse and who, when I handled them, would turn on each other with feral alacrity. I'd open the house on its central hinge, the doll children would swarm from their rooms to exchange fisticuffs in the kitchen, and the two parent dolls would decamp behind a locked bedroom door to shout at each other. The doctor would watch the fracas without comment, jotting his notes. Then I would pummel a giant foam Weeble in the corner, something I could have done at home for free with a pillow. Later, the doctor would report my progress back to my father.

It was a charade—a sick, expensive charade. I know my father only wanted to help and that, being a doctor himself, it was natural to refer me to the appropriate specialist. But I see these visits as the touchstone, the early conditioning that led me to seek out, blindly trust, and believe the therapists and psychiatrists who would come to oversee my near undoing. In time, in any case, my behavior grades improved and my father, as promised, bought the Intellivision. The video games kept me out of trouble for a few years, until I turned thirteen.

Every teenage boy needs his thing, and mine was skateboarding. Other than earning A's, I had never been good at anything until I found skating. Actually, I was no good at skating either; I just liked it. At the peak of my powers, the best trick I managed was the infamous seven-foot acid drop off the bell tower on the UNM campus. I'd skate along the stucco rampart that housed the bell, fall through the ether, and then land on a riser, my knees jarring with the impact. I never progressed beyond acid drops, concrete ditches, parking garages, or streets to half-pipes or swimming pools, but it didn't really matter: Skateboarding meant freedom. Had there been climbing gyms back then, I'm sure I would have found my true calling earlier in life.

As an early teenager, being a skatepunk was all the identity I had, and I ran with a crew of likeminded friends. I'd tried my hand at team sports, but could never align with the competitiveness, the players' egos, and the rabid, frothing, win-at-all-costs coaches. I just don't care about winning. You win one game, and then it's back to square one with the next—and what difference does it make anyway? Soccer I quit after transferring from the fun, recreational American Youth Soccer Organization to a team in the more martial Duke City Soccer League, where the coach, a porcine, buzz-cutted ex-Marine, nicknamed me "Ernie" and kept me perpetually benched. Basketball I bailed on after only three practices, terrified of the nutso coach who kept spittling, "Are we having *fun, everybody*?" in our faces during huddles. Wrestling I was miserable at, winning two matches in sixth grade but just barely, and another in eighth grade against a developmentally disabled kid who would have made mincemeat of me had his reaction time matched my own. I also tried track—the 600-meter—and won a few, sad white fourth-place ribbons. Later I went out for cross-country, at the private school I attended, Albuquerque Academy, but my knees filled with fluid—the painful Osgood-Schlatter syndrome—from pounding the dirt trails. I even tried playing the guitar, and would spend summers at Hummingbird music camp in the Jemez Mountains. That didn't take either: I have no rhythm, talent, nor a willingness to perform. I hate reading music and I have sausage fingers that are better suited to rock climbing.

I'd become a bit of a rebel, perhaps because of the stuffiness of the Albuquerque Academy where I attended grades six through nine. I'd left public school after fifth grade for this elite institution two long city-bus rides across town, in the wealthy Northeast Heights. The Academy was a landed, quiet, serious space with vast soccer fields, tennis courts, grassy quads, and porticoed walkways. It was a school at which our exuberant sixth-grade English teacher leapt up onto his desk mid-soliloquy, like Robin Williams in *Dead Poets Society*, and where a prim system of lights—green, amber, and red—mounted on the walls let you know how much time remained per period. It was a place of privilege and of classical education for the city's wealthiest children; a preparatory school for future Ivy Leaguers. It was a separate reality, a mini-university with buildings that smelled of book-binding glue, tweed, floor wax, and notebook paper, and where docksiders and Izod Lacoste alligator shirts were worn without irony.

I spent three years there as "class scholar," banging out the highest grades by the one-tenth of a decimal point that separated me from the pack, though my efforts soon left me weary, burned out, and tired of all the studying and myriad rules and contrived, faux–East Coast pomp and ritual. My three closest friends and I (all children of divorce, it turned out) took to skateboarding in eighth grade, started listening to new wave and punk rock, wore loud-patterned board shorts, and had our ears pierced. The teachers despised our otherness—we stood out, sassed off, but still earned top marks. One day a math teacher, a fading Southern belle, passed us loitering in the hall and said, apropos of nothing, "You boys will never amount to anything." Maybe not, but how I chose to look had nothing to do with it: I'd become a skatepunk not because I fancied myself as *opposed* to anyone else, but because that's simply one place where outliers end up. As a teenager, then, at an age where physical appearance is *everything*, I expressed my outlander status by sticking out, not disappearing as I tend to do now. However, sporting a Mohawk haircut, safety-pin earrings, leather combat boots, a trench coat, and torn punk-band T-shirts makes you an easy target, whether that's your goal or not.

It all began to unravel at the Academy in autumn of eighth grade, when, in the heedless, destructive way in which teenage boys undo things, a skater friend, Sergio, and I took a purple El Marko marker to the yellow locker bays in our building. The facility was pristine, still smelling of fresh paint and virgin carpet, only in its second cycle on the campus' new middle school. We didn't write "suck me" or "dog balls" on the lockers; no, we wrote people's names, thinking ourselves clever and not realizing that the El Marko was permanent. This the middle-school disciplinarian, also our math teacher, took as a personal affront. The crew-cutted and wattle-necked Mr. Sandwich turned stoplight red and screamed in our faces as Sergio and I sat in his classroom after school, spittle flying, eyes bugging, forehead veins popping as he hollered about "vandalism" and "hooliganism" and "disrespect." By way of punishment, he took us out to the track, plunked down on the bleachers, lit a cigarette, primed his stopwatch, and put Sergio and me through windsprints.

The next year was little better. I made sure to overstay my welcome at the Academy, so that a transfer halfway through freshman year became inevitable. That October of 1985, two of us "liberated" cans of the spray-on athletic adhesive Tuff Skin from a gymnasium storage closet and spritzed it through ventilation holes in the PE lockers. The adhesive turned the clothes inside into sticky, starchy planks. Just for good measure, we did this a few times. I remember sitting sheepishly before the upper-school disciplinarian, Mr. Buck, with his Harry Potter glasses and THE BUCK STOPS HERE placard, and being told that we would need to come to school one weekend and weed planter beds. My buddy and I pulled up thistle and tumbleweeds, and then I told my parents that I could not stay at the

Academy. Some of my grades had even dropped to Bs for the first time in my life. I was rapidly going off the rails.

Not *this* again. Not another "street fight." Wading through my first semester of ninth grade, hating life at the Academy, I'd been jumped for the fourth time in as many months. Fact: Going around the streets of Albuquerque dressed like a punk rocker will get you jumped. Sergio and I had learned this the hard way, paddling along Twelfth Street down in the Valley, when a road crew of juvenile-detention inmates surrounded us with shovels and pickaxes and tried to take our skateboards, the ringleader punching me in the mouth and knocking me to the pavement. A small band of us had learned this at the underage nightclub The Big Apple, when two packs, of jocks and metalheads, converged on us in the rear parking lot over a minor verbal misunderstanding. And I'd learned it again just two blocks from my mother's home, skating alone behind Jefferson Middle School one night when a dozen barrio kids chased after me, trying to steal my deck. There was always an edge of mortal peril to the attacks, an undiscriminating, many-on-few bloodlust forged in the city's hot, dusty crucible. Kids get stabbed and shot in Albuquerque, so I always tried to cut and run. I'm strong, but not street tough. I didn't grow up in the crack-shack ghetto but instead in middle-class neighborhoods in the Northeast Heights, the wealthiest quadrant in town. It barely mattered, because the weirdness goes down everywhere. Albuquerque has a well-merited reputation for crime, racial tension, and random violence—it's an economically and ethnically mixed, sun-blasted, windswept Southwestern mini-megalopolis split by two major interstates—a smaller Los Angeles where evil happens quickly and without apparent motive. (As one friend who also moved away, to Texas, put it, "I hate coming home. Everywhere I go, I feel like I'm looking over my shoulder.") The city's dark undercurrent seeps into your soul, even those of children.

Now, the one time we victims outnumbered our attacker, he had to be some armed sociopath older and larger than ourselves with the saucer eyes of a panicked horse. Mean as a rattler, impervious to reason, an unfeeling killer from some cold, alternate universe. Another thief of skateboards, a creature of the night just like we fancied ourselves to be when we'd steal out of our parents' homes to hit the silent streets.

We liked to do this: sneak out after midnight, rendezvous, smoke cigarettes, drink watery beer, and pop ollies and try wall-rides and acid drops on lots, stairwells, and parking garages where we'd be chased off by day. Night skating was the best. The air had cooled, the asphalt had hardened, and there was no one about to call the police, no cars in the way or grumpy old codgers hollering abuse from their driveways. Our favorite was to street-luge from the four-way intersection at Constitution and Washington boulevards. The streets dropped precipitously to the west, north, and south, all with run-outs onto flatter spans. We'd tighten our trucks with a skate key so the boards wouldn't wobble, lie feetfirst on our backs or face-first on our stomachs, and then bomb down the tarmac, backyard fences whipping by, the asphalt a black blur but inches away, praying a car didn't turn in from a side street. I stood up a few times and realized, from this higher vantage, how fast we were going: thirty mph, maybe more near the bottom. Had you hit gravel or gotten mired in pothole filler, it would have been curtains. Constitution ran out by the Safeway next to Aspen Plaza. We'd coast to a stop there on moon-bright nights of boundless possibility, skid plates grinding as the boards' noses came up, happy to be alive in our private playground, feeling the hermetic specialness of the slumbering city.

But now: "Give me your fucking skateboards!" this madman shouted. "You think I'm fucking around?" He held a length of PVC pipe high in one hand, a switchblade extended in the other. He wore a denim jacket with an AC/DC logo on the back and tight black jeans: the metalhead uniform.

"I've got my bat . . . and I've got my knife . . . and I'll fucking kill you!" he continued, advancing on us four wee skatekids.

We'd seen him in the distance, a tall figure with a wild tangle of dark hair, noodling around a bus stop along Lomas Boulevard by the Bernalillo County Medical Center, kicking over newspaper-vending machines and then weaving an erratic path along the sidewalk, orange with pools of nocturnal halogen. One among us, Owen, had skated past the guy on his way to our meeting point at the Albuquerque Indian Hospital, on UNM's medical campus. Owen said something about "a weirdo down the road," but we didn't think much of it. Down the road meant somewhere else. Flapping about in our trench coats, we lit up Kools, trying rail slides on parking blocks, oblivious as our attacker advanced through the night. When he suddenly emerged from a pine grove on the lawn, I saw the PCP glaze to his eyes and felt my heart skip a beat.

When bad things go down like this—when you're confronted with a physical threat—the "fight-or-flight" reaction kicks in. A primitive, automatic, animal survival mechanism, fight-or-flight activates at the first perception of peril as an azure spot—a brain-stem nucleus called the "locus coeruleus"—sets off a series of physical reactions.[2] The locus manufactures norepinephrine (aka noradrenaline),[3] which is a neuropeptide or neurotransmitter, a message-relaying, mobile protein molecule found throughout the brain and body, and one key to fight-or-flight. At essence, neurotransmitters are the intermediaries between the 100 billion neurons (nerve cells) in our brains, where they relay chemical messages across inter-neuron gaps called synapses, and between all the neurons found throughout our bodies. This transmittal happens when a message travels from each pre-synaptic neuron along a single axon; these axons, of varying lengths, then branch into many terminals from which the neurotransmitter "jumps" to specific, mirror-image receptor sites on the membrane of the post-synaptic neuron. (The neurotransmitter does so by traversing a twenty-nanometer gap called the "synaptic cleft." Received impulses enter the post-synaptic neuron via dendrites.) As Robert Whitaker frames it in his excellent exposé of modern psychiatry, *Anatomy of an Epidemic,* "A single neuron has between one thousand and ten thousand synaptic connections, with the adult brain as a whole having perhaps 150 million synapses."[4] Untold neuron-to-neuron transactions are going on at any given time—the human brain and nervous system are immeasurably complex.

Meanwhile, neurotransmitters are called either excitatory (activating) or inhibitory (inhibiting) in their action, in that they either encourage the post-synaptic neuron to carry out a specific task or they prevent it from doing so. Excitatory neurotransmitters activate the brain by causing neurons to fire, releasing neurotransmitters that then carry the message to other neurons in a kind of domino effect, while the inhibitory ones call a "cease-fire" that stabilizes or calms the brain—though some neurotransmitters carry out both functions. (Neurotransmitters also regulate our bodily functions—they course throughout the immune and endocrine systems, guts, lungs, heart, and so on, and can communicate with cells and organs.) At essence, neurotransmitters serve as chemical mediators of our emotional reality: As Richard Restak, M.D., writes in his examination of anxiety, *Poe's Heart and the Mountain Climber*, "*all* [emphasis added] mental processes result from the release of neurotransmitters from billions of cells in the brain and the reception of these chemicals by billions of other cells."[5] And, as Paul Foxman puts forth in *Dancing with Fear*, neurotransmitters translate our emotions, feelings, and every thought—even unconscious ones—into "physiological changes."[6] Without neurotransmitters and receptors, we would just be switched-off computers.

In a fight-or-flight situation, then, activating neurotransmitters such as epinephrine (adrenaline), norepinephrine, adrenocorticotropic hormone (ACTH), and serotonin flood the bloodstream.[7] More specifically, the adrenal glands release epinephrine as the sympathetic nervous system (SNS)—one branch of the body's autonomic nervous system (ANS)—fires, the so-called "adrenaline rush" during which your muscles tense, sight and hearing sharpen, breathing and heart rate quicken to take in more oxygen, and your posture becomes defensive. It's the process by which, as Foxman writes, "your body becomes charged and energized to protect itself"[8]—either through battling the threat or fleeing it. Only the triggering of the parasympathetic nervous system (PNS), the SNS' counterpart, brings you back down. (The PNS controls salivation, lacrimation, urination, digestion, and defecation,[9] and is like the "brakes" to the SNS' "accelerator." Think about the last time you were confronted with some danger, and the almost holy calm that washed over after the danger had passed: That was the PNS bringing you back to baseline.) The two complementary systems have long helped man to survive—to recognize and then confront and/or evade imminent threats. I would later have a therapist frame fight-or-flight this way: When man was both predator and prey, roaming the steppes and hurling spears at antelope, we evolved the response as a safeguard against creatures like saber-toothed tigers. These days, however, because we have few natural enemies—other than each other—fight-or-flight is almost an anachronism.

For the moment, however, the urge to flee our midnight attacker was perfectly understandable. This guy, after all, had a knife and seemed ready to use it. I'd never been in a proper fight (and still never have). My parents had always insisted that it was wrong to hit anyone, even in self-defense, so I'd learned to bail out even in situations I might have resolved with my fists. They'd told me this in second grade after I'd been cornered and stoned on the schoolyard by two reprobates I'd prevented, days earlier, from beating up a mentally challenged boy down the block.

"We'll get off your turf, man," I told our assailant lamely. I'd just watched the gang film *Rumble Fish*, so this seemed like a thing you might say. The wild man whirled from boy to boy, brandishing his weapons, his face a grim mask of homicidal rage. Clearly, this wasn't about "turf." It all felt slowed and unreal, like some terrible dream. The white glare of a streetlight painted us in a surreal glaze.

"I don't care about turf, you stupid motherfucker!" he said. "Now give me your skateboards!"

None of us were older than fourteen *and* we were a gaggle of whitebread wimps; this guy was eighteen or older, a veteran of the streets. We began backing away just as he brought the pipe down on tall, skinny Owen's head hard enough to shatter the plastic. Owen dropped his board and we fled east through the parking lot, looking back over our shoulders as the metalhead followed, knife hand pumping beside him, eyes flashing. When we reached a cross street, I looked back again to see that he'd returned to the lot to inspect Owen's skateboard. The guy had gotten what he came for, in that Albuquerque way.

I still replay that incident—and the others—in my head. Four of us with skateboards: If we were "real" men, why didn't we just gang up and clobber the guy? Instead of standing there like a useless clod, I picture teenage me raising my pink Alva skateboard, raking the trucks across his face, staving in his flaring nostrils with a jab of the board's tail, and then taking up his knife and exsanguinating him. He lies on the pavement, the PVC pipe clutched to his chest, holding his other hand to a burbling, hissing neck wound. He's fucked with the wrong guy—the guy who will not be a victim. The guy who claims personal power and who chooses fight, not flight. In the days that followed, I replayed the scene that way so many times, I began to feel like I *had* committed a murder. Feeling sharp pangs of guilt, I'd check the papers to see if a body had turned up or the police were looking for suspects.

But it didn't happen that way, not that time and not the others. Not ever, because I'd been raised not to fight; I'd been raised to flee.

Halfway through freshman year, I transferred to Highland High, a public, inner-city high school where most of Albuquerque's core punk-rock kids attended and where, rumor had it, you could dress however you wanted, smoke cigarettes out front, and skate all over the surrounding streets. By then I was a full-bore wannabe punk rocker with a safety pin in my left ear, black combat boots, a long dark-blue trench coat, and a gelled-up Mohawk. To the back of the coat, I'd pinned a bit of T-shirt I'd cut away: cover art for the punk outfit Charged GBH's album *City Baby's Revenge*. It showed a baby wearing a spiked collar and with blood dripping from his mouth who'd taken a hatchet to rats and hung his stuffed-dog toy from a noose in the nursery. I couldn't have stood out more conspicuously. I was a one-man lightning rod at Highland. I'd emigrated with friend and fellow Academy expatriate Jeff, our transfer part of what he, nearly a quarter-century later in an e-mail, would eloquently recall as a "kamikaze brothers' pact," our hopeful launch into a "bitchin' new punk-rock adventure at the cool kids' school" as we left behind the Academy bubble.

Bitchin'.

Mistake. Highland was prison brutal, the halls echoing with the catcalls of the toughs, the rules, boundaries, and allegiances not immediately clear to us newcomers.

Bitchin'.

That first morning I came in through the northeast entrance in my trench coat and "turd-burglar" sweat pants, which had ripped along the seat and which I'd safety-pinned back together, though you could still see my skivvies. I had no idea that each doorway and hall belonged to a certain clique, and that it was best to be selective about where you entered. The halls were jammed, dimly lit, a flood of backs and faces and arms and legs, teeming, vari-ethnic cadres, and booming shouts—a florid chaos so unlike the quiet, orderly Academy.

"See that little motherfucker?" I heard someone say behind me as I punted through the door, eyes glued to the linoleum. "The one with the Mohawk? I'm gonna kick his ass!" The laughter rolled as he and his crew watched me shuffle by.

Bitchin'.

I continued along to the principal's office to get my student ID. The first thing the principal told me, noticing the Charged GBH cut-out on the back of my coat, was, "We don't dress that way at Highland. Don't wear that to school tomorrow."

Bitchin'.

I'm not sure how many days passed before I stopped showing up, but it was no more than a week and change. A mutual friend of Jeff and mine, Josh, shared two classes with me. We all knew each other from skating at the Four Hills ditch, a smooth-sided concrete sluice in the foothills. Josh let me piggyback on his locker and showed me around school, but there was only so much he could do. Even when I was given an assigned locker, I kept my books in a duffel bag. I lugged the bag from class to class, wary of being in one spot, at the locker, in the halls. I would hold my bladder for as long as I could, terrified of heading solo into the bathrooms—the things you do during your first month at a penitentiary.

"I, too, remember feeling that initial fear and shock when we arrived," Jeff wrote in his e-mail, "almost like we'd just landed in prison. Right away it made quaint the little pranky, play-punk stuff we did at the Academy, like slam dancing in the auxiliary gym to a ghetto blaster." The difference was, Jeff endured while I gave up. Those four times getting jumped coupled with Highland's charged, cusp-of-violence atmosphere had conjured in me a critical mass of anxiety—a sick, nauseated bolus that coiled somewhere below my heart. Hypervigilant, scanning for threats, uncomfortable everywhere but home, I'd even taken to carrying a weapon, a butterfly knife with duct-taped handles. I could, in the safety of my own or a friend's house, whip it out and *click-click-click* the blade into place with a hoodlum's flourish of hand. But the likelihood of me stabbing anyone was less than zero. If confronted, I'd surely bobble the knife and see it plunged into my Adam's apple.

Lunchtime was the worst, as I knew almost nobody, didn't want to wander with Jeff and the other punk kids off campus into the sleazy hinterlands near Central Avenue (old Route 66), and was unable to brave the cafeteria. During that hour the various tribes would break off to occupy dominions across the campus, and as fights erupted— seemingly a daily occurrence—the hordes sprinted to encircle and enthusiastically jeer each drubbing. I'd try to find some inconspicuous corner of lawn where I could choke down a sandwich, avoiding eye contact, saying nothing, slouched against my duffel bag, sidestepping the scuffles: a walking mark. The last straw was what I perceived as another hallway threat—this from the biggest, meanest punk-rock kid at school. I'd been heading to class with

Jeff and thought I'd heard the guy say something menacing about my safety-pin earring, but it's doubtful he was even talking about (or to) me, or maybe it was just a compliment. By then I was barely sleeping, locked in a dizzy gray-black fog that smudged day into night. I wanted to be a real punk rocker but didn't have the chops to survive at the "cool school." My perceptions were skewed; the bitchin' punk-rock adventure had become psychological torture.

My parents had always hated the punk-rock thing, and now I get it. I see kids today with black leather jackets and Mohawks, purple hair and Goth eye shadow, tattoos and piercings, and I feel for them. My folks dreaded being in public with me: the comments ("I'd never let *my* kid have hair like that," "Look at that little faggot," "Is that the last of the Mohicans?"), the cross-eyed glances, my own jitteriness in anticipation of the myriad predictable barbs.

Not surprisingly, when I stopped attending Highland, both parents launched in with the "Why do you listen to that terrible, angry music?" spiel. I'm sure they, like anyone with a foundering child, needed a ready scapegoat, but it's not as if a song or two had single-handedly derailed me. As far as I recall, none of the bands I listened to—not Black Flag, MDC, Corrosion of Conformity, the Exploited, the Sex Pistols, Operation Ivy, Poison Idea, Suicidal Tendencies, Killing Joke, Minor Threat, the Misfits, the Angry Samoans, or D.O.A.—had a song called "Get jumped four times, transfer to a scary high school, become agoraphobic, and drop out!" It doesn't work that way, and what a crappy song that would be anyway: The title alone takes more time to say than most punk songs are long!

That final day at Highland, I took myself to the school counselor's office, feigned stomach pain, and called my father to come pick me up. Jeff accompanied me, trying to talk me back into the fray, but I was having none of it. "I would go away to a class and return and you were still there waiting," he wrote me. "[It was like,] 'Come on, kamikaze brother, we've got punk-rock shit to do out here!' Why won't you leave?" I must have waited three hours while my dad wrapped up things at work, my duffel bag at my feet, eyes glued to my boots, not even getting up to use the restroom. I didn't care; I

B eing locked away in a mental hospital: It's not the same as driving past one on the highway or even popping in to visit your mother. When someone else holds the key, everything changes—you cannot leave until *they* say you can. So you do what they tell you to do, and you act like you like it.

The Challenge Program was housed in a school/outbuilding behind Memorial Hospital, part of a gloomy complex at Central Avenue and I-25 that opened in 1926 as a tuberculosis sanitarium but had earlier served as a railroad hospital for employees of the Atchinson, Topeka and Santa Fe Railroad.[1] Today the grounds are empty, enclosed in chain-link fence and on offer for $4.6 million, which buys you the school, a tiny power plant with a creepy smoke-stack, and the vacant horror-movie hospital with its rows of blank windows, gray gargoyles, and two-plus acres of sloped, wooded lot. Here Albuquerque drops toward downtown and the Valley along Central, the city's main artery of funkness, sleaze, and skeeve. I entered Challenge as an outpatient, meaning I showed up at 8:00 A.M. and left at 5:00 P.M. Mornings were spent on lessons: English and literature with one teacher, math and science with another, with a half-hour break between.

Because so much of the program centered on exercise, we all

had to get away from Highland before somebody killed me. It was pure animal terror. Over the next two weeks I refused to leave my bedroom, making half-baked efforts to keep up with my studies remotely but soon giving up even on that. I drew the blinds, left my bed only to visit the kitchen and the bathroom, and slept as much as possible. I'm sure my folks thought I was on drugs—the change had, from the outside, been as sudden as if I'd gotten hooked on methamphetamine. But I wasn't on any drugs, not even pot. As Jeff put it, "Before then, you always seemed so happy-go-lucky, if restless, so this kind of paralysis came on abruptly."

When anxiety and panic set in, it's often that way.

As the weeks passed and my options dwindled, my parents enrolled me in the Challenge Program, one of those outpatient programs for troubled teens, popular in the 1980s. Here I would remain for five months, two weeks of that as an inpatient, until fit to be released into the world again.

wore mandatory sweatpants, so there we were during mid-mornings on our walks: a motley pack of sweats-wearing fuckups shepherded around the local streets, our blue Challenge Program T-shirts on for identification. Afternoons were dedicated to exercise—karate, aerobics, weight lifting, yoga, runs around parks, the occasional hike—and individual, group, or art therapy. When I showed up still wearing my turd-burglar sweats, I was told that wouldn't fly. My mother bought me a pair of fuzzy, blue terry-cloth sweats that were too long, so I cut the cuffs away. The sweats looked tattered like the Incredible Hulk's jeans shorts after he transforms. With those pants on, acne spattered all over my face, and my Mohawk half grown in, I looked as ungainly as I felt.

My favorite instructor, a man who became my friend, was John, our math teacher and also the director of Challenge's outdoor program. His uncle was Warren Harding, who in 1958 had become the first to conquer Yosemite's 2,900-foot monolith El Capitan, the most famed cliff in the world. Some afternoons, John would let us "builder" on the outside of the school. ("Buildering" combines "bouldering" with "building." You seek bouldering-type challenges in the urban environment, from cracks between buildings, to sequences along flagstone walls, to minuscule solution holes—air pockets—up concrete.) Our goal was to circumnavigate the school using a two-inch-wide decorative ledge. We'd shuffle along with our butts pressed out, faces flush to the stucco exterior. Because the traverse crossed over irrigation pipes and big metal sprinkler heads, we'd take turns spotting each other. The most technical bits came when transitioning around the outside corners; you would lean off a window well with one hand, reach the arête with the other, then, as if slow dancing, navigate your pelvis around the bend. I mastered a move—a sort of two-handed vice-grip press on each side of the corner—that held me in place at the crux, poised between "sending" (success) and falling. With form-fitting, specialized rock shoes, which have soft, sticky butyl rubber, the traverse would have been a snap. But we all wore running shoes, which would slop and roll on the ledge. One day a kid careered off at a bad angle and rolled his ankle, putting an end to buildering, which for me had been the highlight at Challenge.

Around this time, my mother enrolled me in the New Mexico Mountain Club's (NMMC) introductory rock-climbing course. She knew that I'd always loved climbing, going back to those earliest Sandias sessions. And starting at age twelve, I'd done at least one week's worth of roped, technical mountaineering and rock climbing in the Cascade and Olympic Mountains of Washington State, where I'd visit my father's college roommate, Bob. A kind, patient, bald-and-bearded mountain man, Bob was my first mentor. He and I, and sometimes his girlfriend and my father, would pile into Bob's eggshell-blue VW van and putter along Washington's tortuous mountain byways to a hotel or trailhead bivouac, and then predawn start on some snow climb, epic hike, or semitechnical peak. I'd even tried Mount Rainier at age thirteen but had turned around two hours shy of the summit due to exhaustion. Bob would pack great, fatty mountain food—Toblerone chocolate, salami, cheeses, and Cotlet fruit bars—that we nibbled on for energy. We'd return from our missions sweaty, depleted, and ravenous, splitting a bag of Fritos or Cheetos as we rallied back to Bob's home outside Olympia. It was from him that I'd first learned to self-arrest on snow, barreling feetfirst, face-first, then headfirst upside-down on a steep slope facing Mount Rainier as I mastered digging in with my ice axe. It's almost impossible to convey the specialness of those early adventures, up among dark, fluted ridges of granite and volcanic rock, skyscraper-high above deep, evergreen-filled valleys, Bob out of sight on a ledge above, the rope snaking upward through protection points as he coached me through the tough spots. Every child should be so fortunate.

I'd return from Washington raving about how much I loved climbing, mourning as I realized it would be another year before I could do it again. My parents had researched local courses at my behest, but you had to be at least fifteen, and there were no rock gyms yet. Skating, meanwhile, was becoming an ever-leaner gruel. During my sad, final semester at the Academy, I'd gaze up from campus at the Sandias with an ache in my heart, at the coruscated pink panels and spires and ramparts in the upper heights only miles away, so close I felt I could touch them. I'd memorized the names of the most prominent cliffs: the Shield, the Needle, the Thumb, massive formations high as the Burj Khalifa and wider than the Hoover Dam. It was up there that I felt I belonged, looking out from some aerie onto the city's flattened grid, safe from the phantoms of random malevolence that roamed Albuquerque's streets.

Other outdoor sports get you out into nature and away from the vicissitudes of civilization, but climbing is the only one that also puts you *above* them. The higher you climb on a peak or big wall, the more your focus on the endeavor becomes total, and the more any life stress drops away. It's why I still do it. For me, climbing is life as it's meant to be lived, in tune with the rhythms of the planet— the flux of the sun, wind, and storms, the flourishing and withering of deciduous plants that spring from the cracks, the changes in air currents—and the true length of the day in rarified places far from mankind and his imbecilic divertissements. There is no feeling of satisfied-tired like the one you get after a full day pushing yourself on the rock. Plus, the kinesthetics of the movement are addictive. In the book *Jerry Moffatt: Revelations*, an autobiography by the top English climber Jerry Moffatt, he shares an anecdote that shows why, to a diehard, climbing is not just sport but lifeblood. Living in caveman squalor in a dingy barn-squat one summer on pennies a day, so that he and a friend could climb nonstop at a nearby crag, Moffatt and company finally take a break one morning and set out to see a BBC Radio 1 traveling roadshow. "There was a couple of open-sided vans with presenters inside, their voices booming out on loudspeakers. They were talking rubbish, but the huge crowd of kids still cheered in all the right places," writes Moffatt. "Some crap band played a song and everyone clapped. They stood around drinking Coke and eating sweets. What were all these kids doing here, I wondered."[2] The climbers promptly turn around and hitchhike back to the cliffs, climbing that very afternoon even though they'd planned a rest day. Once the sport sinks its claws into you, it's like that: Everything else is revealed as crap.

I began climbing regularly at age fifteen. For the first time, I'd found a pursuit that held unadulterated appeal—the competition was against only myself, against my fear and physical limitations. The relaxed, almost transcendental peace I felt at the cliffs, even while I experienced a neophyte's terror at exposure (being up off the ground) and learning to trust the equipment, stood in stark juxta-position to all the urban anguish that came before. My lowpoint in the Challenge Program came during a two-week inpatient stay that February, which I'd requested to escape ongoing discord with my parents. I'd stand at my window come bedtime, bantering with my roomie, waiting for the L-tryptophan the nurses had given me to usher in sleep. I swayed there looking down across Central to where a gaggle of half-frozen prostitutes gathered under the eaves of Milton's Family Restaurant awaiting johns, their breath steam-ing into the night. They'd huff into the cupped bowls of their hands and pace back and forth to stay warm. It was then that I vowed to escape this dystopia and dedicate myself solely to my new love, rock climbing. I threw myself wholeheartedly into the NMMC climb-ing course. It was taught almost entirely by engineers who worked at Sandia National Laboratories and comprised the bulk of the NMMC climbing section. They were a wonky but friendly crew: lots of coke-bottle glasses, tube socks, and groan-inducing puns about the female anatomy.

We pupils began with knot-tying and simulated belay sessions on terra firma, then progressed to toproping, in which the rope is anchored above, meaning you drop only inches in a fall. Toprop-ing is the perfect way to learn the technical nuances of rock climbing, to memorize and apply the different terms for holds— layback, crimp, pinch, fingerlock, Gaston, etc.—the various body positions, and the techniques that let you climb up cracks and overhangs. Climbing gear is expensive, so the club had us use low-cost improvised gear until we were certain of continuing. Thus I climbed in running shoes, a bicycle helmet, my Hulk sweats, and with a "Swiss seat" harness fashioned using twenty feet of nylon webbing. We'd meet on weekends and head for gentle, crystal-studded slabs in the lower Sandias, or out to the dead-vertical black-basalt cliffs near Cochiti Lake or Bernalillo in canyons with Anasazi petroglyphs lining the walls, glum green streams burbling through the depths, and the requisite New Mexico wrecked car or two rumpled in the talus. Slippery beige clifftop silt washed over the rock with each rainstorm, obscuring the white climbing chalk that daubed the holds.

We greenhorns spent hours mastering belaying—securing the rope for your climbing partner. In rock climbing, the "lead" climber goes first, placing protection as she moves and clipping the rope into it with carabiners, or metal snap-links. In what has come to be called "traditional" climbing, the gear is placed in cracks and then removed by the "second" climber, who follows the ropelength (pitch) while the leader belays from above. It's rare that climbers pound in pitons anymore, as nonclimbers might picture with "nails" and "railroad spikes." Instead we use low-impact passively seated gear such as the wired nuts that slot, like chockstones, into constrictions, or actively placed gear like spring-loaded camming devices ("cams") on which you retract a trigger to create pressure between opposing lobes within a crack. Belaying a lead climber requires focus and diligence: Assuming her protection holds, she'll fall at least twice the distance climbed above her last piece of gear. That is, a leader who is ten feet above her last protection point will fall a minimum of twenty feet, factoring in two or three feet more for the stretch of the dynamic rope as well as slack playing through the belay device. The New Mexico Mountain Club imposed belay drill upon belay drill until our final test to become certified belayers: catching a hundred-pound rock dropped from a cottonwood in lower La Cueva Canyon. The instructors would hoist the rock with a three-to-one pulley system, making gleeful, almost sadistic comments, and then drop it repeatedly, having us halt it with a hip belay—in which the rope is brought around the waist—and with a Sticht plate, the earliest mechanical belay device. Anchored to a rock beside the cottonwood, we'd feel the terrible forces upon us and the belay system as we fought to check the fall. So much of climbing is built on this elemental trust between climber and be-layer, roles we exchange fluidly as we move up a multipitch climb or even while "cragging"—climbing on lower, single-ropelength cliffs. You must place a rightful trust in your partner or the center will not hold. In climbing, you become friends for life with people who, as a matter of course, routinely save your bacon.

I can't recall the name of the psychiatrist I saw a few times at Challenge, but he was an old, cold fish whom all the kids hated: pasty and flabby, his mouth full of marbles and ears packed with wax. I'd already begun improving, thanks to the structure imposed by the program, but the doctor nonetheless wanted to try Desipramine, a tricyclic antidepressant like the nortriptyline that was to be my final medicine. The tricyclics are old antidepressants spun off from the infamous Thorazine,[3] a phenothiazine major tranquilizer, or antipsychotic; the major tranquilizers also go by the name "neuroleptic," which means "attaching to the neuron," a term coined by Jean Delay and Pierre Deniker to, as the "antipsychiatry" psychiatrist Dr. Peter Breggin writes in *Toxic Psychiatry*, "underscore the toxic impact of the drug on nerve cells."[4] Tricyclics come with unpleasant antidepressant side effects including cotton mouth, blurred vision, low blood pressure upon standing (orthostatic hypertension, aka a head rush), sedation, lethargy, blunted emotional response, and suppressed gut, urinary, and sexual function.[5] As I'd find out, they're heavy, dirty pills that give you heart palpitations and fatten you like a veal calf. They are also incredibly difficult to taper. Fortunately, I broke into a rash after one week on Desipramine and we stopped the regimen. What ultimately allowed me to be in the world this time was not a pill but desensitization therapy. In my final month at Challenge, I visited Highland twice with the karate teacher, Gerald, and walked through campus to see that nothing bad would befall me. I'd traded in the punk look, too, for a more incognito skate style: maroon Chuck Taylors, a windbreaker, a flat-top hairdo, and simple gold-hoop earrings.

I was lucky I found climbing at this critical juncture. It really could have gone either way. My love for the mountains only deepened after taking a National Outdoor Leadership School (NOLS) Adventure Course in the Big Horn Mountains of Wyoming the summer after Challenge, and the NOLS Mountaineering Course in the Wind River Range the following summer. I kept signing up for NMMC trips, too, and to this day remember the kind mentorship of its core members, who taught me to lead-climb and passed along hand-me-down rock shoes and lead protection. My parents were behind climbing all the way, happy to see me well again; they gladly dropped me off and picked me up at the club's rendezvous spots in town, and helped pay for the expensive equipment. Soon I made a few friends my own age at Highland who were also into climbing, and we formed a little tribe.

I graduated in 1990, a straight-A student despite missing class more and more to go to the rocks. We would tear out of the parking lot after school or cut afternoon lessons to spend half days on the silent, austere vertical panes of welded tuff in the Jemez Mountains, on the bulging andecite of Box Canyon near Socorro, or bouldering in the Sandia foothills. I never felt totally comfortable at Highland and never did keep a locker—I lugged my duffel bag everywhere and spent lunchtime as far from campus as possible—but I made it through without a single fight. Soon, because Highland was academically so unchallenging, I fell into smoking pot, a daily habit from sophomore year nearly until I graduated. High on the Mexican marijuana that flowed freely through town, I'd either read the *Climbing* magazines tucked into my textbooks or sleep with my head on my desk. In a school where I once saw a fistfight, replete with a WWE body slam, break out during a geometry lecture, the quiet, stoned, straight-A kid in the back of the class was the least of the teachers' worries. My high school years were oddly schizophrenic, split between climbing, constant training (road biking, weight lifting, and pull-ups) for climbing, and smoking weed. A few climbing partners liked to burn as much as I did, and getting high on the way to the rocks, at the rocks, on top of the rocks, and beside the rocks was as integral to a day out as making sure your harness buckle was doubled back. Climbing was still a fringe, counterculture sport, and it wasn't uncommon to smell sweet, skunky pot smoke wafting up below the cliffs. The marijuana dulled our pain receptors so that we could climb until our fingers bled, and imparted that single-minded focus you need to "get into the zone" . . . if you weren't too hell-baked to remember where the next hold was. It could also make you unreliable, out of it, and hopelessly scared. You never knew which way it would go until you cashed a bowl and pulled on your rock shoes.

In the mid-1980s, a new style of climbing—so called "sport climbing"—was ascendant in America, having sprouted on the welded-tuff formations of Smith Rock, Oregon, and having also trickled over from France. In sport climbing, the emphasis is on pure gymnastic difficulty, the climbs having left the traditionally protected fissures for the smoother, blanker faces in between. As such, climbers install expansion bolts (construction-grade anchor bolts with stainless-steel clipping hangers), often with power drills and on rappel, a radical departure from the "ground-up" ethos that had dominated since the dawn of mountain climbing, when logic dictated that you begin at the bottom and end at the top. In much the same way that snowboarding split from skiing, causing temporary friction on the slopes, so, too, did sport climbing cause feuding in the climbing world. In the 1980s, sport climbers adopted a punk/new-wave style, wearing garish Lycra dance tights, boasting earrings and flashy hairdos, and either going shirtless or sporting neon-colored tank tops; they might even bring a boom box blasting rap or heavy metal to the crags. These "rads" (versus the "trads") were also known for unapologetic anorexia, in constant pursuit of the perfect strength-to-weight ratio that let them, with less heft to hoist, achieve higher grades. It was considered a badge of honor to be "way honed"—so bereft of body fat that you could see every last rib, vein, tendon, and muscle.

Around that time, my mother and I caught a slideshow from Christian Griffith, a pioneer of sport climbing from Boulder, Colorado. He showed photos and video of a trip he and other Americans had taken to Buoux, France, then the cutting-edge sport "Laboratory" in Europe, and home to some of the first 5.14s. Still wiry to this day, Griffith was open about the radical dieting he saw at Buoux (the Frenchies favored chain-smoking in lieu of food) and his struggle to cut weight to do a 5.13c called *Chouca*. In sport climbing, climbers will rehearse and attempt a prospective climb, or "project," in hopes of a "redpoint": a clean, top-to-bottom ascent without weighting the rope. Much as gymnasts rehearse a single routine for a competition, climbers learn, refine, and ingrain each move (the so-called "beta") such that when that perfect "low-gravity" day comes, when they're feeling snappy and the air is cool, to aid skin-to-rock friction, they put it all together. They might even draw a "beta map"—an informal, hand-sketched topographic outline of the holds and sequences—to study. In trying *Chouca* day after day, week after week, Griffith had taken to starving himself at the cliffs to get leaner; in the throes of his hunger pangs, he'd look longingly upon the plastic bag of dried oats his climbing partner Dale Goddard brought and measured out in precise allotments before each climb. Griffith also took to restricting water, and once even tried *Chouca* in his underwear to cut weight. He would also obsessively tend to his fingers, filing down, gluing, and smoothing them to perfect points that more easily slipped into *Chouca*'s solution pockets.

As he gave his slideshow, Griffith pointed out how unhealthy his behavior had been, and that it was phoning his girlfriend and breaking down to eat a couple of "forbidden pastries" one morning that had finally loosened him up enough to redpoint *Chouca*. But I remember thinking, in this first introduction to real, world-class sport climbing, that I, too, needed to get *skinny* if I were to touch the big numbers, 5.13 and 5.14. And I *wanted* it: In the same way that I'd always pushed myself to get good grades and to exercise, so, too, did it go with climbing. In the early days, in the honeymoon phase, I'd climb five or six days a week, rarely taking rest to let my skin and muscles heal. I'd climb with "flappers" (flaps of skin sliced away by sharp handholds) and "splits" (fissured calluses at the creases in the hand), leaving blood on the rock. I'd climb until my fingerprints wore off, leaving only dewy pink flesh. Meanwhile, cultivating an eating disorder—buliramexia, it turns out—was frighteningly easy, like slipping on an old pair of slippers. Though I'd always been obsessed with exercise and my weight, I started getting truly nutso in the spring of my sophomore year, paring my diet down to the bones. I'd have a General Foods Diet International Café Vienna coffee drink for breakfast, a Diet 7Up and miniature box of Red Hots for lunch, a few corn chips once I came home, and as small a dinner as possible.

To cross-train, I rode my father's old Motobecane ten-speed along the ditchbank paths through Albuquerque, cluelessly hammering in the highest gears for a "better workout" even as the crank barely turned on the hills. At school, I took a weight-lifting class after lunch in lieu of PE; my blood sugar precariously low, I'd feel fainter with each set until my hands shook on the bar. I could sustain starvation for four or five days, then would usually, in a stoned, crazed, late-night fugue, raid the kitchen and devour everything in sight: ice cream, juice, cheeses, bread, Grape-Nuts, the frozen bagels my father kept in the freezer. We liked to go to Dunkin' Donuts on Sundays, my father and I, and if I could make it through the week properly starved I'd allow myself one chocolate-chip muffin. This "sin" would then trigger a "fuck-it-I-broke-the-rules" feeding frenzy until I was so stuffed I had to sleep on my side. After every binge, I was back on the rocks or on the bike, burning off the calories, my stomach glazed in sugars and roiling in protest at having been so rudely shrunken then stretched. And so the cycle continued: bleak, hopeless, unending. Self-starvation is a bugaboo—because you need food to live, it places the brain and the body at odds as food, your sworn enemy, comes paradoxically to occupy your every waking thought as your body cries for nourishment. It's a double torture. All you can think about is cramming sugary, salty, crappy junk into your gob, even as you hate yourself for these cravings, even as you starve down to a skeleton but still see a bloated ogre in the mirror, a mind twist called body dysmorphia. I'd prefer a heroin addiction over one to food: Black tar, for example, has no caloric value.

In my junior year, when I earned my driver's license, our crew started frequenting one of America's first sport areas, Cochiti Mesa, in the Jemez Mountains. Cochiti's welded tuff is dead vertical and apparently blank, the only holds air pockets you can just floss your fingers or toe tips into. The mesa crowns a vast, ponderosa-studded rift on the east flank of the range, the slopes uncoiling precipitously below, leaving you feeling hundreds of feet higher than you actually are. The climbing style is elegant, connect-the-dots movement on which distinctions such as which two fingers you plug into a pocket or at which angle you articulate your ankle dictate success. Contrary to popular belief, rock climbing is not primarily a strength sport. Even physically gifted phenoms—the types who can do one-armed, one-pinkie pull-ups—must move fluidly and with their weight distributed over their feet, as the leg muscles are slower to tire than the forearms. You "crank" upward on the handholds all while pushing off the feet and using your core, or abdominal muscles, and hips to stay parallel to the rock. The permutations of movement are infinite: Every climb might introduce you to some nuanced new move, and only through years of incorporating motor (muscular and neural) programming into your repertoire do you attain mastery. My friends and I loved visiting the Mesa and, safely protected by the bolts, pushing the grades. It was here that I succeeded on my first 5.12, a rounded rib of stone called *La Espina*. With every notch in difficulty, first 5.12a, then 5.12b, then 5.12c, I could feel new horizons opening. It's addictive to chase numbers, to add notches to your belt, but the central advantage is that you get to attempt ever more spectacular climbs—the wild and sequentially intricate 5.13s and 5.14s (and now 5.15s) where the rock is most sheer. I wouldn't do my first 5.14 until 1997, after a long, bumpy, anxiety-filled journey, all totally avoidable had I not been so hell-bent on starvation.

PART TWO

|

PANIC ATTACK

CHAPTER 5

You really shouldn't starve yourself. Limiting calories and depriving myself of certain foods came to have consequences beyond mere hunger pangs; it did long-term physiological and psychological damage. This is because, like the rest of your body, your brain needs proper nutrition in order to function. There are no shortcuts. It all goes down to the neuronal level. Here, starvation can torpedo your neurotransmitters, altering neuron-to-neuron communication and hence how you perceive the world. (Around seventy-five different neurotransmitters have been identified, though the exact number remains unknown.[1]) Our brain's main fuel is glucose converted from carbohydrates, but it also uses amino acids and fatty acids, from protein and fats, to maintain and grow neuronal connections. Eat a diet void of fat, protein, and fresh vegetables, as I did up through my mid-twenties, and you will start to lack the precursors—key vitamins, amino acids, and other molecular building blocks—that neurons use to synthesize neurotransmitters. At which point everything goes wonky.

Published in 1950, one famous—or perhaps infamous—study, the Minnesota Starvation Experiment, tracked a selection of thirty-six young, healthy, emotionally stable men over six months of severely restricted caloric intake. (The men were picked from a pool of one hundred who volunteered in lieu of military service; they ate a pre-scribed average of 1,570 calories per day.) Among the many findings of starvation's curious effects was the revelation that it provoked profound emotional distress. "Almost 20 percent [of subjects] had extreme emotional deterioration that markedly interfered with their functioning," writes David M. Garner, Ph.D., in "The Effects of Starvation on Behavior; Implications for Dieting and Eating Disor-ders."[2] In fact, according to Garner, most subjects "experienced periods during which their emotional distress was quite severe."[3] To escape the experiment (and hence his anguish), one participant, Sam Legg, weighing only 113 pounds at the time, had a car drop onto his fingers in an "accident" and then amputated three fingers from the same hand with a hatchet while chopping wood several days later.[4] Evident among the men was a depression that wors-ened over the months, as well as irritability mixed with frequent irascible outbursts. Most subjects also became anxious, smoking and nail biting to calm their agitated nerves. And they excessively consumed coffee and tea, as well as chewing gum (forty packs a day with one subject, until he developed a sore mouth).[5] Mean-while, one subgroup developed a tendency to binge-eat, in some cases for months after the study had ended. Overall, the men had grown obsessed with food in a dark and unhealthy way.

Coffee, gum, bingeing, food obsession, depression, anxiety, angst—I know these devils. I conducted my own one-man Minne-sota Starvation Experiment until my world broke open. As one friend, a dietitian, Lisa Lanzano, M.S. R.D., who has worked with eating-disorder patients for the last sixteen years, told me, "If you weren't eating anything, it's not surprising that you had the kind of exacerbations of those mood states."

In 1980s and 1990s sport climbing, and certainly also today, "stay-ing light" was seen as the key to performance—our sport's dirty little open secret. In *Jerry Moffatt: Revelations*, Jerry Moffatt con-fesses as much as he ponders retirement after twenty years at the top: "It was feeling like a young man's sport. For years, I had been living on 1,500 calories a day. I was training nearly every day as hard as possible. My immune system was beaten down from all the work. . . . Because of this I was often ill or injured."[6] Moffatt always appeared preternaturally ripped in photographs, his legs with the twiggy look coveted by sport climbers. Given that Moffatt's intake was only 1,500 calories on days during which he probably burned 4,000, his honed physique is hardly surprising. When I look at photos of myself climbing shirtless from my early twenties, I likewise marvel at the fine striations of back muscle, the coils and bindling of ligaments and tendons popping from my shoulders, my breastbone close to the surface, skin papery, rib cage visible, blue webs of vein popping off my hip bones: Climborexic perfection.

Like all obsessed climbers, if Moffatt had a particular goal he might diet even harder. In 1993, Moffatt established one of Yosemite Valley's most difficult boulder problems, *The Dominator*, a concatenation of wicked "power" moves—which recruit explosive muscular force—on fingertip holds out a bald, ten-foot overhang. To succeed, he went on a strict diet. "As a pure power problem, I didn't need any stamina, so didn't need any carbohydrates," wrote Moffatt. "I was keen to lose the weight to give me the edge on that first move and I was so excited about doing it that I could hardly eat anyway."[7] Moffatt ate only salad for a week. His stomach was a "void," and he lay awake come night with his belly grumbling, picturing the moves on *The Dominator*, reckoning that he could eat properly after he succeeded—which he did. I couldn't tell you how many nights I've passed just like this at climber campgrounds, my stomach so braided in knots that I hovered in a twitchy nightmare state just shy of sleep. Or plain awake, I was so hungry. On the worst nights my heart palpitated, spitting spare beats, fighting to find a rhythm even as I deprived it of electrolytes and my body consumed its own fat (not glucose, from carbs) due to ketosis.

My friend Jim Karn was America's top sport climber in that epoch, winning a World Cup event at La Riba, Spain, in 1988 and taking third overall in the World Cup some years later. Karn is tall, lanky, and dark-haired, a whip-smart overachiever who since retiring from the sport has gone on to help design a host of innovative climbing equipment with Metolius Mountain Products. Back in the day, he onsighted 5.13 (did it on his first try, with no prior knowledge of the route) and redpointed 5.14 when such standards were exceedingly rare. (America's first 5.14 was climbed in 1986, a blank, 140-foot vertical wall called *To Bolt or Not to Be*, completed by the French climber JB Tribout at Smith Rock, Oregon.) At six-foot-one, Karn, today an avid mountain biker, weighs a healthy 175 pounds, but at the first World Cup on American soil—in Snowbird, Utah, in 1988—he weighed 142 pounds and was sub-3 percent body fat. Most of the other competitors, who volunteered to be measured, were similarly emaciated. It was almost a point of pride.

"There was a big period of time where people approached the strength-to-weight equation more by reducing their weight," says Karn. "There was a huge culture of that, and like any other trend, you copy it." Everyone knew who was thinnest—you could see it at the cliffs, our shirts off and ribs poking through, giving each other nicknames like "Skeletor" and "The Human Tendon" and "Stick Insect." At the grades of 5.13 and higher, it was hard to escape. Once, watching a competition in Torino, Italy, I noticed a woman competitor so thin that her elastic-banded running socks bagged around her ankles; brittle with starvation, she sat sobbing beside the wall upon being knocked out of the semifinals. Apocryphal tales abounded of self-induced vomiting, of laxative abuse, of a European at the Smith Rock campground downing a packet of crème-filled cookies then showing other climbers how to puke them up in the bushes. Of one climber, who you'd see surviving on chewing gum and cigarettes at the crag, eating then regurgitating his food, pushing the cud around his plate before re-swallowing it. Of a European woman who taped glucose tablets to a hold halfway up a 5.13 at Smith Rock so she'd have the energy to reach the top.

A host of bizarre, fucked-up behaviors.

Karn, living and training much of the year in less Calvinistic Europe, says that he missed the worst of it. Yet he recalls subsisting for a time on a diet heavy in steamed vegetables, without meat or eggs, and that, like so many climbers, he avoided fat altogether for a while. "I started getting wicked flappers [skin tears]," says Karn, "and I figured out that it was because there was no fat in my diet." As soon as Karn added fat back in, his skin issues cleared up. Climbers similarly fell prey to the delusion that having pencil legs was the key to overhanging routes—that leg muscle was undesirable. (While you don't want power-lifter quads, having strong legs and a good aerobic capacity trump having a prepubescent's thigh diameter.) Some climbers thus refused to run or ride bicycles for cross-training, or visit cliffs with long, uphill approaches. Meanwhile, many of us overtrained into chronic exhaustion, with the top Europeans putting in twelve-hour days at the cliffs and then coming home to climb *more* on a home-wall plywood "woodie," running circuits until 2:00 A.M. to up their "volume." Karn recalls pushing himself like a "circus monkey" to his physical and mental limit for three, four, five days in a row, taking one rest day, then going right back to it.

"If you weren't completely exhausted, then you weren't trying," he says. That's just how it was. Karn has since experienced ongoing chronic-fatigue issues, and concedes that undereating and overtraining probably hammered his immune system. "I'm absolutely convinced that I did some type of long-term harm," he's told me.

A byproduct of or at least analogue to 1980s and 1990s Climborexia was a collective dark cloud of rage (see the Minnesota Starvation Experiment). So many of us labored to project a bleak, detached, sarcastic outlook, punctuated only by tantrums—throwing fits, pitching "wobblers"—when we didn't succeed. It was punk-rock nihilism, a natural outgrowth of sport climbing's "rad-boy" schism from the traditional-climbing world. As the logic went, if you didn't get psychotically enraged when you fell, you just didn't care. By the same token, hanging on the rope screaming, "Fuck, I was fucking robbed! I fucking hate this route!" also telegraphed to nearby climbers exactly how "rad" you were: that by all rights you, an amazing talent who of course climbs 5.14-whatever, should have redpointed said route. And that only some exterior factor—the air was too warm; the rope got in your way; your belayer didn't feed slack quickly enough—provoked this undeserved failure. One friend and 1990s survivor, Will Gadd, e-mailed me an unpublished essay he wrote called "The Kids Are Alright" examining the foibles of our miserable generation. He, too, attributes much of our blackness to starvation, what I jokingly referred to as desperate, erratic "concentration-camp" behavior in an e-mail exchange. "A lot of our anger was probably dietary in origin," writes Gadd. "In our attempts to climb harder we decided that every ounce of weight on our bodies was just one more ounce for gravity to act upon." Gadd recalls the omnipresent rice-cake-and-mustard diets, and that "only those who weren't committed to climbing hard used jam or butter, and pretty much nobody with any talent ate anything with fat in it."

No fat equals angry, anxious brain equals raging, psycho fits.

In that epoch, I had so many wobblers that I stopped counting. It didn't help that I didn't lose my virginity until age twenty-two, after five loser years without so much as a date. Though sexual frustration can be a great motivator to achievement in other nonsexual areas of life, I was too callow to see how counterproductive was my anger, how it held me back. Even top climbers might see only one good day in four—it's a difficult sport and climbers are notorious for not resting enough, which leaves your muscles shredded and consigns you to further failure. On routes at your limit you might spend days figuring out the most efficient sequences, then weeks more pushing a new "high point," falling higher on each redpoint attempt. Climbers have, in some cases, spent months mastering a single move, and years mastering a single route. All that failure for a moment of success: It's an idiot's game, and if you can't laugh at yourself you'll become toxic with frustration.

I developed a reputation as an enfant terrible during my formative years in New Mexico and beyond. I once ripped the sole off an expensive rock shoe after failing on a climb my friend Randal had fired as he taunted me with, "Ooh, hardman takes the whipper!" Later I winged a quickdraw (a bartacked nylon runner with a carabiner on each end, used to clip the rope to protection) so hard that it ricocheted off the rock and hit my belayer Scott in the head. I kicked, punched, and chased a two-liter soda bottle through a tangle of ferns, nettles, and deadfall below a Rifle cliff while screaming, "Fuck, fuck, fucking FUCK!" until I'd driven the other climbers away. And most hilariously, I tried to throw my rock shoes into the highway from the hillside bouldering area above Morrison, Colorado, but lacked the pitcher's arm to do so; I had to search for the shoes in a filthy snowbank while my friends mocked me from above. Apparently, I cared a lot. So many of us acted this way, a cadre of irate knuckleheads roiling in our own self-made pressure cooker. Karn, at Rifle, once became so angry upon falling off the last move of a 5.13c that we could hear him screaming a half mile up canyon. Karn's equally talented brother, Jason, broke his toe kicking a wall after he fared poorly in a competition. One friend—name withheld—had a fit that's become lore, becoming so testy with his wife/belayer that she tied the rope off and walked away, leaving him hanging like a piñata until he calmed down. We were all so hungry—for greatness, but also for food.

After high school, I spent a year based out of Albuquerque, applying to colleges—a requirement for living at my father's house—and working as a mover, interspersed with one- to three-month road trips. Basic economics made it easy to stay thin: Paying only nominal rent ($150/month) at my pop's, I'd save up what I could and then once on the road put every last penny toward gas, campground fees, and then, at the bottom of the pyramid, food.

In some strange way, this gypsy lifestyle felt ennobling, from buying canned-goods seconds at dollar stores, to camping down back roads, to taking $2 showers at the KOA. For accommodations, I had a beater REI tent with a busted rainfly I was too cheap to replace, spending stormy nights sloshing in its smelly, wet cocoon. My sleeping pads were just as ghetto, one a thin strip of Ensolite, the other a leaky half-length Therm-a-Rest that I was, again, too miserly to repair. Finally, to combat the cold, I broke down and bought a $10 thrift-store sleeping bag, a cotton bedroll with little deer on the lining. This I wrapped over my synthetic bag for "double protection," or added an itchy red smallpox blanket ($3 at the

Las Vegas Salvation Army store) for triple layering. On nights when the tent became unbearable due to wind or driving rain, we might sleep in my Toyota Tercel wagon, my travel partner and I each dozing upright in the front seats. During a two-day windstorm that drove red sand into my eyes, teeth, and throat at Red Rock Canyon, west of Las Vegas, I finally grokked that I could fold down the Tercel's hatchback seats and stretch out away from the elements. I now had a fine "dirtbag RV," replete with pine-tree air freshener. I crisscrossed the American West with various friends, from New Mexico, to Colorado, to Arizona, to Nevada, to Utah, to California, slumming and climbing five, six days a week, as much as my fingers could handle.

Dirtbag life was good.

"Dirtbag" is a term climbers love: It implies self-inflicted poverty and career avoidance in the name of screwing off to climb full-time. The term has its romantic connotations, evoking images of self-sufficient outlanders with no need for society or its trappings, but instead only the company of "the tribe" and the rocks. In the 1980s and '90s, before America's current explosion of outdoor recreation, before swelling climber numbers put us on land-managers' radar, you could dirtbag more easily. All you needed was some Forest Service or BLM land and you could squat for months. For years at Rifle the favored free doss was the "Dirt Pile," a pullout behind a scary yellow-white tailings heap. I met a consummate dirtbag down at the bouldering area Hueco Tanks, near El Paso, Texas, who survived by resoling fellow climbers' rock shoes out of his van, and another ubiquitous character who squeaked by selling customized climbing T-Shirts and hardware out of the trunk of his car. In Yosemite, the historical heart of American rock climbing, climbers have long survived by "scarfing": risking arrest as they steal half-finished food off tourists' trays at the Lodge cafeteria.

Climbers hate paying for anything. I have friends who've lived for years in tents, caves, or vans rather than deign to work a proper job. I suppose I was only a "half-dirtbag" in the sense that I had my father's house as a home base, though I still embraced the parsi-

mony. Poverty also gave me a handy excuse to do the bare minimum to fuel myself, and I became notorious for my execrable nutrition. Even while friends had tidy food boxes and Igloo coolers full
of produce, cheese, and yogurt, I skitched by with a couple grocery
bags stashed behind the driver's seat filled with whatever crap was
on sale. Usually ramen noodles, Parmesan cheese, store-baked
French bread, Cheez-Its, off-brand Dijon mustard, vanilla-crème
cookies, red vines or Twizzlers, tortillas, refried beans, moldering
cheese, diet hot cocoa (for appetite suppression), and powdered
Café Vienna. When I couldn't take the hunger anymore, I'd power
down a "Cheez-It hoagie": half a loaf of French bread slathered in
mustard and stuffed with crackers. But most nights, too lethargic
from climbing to fuss with my cranky camp stove and boil water
for Ramen, I'd slump in my lawn chair and silo cold beans from the
can, staring at the dirt, saying little. About once a week, we might
hit up an all-you-can-eat salad bar or buffet, shoving rolls into our
pockets to eat back at camp.

I organized my road trips to scope the climbing around prospective Southwest university towns. I had to be near climbing. I'd
passed through Boulder the summer before my senior year in high
school and fallen in love with it. As you near town on US-36, the
Boulder Turnpike from Denver, you crest Davidson Mesa and the
city fans out below, framed by the Boulder Mountains with their
iconic Flatirons, the summits of the Indian Peaks looming behind,
and then Longs Peak, a dark, diamond-tipped hulk to the north. On
the Boulder Mountains' south end, a deep cataract named Eldorado Canyon teems with sandstone cliffs up to eight hundred feet,
while on the north, past the bouldering haunt of Flagstaff Mountain, you'll find Boulder Canyon, a winding defile full of ancient
gray granite. North again stretches gentle Mount Sanitas, its spiny
southern ridges comprised of beetling backbones of maroon and orange Dakota sandstone. Everywhere you look: fields and meadows,
cottonwood-lined ditches and streams, rocks, and mountains. It was
late June and Boulder's many beauties were out in force, wearing
clingy T-shirts and high-cut summer shorts, strolling the sidewalks,

riding bicycles. A young man could be happy here, so I was delighted to learn, in spring 1991, that I'd been accepted into the University of Colorado–Boulder. Like so many climbers drawn by Boulder's reputation as ground zero for American climbing, I emigrated both to pursue my passion and, with the brashness of youth, make a name for myself.

At first blush, Boulder was intense. Even as a college freshman, consigned to the dorms by night but out at the rocks every free hour, I quickly found myself rolled into the fray, bouldering up at Flagstaff and trading belays with famous climbers I'd seen before only in magazine photos. (Boulder had only one gym—today it has *five*—so you'd see everyone either there or at Flagstaff or Eldo after work.) I met personal heroes like Christian Griffith, whose slideshow I'd attended in Albuquerque, and Derek Hersey, a British wild man known for his free-solo (unroped free-climbing) exploits in Eldorado Canyon. Derek, whose mane of dark hair blew upward in Eldorado's drafts as he trusted life to fingers and toes, his wool socks pulled up to his calves, his rock shoes two sizes too big so he could leave them on throughout his all-day climbing binges. And Bobbi Bensman, aka Madame Muscles, a woman so enviably buff and talented that most guys were scared to rope up with her. Or Colin Lantz, tall, wiry, with finger tendons like steel cables who could do Flagstaff's hardest boulder problems in Tevas with a cigarette in his mouth, pulling on holds the size of lima beans. I'd scored a shoe sponsorship in New Mexico to the tune of a few free pairs a year, but my connection at the bootmaker La Sportiva said I might lose it in Boulder, since "there were so many other good climbers." And he'd been right: Whereas in New Mexico in the early 1990s maybe ten people could climb 5.13, in Boulder I stopped counting after my twentieth "honemaster." If I wanted to keep getting free shoes, which cost $150 at the shops, I needed to step up my game, which meant no more food, preferably ever.

I wanted to be just as ripped, just as honed as all the top dogs I was meeting and to whom, in my bottomless insecurity, I felt I'd never measure up. Hell, I wanted to do them one better and be the skinniest and strongest myself. So many climbers move to Boulder with that very notion. Twenty years along, I see younger versions of myself at the gym, freakishly low body fat, shirts off, making "dig-me" grunts as they throw down on some 5.13. I miss that youthful yen to climb hard—in most of us it fades with age, especially as old war wounds creak and ossify. I miss that boundless sense of possibility that comes with athletic improvement at one's physical prime, of feeling the near-godlike potency of "levitating" on microscopic grips out an overhang, the ground skewing away, swifts and pigeons darting past in the ether. I feel fortunate to have even tasted it, even if I was to pay a terrible price.

Conveniently for my Climborexia, I loathed the starchy carnivore fare at the CU dorms, hated eating in the cafeteria with all the cliqueish dipshits, and often returned from climbing so late that I'd missed dinner anyway. Everyone says college is better than high school, but it's not: It's the same tired adolescent crap, only with the volume turned up to eleven because there's no adult supervision. Campus, with some twenty-five thousand students, felt like a teeming mini-opolis that would swallow me whole, brimming with undifferentiated sexual tension, macho posturing, and alcohol-fueled hostility. I never clicked with its party-bro rhythms, and always hated the throngs on campus even though I ended up spending eight years there before I'd completed my master's. Infelicitously, my first roommate was a hard-partier, and also an achondroplasic dwarf—he snored so loudly when he'd been drinking (he slept on his back because of his physiology, though he *could* vomit into trash cans while standing) that I'd try to sleep in the hall, where some drunken hooliganism was usually going on and the lights shone in my eyes. One night as a "prank," one of the besotted morons on my floor soaked my roommate in lighter fluid and tried to ignite him; that was the caliber of behavior. I never fit in—I had no interest in drinking, football games, chasing girls, the Grateful Dead, weed, concerts, fraternities. I wanted only to climb and get on with my studies. Once, as I used the bathroom at Norlin Library, I saw that someone had penned "Hate weed, hate beer, hate parties, hate college" in the stall, which pretty much summed it up.

I was also horribly self-conscious, locked, thanks to Climborexia, in a severe case of body dysmorphia. Attending a friend's party with my dwarf roommate that fall semester, I felt the eyes of my friend's housemates upon us as we approached. Surely they were looking at *me*, repulsed by my hideous, bloated form as I waddled up to the fence (I weighed only 135 pounds). Only twenty years later do I realize that the "spectacle" was my roommate, four feet tall and wearing a loud tie-dyed T-shirt that hung past his knees. And I could barely talk to girls, having spent so much time solely in the company of dirty, sweaty, gassy dudes—unlike today, which edges closer to a 50-50 split, women numbered about only one in ten climbers at the time.

It was better to throw myself into climbing.

Boulder is a magnet for top outdoor athletes, not only climbers but also cyclists, triathletes, runners, mountain bikers, skiers, and so on, who come to train at altitude (a mile high) and for the easy access to open space. It can be overwhelming, confirmed by a trip to the eternally clusterfucked Whole Foods at Pearl and 28th Street, where shoppers' net average body fat hovers around 3 percent and where spandex and GORE-TEX are more prevalent than cotton. Just this morning, my wife and I were walking the dog when a kangaroo-legged runner couple passed by on the path. They trotted at an almost recreational pace, not cantering or sprinting, and Kristin and I turned to each other wondering the exact same thing: Why weren't they running *faster?* That's how it is in Boulder: You get so used to seeing exercise junkies engaging in constant, insane, high-octane workouts that you forget it could be otherwise. It was the perfect place for a fiend like me.

By the end of freshman year I'd starved myself down to 125 pounds. Climbers had just begun developing Rifle in autumn 1991, and I'd gotten on board from the get-go, driving out with friends all autumn, even venturing out in the dead of winter to "stake a claim" on the primo lines by bolting them while it was still too cold to climb. We'd tie red string through the first bolt to mark each "red-tagged project," warning other climbers off. By spring I had bolted and climbed my first 5.13c, a radical sixty-foot climb out a pendulous overhang I named *Fluff Boy*. So clueless was I to just how much my weight loss had made climbing easier that I graded the climb 5.12d, three notches below its true difficulty: a "sandbag rating." Meanwhile, my climbing partners had taken to calling me "Auschwitz Boy," a nickname I embraced.

I don't track what I weigh today—I avoid scales, and will shut my eyes and ask them not to read my weight out loud at the doctor's office—but at last check I was a buck sixty. I'm five foot six and a half, bowlegged, Slavic-stocky with dense slabs of muscle. I don't have the typical lithe "climber's build," but I don't care. I can still climb 5.13, even onsight, which might put me in the top 5 percent of climbers. Good enough. I eat three meals a day, snack when I'm hungry, and eat dessert, every night. If my harness gets too tight or I have a project in mind, I'll drop the dessert for a week—this is as far as the dieting goes. I do not deprive myself of food anymore. I can't afford to.

Here's a typical day from freshman and sophomore year: black coffee for breakfast (10 calories), an apple (100 calories) for lunch, and then Big Red chewing gum for afternoon appetite suppression, a carrot or two for a late-afternoon snack (50-100 calories), and for dinner one strip of fat-free Saltines (20 crackers; 200 calories), rice cakes with salsa (400 calories), and a diet hot-cocoa bonanza (100 calories for, say, four servings) to fleece my stomach into feeling full. A measly 910 fat-free calories, nowhere near even Jerry Moffatt's spartan regimen of 1,500 calories a day. Every fifth or sixth day, I would break down and binge—I would have to, to build up fuel reserves and to stop from obsessing over food—then feel guilty and go back to starvation and exercise. On climbing days, I'd be out all day, come back to my dorm room, do one hundred sit-ups and one hundred push-ups, and perhaps visit the weight room. On rest days, I took solo hikes in the Flatirons, combing through gullies, thrashing through fern groves and poison ivy thickets in search of boulders, a one-liter Nalgene bottle clasped in one hand and not a lick of trail food on me. More than once I found myself dizzy, near passing out high on some hillside as I cast around for errant, early season raspberries.

Never once did I consider that this extreme dieting was not sustainable.

CHAPTER 6

Y ou've had a panic attack," the nurse told me. A stern, middle-aged woman with her hair pulled back in a bun, she held my file in front of her, frowned, looked at me, looked down at the file again. We were at Boulder Community Hospital's emergency room. "Go home," she said. "There's nothing more we can do for you." I sat atop crinkly hospital-bed paper in a little gown, my ass freezing, an IV jammed into my arm, quivering with the chill fluids that infused my veins. The nurse had drawn the green loop of curtain that enclosed the bed, separating it from the others so she could deliver her diagnosis.

A what, now? A "panic attack"? I'd never heard those two words strung together before. The phrase sounded somehow clinical yet Victorian—whitewashed doctor-speak that also connoted a hysterical fit, a swooning away or case of the vapors. It conveyed no hint of the emotional trauma, the raw nerves of the sufferer. A *panic attack:* an *attack* of *panic.* I had no idea that I'd experienced a relatively common anxiety event, and that all of us might at least once, due to some life stressor (lack of sleep, grief, job stress) experience one: the body reacting, writes Foxman, as if "there is a life-threatening situation when in reality no danger exists"[1]—the fight-or-flight reaction pumping adrenaline through your system absent any tangible threat. Hell, even my wife, a sunny blonde, has had one. One night in 2009, she called me from a South Boulder gas station, terror in her voice as she chattered over herself, near-screaming into her cell phone that she was dizzy, couldn't breathe, and had felt herself blacking out on the highway. It turned out she'd visited a chiropractor's office earlier that day, and he'd manipulated her neck too aggressively. Hours of post-visit pain had triggered the attack: the fit arisen seemingly "out of the blue," reaching its full intensity within ten minutes and arousing in "[its] victims fears of impending death," as Restak puts it.[2] With panic attacks, common complaints are a too-fast or erratic heartbeat, sensations of suffocation and the throat closing up, numb extremities, and fear of "freaking out" or "losing control." But a symptoms list will never capture the helplessness and horror. You truly feel like you're going to die.

Physical fear without origin. The first time you feel it, it's a terror like no other, a sourceless and inexplicable wave breaking over you. I'd called the ambulance, this December 1992, from the condominium I shared with two friends, Scott and Amit, east of campus because I was certain I *was* dying. Returning salt-lipped and thirsty from the complex's health club where I'd flogged myself on the StairMaster, I'd gone into the kitchen for a drink and succumbed to a sudden vertigo as I reached for a glass. *Last time I reached in this cabinet, I started to pass out*, I remembered. *Just like this. Reaching for a glass. Then I almost died. Really died. Just two months ago.* Home alone, my heart slamming, gut high and sick, I felt as if death itself had invaded the building. I backed out of the kitchen and fumbled for the telephone, hands shaking violently.

"I'm passing out—I-I think I'm dehydrated," I told the 911 operator, whimpering like some scared old crone. "I'm dying. Please . . . help, send help!" The woman told me to stay calm, that emergency services would be right there. I wrapped myself in a comforter and sat on the couch, Richtering with interior ice, my hands and feet unfeeling. We had a dark, north-facing living room that was swollen with shadows.

A panic attack?

Even though an EKG and a blood test at the hospital had found nothing amiss, I still wasn't ready to leave. I felt so fragile, like I might just walk out the door and spontaneously die. I asked the nurse to clarify "panic attack" and received only a brusque, "It's when you feel anxiety for no reason," by way of an answer.

"But are they dangerous?"

She gave me a look, this harried ER nurse, one that said *I have real patients to attend to.*

"No. It only feels like it. You might want to see a psychologist."

A psychologist? Shit. Really? I hadn't almost died again?

That October, I had nearly snuffed it after Scott and I drove to Rifle for the weekend. Over the summer, he and another friend, Ryan, had sunk bolts in a wild, thirty-foot blue-gray overhang, a feature we named the *Crystal Cave* for the white quartz littering the scree below the cliff. Overhanging 30 degrees, the wall offered features typical of Rifle's Leadville limestone: square ribs of rock, hanging blocks, and strange, almost polygonal facets. Scott and Ryan had made little progress, so Scott suggested I try this difficult climb. That year, a now-defunct British climbing publication, *On the Edge*, had run an article about the country's young guns, one of whom, Malcolm Smith, had trained and dieted monkishly to repeat a 5.14c named *Hubble*. In his interview, Smith copped to eating only greens for months, and the piece was adorned with clip art of broccoli. If veggies had worked for Smith, then they would work for me, too. I took to eating cold green beans from the can, Progresso vegetable soup, fields' worth of celery and carrots, and Pace Picante salsa, which came in gallon jugs, poured over rice cakes.

In late September, I'd started to put the climb together, dialing in its crux leap for a small, square-cut "cigarette pack," karate-chop slaps for blocky sideways holds ("sidepulls"), brutal "underclings" (in which your hand turns upside-down, like a waiter bearing a tray), and a technical "pinch" move, in which the thumb has to oppose the fingers just so. The line had only one real rest—a one-handed shakeout, in which you take an arm off and flick your hand to flush trapped blood from your forearm—so I had to climb quickly, almost at a sprint. Climbs like these are known as "power-endurance" routes, hold-to-hold races in which each move recruits at least 50 percent of your power yet you never encounter a two-handed resting "jug"—a friendly, incut handhold on which to pause, hang straight-armed (off your bones), and recover both arms. On my first real redpoint attempt, I'd made it to the third bolt about twenty feet off the ground powered down but with only five hard moves left. I pulled up rope to make the clip even as my arms "chicken-winged," elbows lifting sideways and out as my muscles failed. Just as I was poised to drop the rope into the carabiner, my hand opened and I whipped off, coils of loose rope falling beside me. As the ground rushed up, Scott sucked slack through his belay device and I came to a halt only six inches above the scree.

It had been worth it, however. I'd tried my hardest.

Scott and I would name the route *Dumpster BBQ*, a nod both to its violent sequences as well as to an incident at the Rifle rest stop along I-70 down in town: Here, a psychopath had "Dumpster barbe-cued" the bodies of an elderly couple he'd slain in Las Vegas, where he'd commandeered their RV and lit out for Denver. We would lis-ten to the dark, pounding, industrial rhythms of Ministry as we drove out to the canyon, making jokes about the Dumpster barbe-cue, and the name had stuck. Even if I felt safer in Colorado than in New Mexico, I still fixated on random, psycho violence this way, as if it posed some personal threat. Rifle wasn't Albuquerque—the violence was tangential to us climbers—but I remember dwelling on this heinous crime all autumn as my mind took a turn toward darkness. In general, climbing areas are out in the boonies where weird things happen, where rednecks, drifters, and other fringe ele-ments go to shoot guns, burn old cars, four-wheel, and drink rotgut. You're out there, out in the Wild, Wild West, and you always need to be aware of who is around you.

That October morning, a Saturday, Scott oozed from his sleep-ing bag in the "Ghetto Meadow," a big, open campsite above the canyon in which we climbers would jam as many cars as possible.

A cesspool of mud, horseflies, and unwashed dirtbags, the Ghetto Meadow also caught good morning sun and had a stream below it, for washing your cooking gear, hands, and face after a long day of climbing.

"Dude, I was up all night puking," Scott said, half-draped out of his bag. An ex–ski racer, he'd shaved off his dreadlocks aka "Rasta pasta" by then, and his curly hair lay matted to his scalp. Scott pointed to a few motley piles near his bedroll. "I don't think I can climb today, but I'll try to belay. Man, I need some water."

"Did you pick up a virus or something?" I asked. Scott took a slug of water from one of the orange-juice jugs he used, and then made a face. He set the jug back beside him. I felt okay, but worried I might succumb myself, *before* trying *Dumpster BBQ*.

"Not sure," he croaked. Scott pointed at a Pace salsa jug we'd left out on the picnic table. "Maybe I had too much salsa, or maybe it went bad."

Shit. I recalled the four salsa-topped rice cakes I'd had for dinner and began to feel queasy—surely just a psychological reflex. But by the time we'd hiked up to the *Crystal Cave* and I put in one doomed-from-the-start, watery-muscled attempt on *Dumpster BBQ*, it was clear that I'd also fallen ill. I'd been in ultra-starvation mode for weeks, my morning coffee had left me desiccated, and any remaining water in my body had been sucked into my intestines. Scott and I retreated for Boulder, feeling pallid and febrile, and with black rings encircling our eyes. A marcid Matt-ghost glared back from the rearview mirror every time I checked on him. I felt too nauseous to drink, and had a splitting headache that increased with my thirst. By the time we pulled in to the condo parking lot, I was unsteady on my feet and bathed in cold sweat. Scott and I stumbled inside, leaving our gear in the car. I beelined for the bathroom, where my bowels voided in a hot, stinking torrent; as I perched sweaty and ignoble on the pot, the screen of my vision went black.

I moaned for Scott, but he'd already retreated to his bedroom. Then, slowly, my vision returned and I wiped myself, flushed, and pushed off the toilet. They couldn't find me this way, dead in the bathroom, awash in my own filth. I needed to get to the kitchen and fetch some water. I weltered in that direction, pushing off the walls, and reached into the cupboard for a glass just as my sight dimmed again. Something had broken inside me, and badly. Fumbling, I set the glass on the counter and staggered into the dining area, where I collapsed to the carpet.

THUD.

"Scott, ermmm, hmmmm, Scott, man, I—" I groaned as I fell. "Help me, help . . ."

The room had gone dark, stars beetling, uncoupling, then recoupling in internal nebulae like when you squint too hard. I needed to shout, to rouse Scott, but I was too weak! By some turn of fate, Scott came out just then to fetch his own glass of water and saw me prone on the floor.

"Dude, should I call 911?" he asked. I could only groan incoherencies, and then managed, "Yes . . . yes. Scott, man, I can't see. *I can't fucking see.*"

"Here, let me help you up," Scott said. He moved me onto a dining-room chair, a cheap, wobbly-legged thing. I felt its upholstery cool beneath my hamstrings.

"I need water," I managed. "So . . . thirsty."

Scott called 911, then brought water. I slouched in my personal darkness, raising the glass feebly to my mouth, dry enough to drink a lake yet only able to take anemic sips. Only had someone shoved a garden hose down my throat might it have made a difference—between the ambulance ride and the ER, they would push six bags of saline drip. With help on the way, I seized on the blindness. Bargaining with God, as one does at these times, I said that I'd be willing to sacrifice my vision if He just let me live. That I could adjust to this. I was *so thirsty*; perhaps if I took just another sip everything would be okay. . . .

The EMTs arrived in minutes and laid me flat on my back. I could hear them bustling around, and felt something cold slide into my arm. Slowly, my sight returned.

"Has he been drinking?" they asked Scott. "Drugs?"

"No," Scott said. "We both got food poisoning or the flu or something."

"No bingeing? You sure?" They busied themselves holding up the IV bag. While I knew they meant bingeing with alcohol—we *were* CU students—I felt guilty, like maybe I needed to confess that yes, a week ago I had eaten an entire Domino's large pepperoni pizza followed by a quart of ice cream. However, it had only been rice cakes and greens since then, so I'm not sure "bingeing" factored in. As I cogitated on this minor semantic distinction, sizzling rods of pain began to shoot through my limbs, especially the big muscles of my buttocks, quadriceps, and biceps, and along my spine.

"Nice veins," one said. "You're strong."

"Yeah," I croaked. "I'm a climber." It was a lucky thing; anyone with less pronounced vasculature would have been a harder stick.

"No. No drinking, no drugs," said Scott. "We were out climbing and drove home because we got sick."

The pain quickly grew worse, forming itself into some cruel entity, a shadow body trying to crowd me out of my skin. "It hurts!" I groaned at the EMTs. A few firemen stood behind them in full garb, ready to help with the carry. Then my back arched off the floor. "It really, *really* hurts!" I said.

"It's okay," someone said. "What you're feeling is shock. Just try to breathe and stay calm. Just try to breathe through it."

My hands and feet had gone icy white, stone-dead numb. All of my muscles were cramping and seizing. It felt like something was trying to crack me open from the inside while another something clenched me in its colossal fist. I took sharp, shallow, hiccupping breaths, my eyes tearing up.

"Fuck . . . just fucking hurts *all over*," I said. "I can't get a breath."

"Let's get him out of here," one of the EMTs said. "We gotta go."

The firemen held the condo doors open while the EMTs carried me on a stretcher to the ambulance. Lying there scared and helpless, I looked closely for the first time at the two men. They had buzz cuts, gym builds, clean-shaven faces: macho types who probably rode Kawasaki Ninjas up the canyons on weekends, who thrived on the ripping adrenaline of situations like this. In a way they were the polar opposite of climbers, who practice our art with as much *control* as possible, who aren't, despite media portrayals, "thrill seekers." We avoid adrenaline rushes and instead consider them the hallmark of bad form: of pushing too hard on a dangerous lead, of going too far into the danger zone on a mountain. Climbers instead crave the sense of accomplishment and *relief* we feel after resolving a hairy situation, having shown poise and mastery despite the possibility of death. We like to sidestep, not confront, the reaper in what is actually a methodical and meditative dance. In climbing, risk is acknowledged—but rarely courted without forethought and preparation. That's another reason I love the sport—it's a fear you can understand and control.

The paramedics loaded me into the ambulance, and it's here, at some unseen intersection, that I almost died. With the vibrations from the siren pinging through the metal, my heart slowed to fifty, forty, thirty beats a minute, *bip-bip-bip—bip—bip—bip* on the little green screen and my blood-pressure dropped precipitously: 90/60, 85/55, 80/45, 70/40. The EMTs shared a look, and I sickened with panic as I saw a grim message transit wordlessly between them: *We're losing him. He's going. He's not going to make it.* I heard their hushed conversation as they worked over me and urged the driver to go faster, faster, *faster!*

Bad salsa had toppled me.

Not this way, not now, not at age twenty when I'd barely lived, when I hadn't yet slept with a woman—or redpointed *Dumpster BBQ!* I could not allow it. A steel cladding of fear from eyebrow to toe tip, then anger: *This will not do! Piss off! Go find someone else!* A transparent death-cloud hovered in the cramped ambulance space, all of us trying to swish it away like a swarm of hovering gnats.

Shoo, shoo, beat it!

One of the EMTs changed out the IV bag and fussed with the tubing, to speed up the flow, while the other said, "Hang in there, buddy, you're doing great," though clearly he meant anything but. The ambulance rattled over the city streets as I spooled back toward blindness, the pain slipping away, looking up at the white metal roof and tiny gold running lights along the equipment bays, seeing them fade, feeling colder, thinking, *This is the last thing I will see, and it's not so spectacular.* The gnats aggregated into an oxygenless miasma, the ambulance interior flattening into two dimensions, cartoonish, derealized, and distant as if projected onto a receding movie screen.

This cannot be happening. And then: *Here we go. This is it. You win.*

Then suddenly I felt a shifting, a crystallization, the running lights becoming crisp again. My heart began to pick up as did my blood pressure, and I felt one EMT squeeze my forearm as he said, "We're almost to the hospital, buddy. You're doing much better. Hang in there, keep fighting." This time he spoke with conviction.

At Boulder Community Hospital, they pushed fluids, had me void in a big steel bowl so they could test for pathogens, and then sent me home with a diagnosis of food poisoning. Another friend, Pete, came to collect me and I had him stop at Walgreens so I could buy three one-gallon jugs of Gatorade. That night I hardly slept I was so waterlogged with the sports drink, up every ten minutes to pee, terrified of dehydrating again. I'd seen just how fragile I was, how suddenly death could bust down your door. I walked around campus for the next two weeks like I was made out of glass—tentative, shambling, a one-liter Nalgene bottle in my book bag, hyperattuned to any minor thirst or dizziness, constantly guzzling fluids. (To this day, my climbing pack is often heavier than my partners' because I pack so many water bottles.) It never occurred to me that I'd fallen ill due to privation and overtraining—that my body and immune system, depleted of vitamins, minerals, and electrolytes, stood little chance against the invasion. And so I went right back to starvation. Two weeks later, I redpointed *Dumpster BBQ* and almost climbed another 5.13c the very next day. I kept on limiting food well into the winter, ever pushing toward 5.14. And then I had my first panic attack.

A "panic attack." I'd had a panic attack. Five weeks would pass before I sought treatment, during which time it flared into a "panic disorder."

Put clinically, a panic disorder is a type of anxiety disorder in which you suffer recurrent panic attacks—or, in the words of the National Institute of Mental Health (NIMH), "an anxiety disorder characterized by repeated episodes of intense fear accompanied by physical symptoms that may include chest pain, heart palpitations, shortness of breath, dizziness, or abdominal distress." Most people will never know this hell: According to NIMH, only 2.7 percent of adults in the United States will, over a twelve-month period, experience a panic disorder, with 4.7 percent experiencing one over their lifetimes.[3] Panic disorders feed and are in turn fed by an insidious fear cycle: You have an attack, obsess over the possibility of the next attack until you're worked into a snit, predictably have that next attack, and so on. I don't care for psychiatric labels, but in this case they're useful in understanding where panic disorder falls on the anxiety spectrum: It often occurs in conjunction with depression and other anxiety conditions like generalized anxiety disorder (GAD: a diffuse, nameless dread that leaves you constantly fretting over routine life events), obsessive-compulsive disorder (intrusive, repetitive thoughts that drive ritualistic behaviors), and post-traumatic stress disorder (PTSD: an agitated, irritable, flashback-prone state upon surviving some profound trauma).

Almost worse than the attacks themselves is the hypervigilance cultivated in sufferers, like Londoners cowering in air-raid shelters during WWII. *When will the next attack occur? What if it's worse than the others? What if my heart gives out? What if this is the one that finally kills me?* are common refrains, and are certainly thoughts that I've had. The sufferer muddles through his days beset by a simmering, low-grade terror that threatens to boil over at any moment—the anticipatory anxiety before the next attack, plagued by racing, obsessive "what if" thoughts. He might complain of body aches, muscular soreness from unconsciously tensing, or a twisting, hollow gut. He might grow further depressed over his lack of control, the way the attacks have shrunk his world to the borders of his home or the few places in which he still feels comfortable. Keen to defuse what feels like an overwhelming situation, he'll begin to pay undue attention to normal, autonomous physical processes like heartbeat and respiration, monitoring for abnormalities or any spike in "attack symptoms." In my case, it manifested as constantly checking my distal pulse and feeling that I had to breathe for my body. Restak nicely describes this shift from the "outside to the inside world," and how it perpetuates panic anxiety: "Even a slight shortness of breath leads to the fear that one's 'throat is closing over'; [and] a minuscule increase in pulse rate foreshadows a deadly heart arrhythmia . . ."[4] When the next attack inevitably comes, fed by the fear cycle, the sufferer gains further proof of his frailty. In time agoraphobia can develop and you can find yourself confined to your home.

On the drive home to New Mexico that Christmas break, 1992, I had another attack, a big one: a panic storm that waxed and waned for hours. Finals-week chaos came on the heels of my ER visit, so I hadn't looked for a psychologist. As I drove through the long, black solstice night, having starved all day, I sank into a deep blood-sugar trough. (Foxman asserts that underreating and bulimia increase anxiety via episodes of low blood sugar "experienced as weakness, irritability, visual fluctuations, impaired attention and concentration, headaches, and fatigue," all cues for an anxiety reaction—think of the last time you subbed coffee for lunch, for example, and how edgy you felt all afternoon.)[5] Somewhere on the inky plains north of Las Vegas, New Mexico, I began to sense an intruder—almost a form or presence—surrounding the car, keeping pace with it. My heart sped up until it was slamming perceptibly, and my hands shook as they gripped the wheel. I felt so far from help, from any hospital where they might "save" me. I was hypoglycemic; I'd probably been hyperventilating for hours, a classic trigger—paradoxically, the more you overbreathe, the higher your body's CO_2 levels and the more difficult it is to draw a full breath, producing a cascade of "air hunger" and suffocation sensations.

Pleading with God, making pacts and promises as I would do so many times, I rolled down my window and stuck my head into the night. A wintry blast lashed my face, a black fist that pummeled the car. *Must. Get. More. Oxygen.* I weaved across the vacant lanes, gulping frigid night air. *Had I become dehydrated again? Would I pass out and crash? Was this another, what was it called . . . a panic attack?* I was too poleaxed to pull over, terrified that I'd simply perish alone in the breakdown lane under a cold bath of stars. I counted the miles to Las Vegas, pulse hot in my throat, my heart thrashing against my rib cage, marking off mileage numbers white and garish on the green highway signs. There I pulled into a gas station, wobbling inside to buy brownies and a Gatorade. The food helped, a little. I got back on I-25, quivering again mere minutes along, my head half out the window for the final 120 miles.

Mortal terror most aptly describes a panic attack: I was sure I would perish at any instant. Until you understand what panic attacks are (and that they don't just come from nowhere) and perhaps even once you do, this will be their imprint; they're that powerful. Your body screams of imminent threat while it floods you with fear chemicals, leaving you no choice but to listen. You're certain you're about to die. For comparison, let me share a true near-death experience in which I felt the same sensations, both physical and metaphysical. It was on a Boeing 767 over the North Atlantic in 2008, the night of July the fourth. That evening, my wife, Kristin, and I had boarded a plane from DC to London, en route to a week's vacation in Ireland. As we dozed around midnight, the captain's voice came over the intercom.

"Well, folks, I have an announcement," he said, in that chummy, Midwestern drawl they all have. "In case you didn't notice, I've turned the plane around and we're headed back toward land. It looks like we've developed a hydraulic leak of some sort—we're not sure where—and we need to get back to an airport pretty quick here, so we're headed to Logan International in Boston. That's about an hour and twenty minutes." Then he added, "I'm sorry for the inconvenience, but had we continued we would not have made it. . . ."

Pause. Pause. Pause.

"Anyway, we'll have you on the ground shortly." And then: "And we anticipate a normal landing."

A normal landing.

Kristin turned to me, her eyes wide, and said, "I love you." I said the same thing. We locked hands and squeezed hard, both of us staring out the porthole at the black ocean and sky death-world whipping by at 500 mph, at this unchanging eternity surrounding our thin tube of thrumming aluminum. We avoided eye contact after that—it just magnified our terror, bouncing it from one of us off the other. The cabin had gone silent, the passengers whispering if they talked at all. The frenetic (and frankly, terrible) Michel Gondry film *Be Kind Rewind* played on the seat-back screens, and Kristin and I tried to distract ourselves with its inane movie-parody skits, though I just kept thinking, *Am I really going to die watching this piece of shit?* Every ten minutes or so, the pilot would interrupt the audio feed to announce things like, "Well, ladies and gentlemen, just four hundred miles off Boston now, and we're still looking good," or, "The folks at Logan know we're landing soon, and are standing by. We still anticipate a normal landing."

We still anticipate a normal landing.

Consider it: 4,800 zombie seconds during which you might, with each one, coast toward oblivion. You look at your watch every five minutes and will the time to pass, or flip to the on-screen sky map to track landward progress. Time oozes stubbornly, if at all, like an oil slick through mangroves. At long last you feel the plane shudder over Boston Harbor, the flight attendants frantically clearing the exit rows because, as you overhear one steward tell a passenger, "We don't know what's going to happen." Twinkling orange sodiums to the side and below, and then, the velvet peninsula of Deer Island slips by on the right: landfall. Bonfires and fireworks in the park, people celebrating the Fourth of July, oblivious to your foundering jetliner.

We don't know what's going to happen.

We touched down as the 767 imperceptibly lost velocity, a banshee howl coming off malfunctioning ailerons that had raised but barely. The crosswise runways were blocked by ambulances and fire trucks, red and blue lights flashing off skid-mirrors of tire rubber. The plane lumbered to a taxi much too far along, well past the airport, everyone on board applauding when we finally slowed. Eighty minutes of *We don't know what's going to happen.* That's a panic attack: X number of minutes of *We don't know what's going to happen,* of an unending fear-filled present. As with a bad fever, you cannot imagine feeling any other way, whether reaching into your deepest past or on into the future: It's a moment in which you're sure, no matter how much evidence is produced to the contrary, that you've locked horns with the reaper himself.

The June 13, 2011, issue of *The New Yorker* ran a heartrending piece by Aleksandar Hemon about his infant daughter's rare pediatric cancer. Meditating on mortality, Hemon devotes a paragraph to the psychological barrier we erect between ourselves and imagining the instant of our own passing—we must, Hemon argues, in order to live, to avoid the paralyzing "attendant fear and humiliation of absolute helplessness" in the face of being eternally but one breath from oblivion. "Still, as we mature into mortality, we begin to gingerly dip our horror-tingling toes into the void," Hermon writes, "hoping that our mind will somehow ease itself into dying, that God or some other soothing opiate will remain available as we venture into the darkness of nonbeing."[6] As I've grown older, lost friends—even had one pass as I held his hand after a battle against lymphoma—and had the myriad near misses of any lifelong climber, I have, in Hemon's words, "matured" into my mortality; I now accept it. But the panic-attack sufferer has no such luxury. Before I beat this thing, every attack, no matter how many others I'd endured, felt like the end—like being back on that 767 but one breath from oblivion.

It's no wonder that panic sufferers will do anything for a little peace.

Home that night in Albuquerque, I sat at the kitchen table trying to explain what I was feeling to my father and stepmother. I could see the concern writ in the creases of my dad's brow as he asked questions. Though he was only in his mid-forties, his hair was almost totally white. My father had originally wanted to go into psychiatry, and I'm sure feared I'd had a psychotic break. Was I seeing things? he wanted to know. Hearing voices or commands?

No, of course not, I told him. I just felt tides of tremendous, sourceless fear that seemed to worsen when I was alone. And maybe, also—it was time to confess—I wasn't eating very well. Which, of course, having seen my mother's eating disorder and how skinny I could get on climbing trips, my dad had suspected all along. "You don't have much subcutaneous fat," he'd say when I returned from the road gaunt and ravenous. "I worry that you're not getting enough calories for being out climbing all day."

Christmas break 1992 was a nightmare, a nauseous, tortured, insomniatic nightmare. Not only hadn't I been eating, now I had such a nervous stomach I barely *could* eat even when I wanted to. I canceled plans to spend two weeks bouldering at Hueco Tanks and tried to climb only once, a jaunt with a friend to Socorro only an hour away during which I had to bail midday as "it" came shimmering over again like toxic drizzle. I'd also come to associate exercise with the fear—with that StairMaster session and ER visit—and refused to get my heart rate up. I stopped jogging. On bad nights, in my peripheral vision, I'd see shadows shifting along the walls, creeping upward like spilled paint in some upside-down mirror world. My best friend, Sky, a nonclimber, was home from Georgetown, so I'd either hang out with him at his dad's house or hole up in my room playing Super Mario Bros and trying to will away the terror. With Sky, I went out once to a record store and again to the movies, and felt "it" happen: In these confined spaces, breathing forced, heated air, I'd begin to "suffocate" and have to run outside to regroup. I had another huge panic attack one night coming back to my dad's while he and my stepmother were out to dinner. Alone in the house, juicing with adrenaline, I called 911 again, my voice so reedy that the EMTs were shocked to find a scared, healthy young man and not an old woman having a myocardial infarction when they rang the doorbell.

Before winter break had ended, I'd agreed to visit my old psychologist in Albuquerque, "Dr. Smith." He was an empathetic, low-key soul who'd counseled me during the Challenge Program years, hip enough that he kept Carlos Castaneda books in his office and would let me borrow them. Dr. Smith was a good listener and engaged in a dialogue of equals, the definition of a solid therapist: someone who cares about *you*—not just your diagnosis—and, without judgment, leads you through the tangled web of your broken thinking. Dr. Smith referred me to his mentor, a professor in CU's psychology department, and I began to see this new therapist, Jack, twice a week. Jack in turn referred me to a psychiatrist, which is often how these things play out—two complementary therapies. Unlike psychologists or therapists, psychiatrists are medical doctors generally focused on a *diagnosis* and on medicating symptoms, who might see you for a quick, fifteen-minute med check-in every three months and tend not to tangle with sticky issues like feelings. This doctor had the standard-issue sleepy demeanor and Sigmund Freud beard. We began experimenting with different antidepressants. The notion was that to treat anxiety you must first address any underlying depression. I tried Pamelor, the name-brand version of nortriptyline, but couldn't deal with the dry mouth, palpitations, and orthostatic hypertension. I quit after a week. We tried Trazodone, an atypical antidepressant, but it made me logy and glassy-eyed, as if I were taking horse tranquilizers; I stopped this drug after only two days. Finally we settled on a low dose (10mg) of Paxil, a selective serotonin-reuptake inhibitor or SSRI, in the same family as Prozac, Luvox, Lexapro, Celexa, and Zoloft. We've all heard of SSRIs, the supposedly cleaner second-generation antidepressants—since 2004 with an FDA black-box suicide warning for children and adolescents—that allegedly outperform the old pills. The party line is that, instead of barraging *all* the neurotransmitter systems, SSRIs are superior because they target only one—serotonin—and thus cause fewer side effects than the old tricyclics and MAOI inhibitors. (SSRIs are thought to increase the bioavailability of serotonin by inhibiting its removal from the synapses—that is, they inhibit the "reuptake" or re-absorption of serotonin by the presynaptic neuron such that more can bind with the postsnynaptic neuron.[7] However, no demonstrable link between this specific chemical action and the treatment of depression has ever been established.) I took Paxil on and off for years, but could never go beyond 10mg without feeling "off"—sped-up, agitated, queasy, and effusive, which is against my nature. It also had undesirable side effects, including an emotional iciness if not a downright aggressive streak, difficulty reaching orgasm, and no longer being ticklish, all of which created issues in romantic relationships. Finally, in 2005, in the throes of benzo withdrawal, an updose in Paxil caused me to be labeled "bipolar" and nearly killed me. I have not taken an SSRI since.

In truth it was a person—Jack—who more than any drug helped restore me to sanity. Together, Jack and I worked through a panic-disorder workbook that tracked things like mood and anxiety levels, correlating them with time of day, food intake, situation, thought patterns, and so on. I also had to note the time of each panic attack, and what was going on in the hour precedent. Fortunately (or unfortunately), the attacks kept coming fast and furious, usually up on campus where I felt surrounded and trapped by my fellow students. As the weeks wore on, I began to see a pattern: low blood sugar, a hot, claustrophobic classroom or lecture hall, an elevation in hyperventilation, and then, finally, an attack. In seeing the pattern, I felt a renewed sense of control: If I could keep my blood sugar stable and learn to recognize and defuse escalating symptoms, then I could derail an episode. I could have my life back. I quickly learned to block catastrophic what-if thoughts and substitute in more sensible notions like, *No, you're not dying of dehydration again—look at how many times you've peed in the last hour.* And *No, you're not having a heart attack. You're young, your heart's strong, and it's just beating more quickly.* I could also adjust my breathing by taking slow, circular breaths in through my nose and out through my mouth. I could place my hands over my belly to bring my attention there and ensure I drew air down deep using my diaphragm, instead of taking hiccupping, upper-chest anxiety breaths. And I could run through the toe-to-head muscular clench-and-release that promoted a sense of calm, even while sitting in class. Soon I even stopped monitoring my distal pulse.

And on days when things were really bad, I could take one of the one-milligram Ativan (lorazepam)* pills the psychiatrist had pre-scribed, tiny white disks barely larger than cupcake sprinkles or spider mites. Like Klonopin and Xanax, Ativan is a fast-acting ben-zodiazepine.

"These are strong, Matt," the doctor told me. We sat in his office, a sunny, upper-floor space in a tony building downtown, the mouth of Boulder Canyon white with snow-frosted pines through the win-dow. "So I'm only going to give you ten a month. They can be addic-tive, and I don't want you taking them all at once."

"Okay," I said. "I'll be careful." I'd never been much into pills, so the idea scared me a little—this notion of their potency. "How, um . . . well, how do I know when to take one?"

"Just keep them with you, and if you have a strong panic attack take a half or a whole pill. Or perhaps on really bad nights if you think you won't get to sleep, take a whole pill before bed."

"Okay."

I filled my prescription at the supermarket and brought home the bottle. It had a droopy-eye drowsiness sticker and a warning not to operate heavy machinery. The pills looked innocuous, so small you'd scarcely notice them going down. They didn't *seem* dangerous.

---

* Here, again, although I often took the generic form of the drug, lorazepam, I refer to it by its brand name to reflect the vernacular usage among psychia-trists and patients.

And yet, if taken too long and/or at too high a dose, and especially if stopped abruptly, benzos can be exactly that.

Benzodiazepines lie in the family of minor tranquilizers, a class of drugs with which America has a long, tangled, love/hate relationship going back to Miltown, the first of the genre, discovered in 1950 and FDA approved five years later.[8] (Pre-Miltown, to squelch anxiety doctors might prescribe alcohol, barbiturates, or opiates. Despite being fundamentally useful and even lifesaving in measured doses, anxiety is also a condition man has long sought to eliminate, and many substance abusers are thought to be self-medicating against it.) Andrea Tone's authoritative *The Age of Anxiety: A History of America's Turbulent Affair with Tranquilizers* gives a great sociocultural recounting of tranquilizers' history, benzos and non-benzos alike. My takeaway from it is that each new anxiolytic (anxiety-reducing) medicine undergoes a boom phase of lavish acclaim and widespread prescription, followed by revelations of addictive properties, and an inevitable backlash. *Huzzah*, we think. *We've finally found the cure for fear.* Then: *Boom, backtrack. The cure, yet again, is worse than the disease. . . .*

Benzodiazepines came into being thanks to Dr. Leo Sternbach, a Polish chemist who developed Librium for the pharmaceutical giant Hoffman-La Roche; this proto-benzo hit the market in March 1960,[9] and by October of that year doctors were writing 1.5 million new prescriptions a month for what was billed as the latest panacea against anxiety.[10] Librium went on to become America's most widely prescribed drug through 1968 and the dominance of its more potent sibling, Valium, another Sternbach creation and the world's most infamous benzo.[11] Valium, aka "Mother's Little Helper" as per the eponymous Rolling Stones song, had hit the market in 1963. It was, writes Tone, "the most widely prescribed pill in the Western world from the late 1960s to the early 1980s"[12] (1968 to 1981). In Valium's banner year of 1973, sales in the United States held at $230 million, or $1 billion in today's dollars,[13] and in 1978 alone Roche sold 2.3 billion tablets.[14]

Over the years, however, it became clear that patients were

becoming addicted to benzos (an estimated 10 million American Valium addicts in the 1970s[15]) and that poly-drug abusers were adding Valium to their quiver, and the pill slipped into disfavor. Then, in 1986, the heavily marketed Xanax (alprazolam), a fast-acting, high-potency benzo, took over as America's most widely prescribed medicine.[16] Never mind that the faster-acting strains are typically more addictive; today, worldwide benzo prescriptions number in the tens of millions. In 2007 in the United States alone, doctors wrote more than 82 million prescriptions for benzos,[17] up from 69 million in 2002;[18] and in 2010 alprazolam was America's eleventh-most prescribed drug, with 46.3 million prescriptions.[19] (After 2000, benzos still represent the leading class of drugs prescribed for anxiety disorders: 38 percent of the top ten drugs prescribed for anxiety, as opposed to SSRIs, which come in second at 21 percent.[20]) Benzos remain ubiquitous, often cited as the most commonly prescribed family of psychiatric medicine, though they do have other applications outside anxiety: for insomnia and seizure disorders, and as muscle relaxants. Physiologically, benzos have five main mechanisms of action: 1) As *anxiolytics*, for anxiety and panic disorders, and phobias; 2) As *hypnotics*, for promoting sleep; 3) As *myorelaxants*, for muscle spasms and spastic disorders; 4) As *anticonvulsants*, for fits due to epilepsy or drug poisoning (they are also administered to detoxifying alcoholics to prevent seizures, and given for acute psychosis with hyperexcitability and aggression); and 5) For *amnesia*—to block short-term memory during premedication for surgery or as sedation for minor procedures like wisdom-tooth extraction.[21] In layman's terms, they knock you flat on your backside. It's precisely because of this potency that benzos can be perilous.

Like the other consummate downers—barbs, alcohol, and Miltown, with which they are cross-tolerant—benzos act on the receptors for gamma amino butyric acid (GABA). GABA, according to Tone, is the brain's "chief and most prolific inhibitory neurotransmitter"[22] and one to which, writes Dr. Heather Ashton, an emeritus professor of psychopharmacology at Newcastle University in the

United Kingdom and the world's leading benzodiazepine expert, about 40 percent of the brain's neurons respond.[23] Indeed GABA, found throughout countless systems in the body, is what our brain and nervous system use to calm themselves—it's "inhibitory" in the sense that it decreases nerve-membrane excitability, reducing the rate of neuronal firing, or the "activating" messages that speed across the synapses like a crown fire through a parched aspen grove. (Restak writes that seizure and anxiety disorders alike are thought to result from too much of such overexcitation in the brain.[24])

On a baseline chemical level, GABA inhibition begins when a nerve impulse releases the neurotransmitter from the presynaptic neuron; this GABA then crosses the synaptic cleft to bind with special GABA-receptor sites on the postsynaptic neuron.[25] (GABA sites, writes Tone, "modulate the emotional states associated with anxiety"; the brain's highest concentration of GABA receptors is in the amygdala, a limbic-system component key to emotional regulation.[26]) This transmission causes the receiving neuron to open and let a negatively charged chloride ion enter, while a positively charged potassium ion escapes. As Jack Hobson-Dupont puts it in *The Benzo Book*, ". . . the electrical potential of the membrane is [thus] increased, which then counteracts any electrical stimulation of the neural receptor."[27] Or as Dr. Ashton frames it, the negative chloride ions "supercharge" the postsynaptic neuron, "making it less responsive to other neurotransmitters—like noradrenalin and epinephrine—which would usually excite it."[28] In other words the activating neurotransmitters that trigger fight-or-flight, and hence panic attacks, are inhibited from spreading their message.

Benzodiazepines, however, are not synthetic GABA: They don't work by binding directly to GABA receptors but instead ligate to benzo-specific subreceptors along the GABA sites, with each subreceptor doing a slightly different duty (e.g., alpha 1 subreceptors are responsible for sedation, alpha 2 for antianxiety effects, and alphas 1, 2, and 5 for anticonvulsant effects, etc.)—though all benzos synch up to varying degrees with the various subreceptors, and all, writes Ashton, "enhance GABA activity in the brain."[29] Taking a benzo can thus be said to *potentiate* GABA, increasing the strength with which the neurotransmitter binds to the GABA receptors. Benzos are therefore "GABA boosters," allowing a greater number of chloride ions to enter the postsynaptic neuron and ultimately make it more excitation-proof. The pills aren't putting anything in your brain that's not already there, but are simply working with what you already have. (As Ashton phrased it in a phone interview, "All benzos do is enhance the action of GABA—they don't work on their own.") Do you recall the locus coeruleus, the little blue spot in the brain that initiates the fight-or-flight response? Well, as Restak writes, "Drugs that decrease the firing rate of the locus stop the panic."[30] And benzos, it turns out, are one of those drugs—by boosting GABA, they have a synergistic dampening effect on norepinephrine, which helps halt the panic response. That's why taking a fast-acting benzo like Xanax or Ativan or Klonopin mid-attack will knock it out—in that sense, the drugs are effective.

At least, that is, until they stop working. The problem is that if you consistently take benzos for too long—more than two to four weeks is a commonly cited time frame—something called downregulation of the GABA receptors can occur. In this process, because the benzos have come to do so much of the receptors' work, the latter's ability to attract GABA, or GABA affinity, diminishes. The GABA receptors become less responsive, "so that the inhibitory actions of GABA and benzodiazepines are decreased," writes Ashton in a scholarly paper.[31] In a conversation with me, Ashton framed it as GABA receptors essentially getting absorbed into the inside of the neuron so that they are no longer on the surface and accessible to the neurotransmitter. In essence, having been phased out by a robot down at the plant, they no longer show up for work and instead stay home to watch TV and eat Doritos. Meanwhile, the robot itself—benzos—needs more and more fuel to do its job.

You're now strung out; you're officially dependent. You "need more and more benzos to get this calming effect," says Ashton. "Or, if you stay on the same dose you go into withdrawal while you still take the benzos"—a bleak phenomenon called *tolerance with-drawal*. In this closed feedback loop, doses climb and receptors invert until your baseline anxiety level is higher than ever, perhaps with thickening storms of panic attacks. You might see tempo-rary relief at each dosage increase, but it's short-lived as down-regulation continues apace. Neither can you keep upping your dose indefinitely, milligram by milligram, for the rest of your life—at a certain point you'll become toxic. Meanwhile you might start to feel "interdose anxiety," common to the fast-acting benzos like Ati-van, Klonopin, Xanax, and Halcion. These pills bind more tightly to receptors and have a shorter half-life than, say, Librium and Valium—they're metabolized much more rapidly, increasing anxiety symp-toms between doses and inciting a "craving" for the next pill. (I say "craving" in quotes because, unlike pleasure-center drugs like co-caine and heroin, which flood the brain with serotonin and dopa-mine, benzos are what Ashton calls "depunishing drugs." Through their GABA-ergic action they "protect against punishing stimuli"[32]—namely anxiety—but won't necessarily get you high except if abused in large doses. They're not really much fun to take.)

The first benzo I took was in February 1992, that spring semes-ter back in Boulder. I'd gone over to some friends' house to watch *Blade Runner*, buying a gallon jug of Carlo Rossi white for us all. Still edgy with free-floating anxiety and also a little bit curious about the pills, I popped one as we cued up the movie. It hit ten minutes later as we watched Harrison Ford track his Replicants, a warm, billowing fog that swelled to fill the room. The Ativan im-parted a feeling of *everything is fine*. Not, *everything is GREAT!*, as you might feel after a rail of coke or a few Vicodin. Just, *every-thing is fine*, as in nothing is wrong, and everything always has been and always will be okay. For the first time in months, my con-nection to the bodily scrutiny and catastrophic thoughts had been severed. I could not have had a panic attack had someone held a gun to my head.

The Ativan was very seductive. In a way—and perhaps because of the alcohol—I did feel "high." It reminded me of the first time I'd been stoned on marijuana, one July night down in Albuquerque, the summer after I'd graduated from the Challenge Program. Leaving The Big Apple, a few of us punks had snuck into a dirt lot across the way and hidden behind a berm. I'd been around weed before but never inhaled, though this night someone explained how I needed to take the smoke down into my lungs and hold it. I did so, coughed, and then did it again. A few minutes later as we walked back toward the club, the world began coming in frames, like over-laid snapshots of itself stitched back together. I felt happy and giddy—almost reassured by the hallucinations. This was a better, more interesting version of reality: the siren song of any psychoac-tive substance. As my feet crunched tangibly over the dirt, I could pick out every pebble and grain of sand, elucidated in crystalline whiteness by the security lights across the way.

Benzos and weed, they didn't feel so different. With both, that initial message that the world was a warm, secure, glowy place and that I was safe in my body was impossible to ignore. I could see why the psychiatrist had urged caution: Notwithstanding the chem-ical component of addiction, on a purely psychic level if you pick up that smooth, laidback, easy-listening station over the airwaves once you'll want to tune in again, even if in trying to banish anxiety forever you end up worsening it beyond your darkest imaginings.

CHAPTER 7

With the benefit of hindsight, my first experience with benzo-diazepine withdrawal came in Italy and Greece, in the summer of 1995. I'd been taking too many pills, and then ran out. I'd been living in Torino (Turin) in northern Italy that spring semester, junior year, for a study-abroad program, but had come mainly to be with my girlfriend, Luisa, an Italian five years my junior. I'd met this lovely girl with bright brown eyes, a rich laugh, nose ring, and dark, lustrous hair at a Christmas dinner at my father's over winter break 1993–94. Luisa lived with close family friends in Albuquerque as an exchange student. As dinner ended, I'd asked Luisa—bored to death, she said, in Albuquerque—if she wanted to ski in Taos, and we'd hit it off on the slopes: my first "date" in five years. Smitten not only with her but certainly also with the notion of female company, once she returned to Italy I'd begun sending Luisa frankly embarrassing missives that professed my infatuation. We started talking weekly by phone. She must have felt something, too, because she agreed to a one-month Eurail trip in the summer of 1994 despite having spent only one day with me. Never mind that she had a boyfriend, who came stumbling into her house drunk and peevish the day I arrived in Torino. By the time Luisa and I hit central Europe, midway through our trip, I'd convinced her of the superiority of the American male. It was either that back-rub in Berlin's Tiergarten or the white wine straight from the bottle one night in Prague's Centre Plaza, but I'd convinced her in my own awkward, fumbling way.

Before I left for Italy, I'd visited the psychiatrist in Boulder to stock up on Paxil and Ativan. He wrote a prescription for sixty Ativan, but the two-milligram size this time, with the idea that it would be easier to travel with fewer pills that I could break in half. I must confess that, with the Ativan, I'd begun to blur the distinction between use and abuse: I'd horde pills the first few weeks of each month, and then wash down one or two a night with wine over the final week. (I dozed through more than a few survey classes the day after my one-man "parties.") It was just like it had been with food: Deprive myself five days out of seven, then indulge to excess the other two. By then I had so few panic attacks that I felt comfortable monkeying around with the pills—I'd even gone off Paxil once or twice, when I didn't feel like I needed it. An improved diet helped as well: I now tried to eat three square meals a day.

That spring in Italy, however, I had had a panic flare-up—heart palpitations, sleeplessness, and night terrors. It would be easy to blame living in a foreign city, or to blame struggling with a new language and culture shock, but that just wasn't the case. I lived only two blocks from Luisa and her family in central Torino, renting an attic room from a mother-and-daughter pair who happened to be friends of Luisa's family. The Italians took great pains to include me in their lives and to help me learn the language. Luisa's parents also had ties to the climbing world—Luisa's father, Luigi, was the director of an Italian publishing house—and he and Luisa's mother, Sandrina, had introduced me to the Torinese climbing community. I had regular partners whom I'd meet weekly at a giant artificial wall at the Palazzo a Vela velodrome or with whom I'd load into tiny Euro-sedans and zip up to cliffs in the nearby Alps. Sandrina loaned her two-door Renault to Luisa and me, and we took weekend trips to Finale Ligure, a spectacular place with pocketed bellies of white limestone dotting lush canyons above the Riviera.

The real problem was that I was starving myself again. The Italians are small, thin hobbit-people, the climbers even more so, and with my thick musculature I'd garner the occasional blunt but well-meaning, *"Sei un po' più grosso di noi Italiani, pero scali come un animale!"* ("You're a little bigger than us Italians, but you climb like a beast!") This only fueled my Climborexia. My main partner was a sometime motorcycle racer, Freddino, a thin man with a moustache who drove like a maniac on the *autostrade* and loved a cliff called Campambiardo, a gneissic plug levering out over a chestnut-covered hillside in Val di Susa. Freddino lived in an apartment building with his extended family and seventeen adopted stray cats, and peppered his speech with colorful, made-up slang like "tanardi" (little cliff critters, like chipmunks). Freddino, at age fifty, could climb 5.13 and had legs twiggy as an ostrich's. "Ciao, big!" he'd say when he greeted me. "Ciao, strong American boy!" It was the only English he knew. With Freddino, I onsighted my first European 8a (5.13b) at a crag called Donnaz in Val d'Aosta, an overhanging face tilted out over an ancient Roman viaduct.

On the hungriest nights I lay awake in bed, the attic ceiling close above as predawn trolleys clacked and echoed along the cobblestone canyon of Via Carlo Alberto outside. Heart palpitations came in waves, quieting only after half an Ativan and a ball of mozzarella scavenged from the kitchen. I was in Europe, the birthplace of hard sport climbing, and I needed to *perform*, which meant staying skinny. And I was climbing harder than ever: I'd redpointed a 5.13d, a few 5.13c's, and was routinely onsighting routes up to 5.13b, which among Torino's rock jocks conferred an intoxicating semistardom as *L'Americano forte* ("the strong American"). The study-abroad program demanded little more than reading art-history books and visiting local castles, so I had plenty of time to frequent the cliffs. One day amidst this manic climbing fest, I became so malnourished that, as I lowered off a 5.13, I could feel my heart squirting dull, barely-there beats, then pounding fiercely to catch up. *Thudda-thud . . . retreat . . . pause . . . pause . . . pause . . . THUD-THUD-THUD-THUD-THUD.* Frightening stuff—a group of us were up at the shadowy black shale plug of Gravere high in Val di Susa, springtime cherry blossoms on the breeze, larch and chestnuts budding along an aqueduct below. My Italian friends talked *frichet-tone*, climber slang, at the base of the wall, oblivious to my plight. Postcard-perfect Alps shimmered snow-covered across the way, mammoth waterfalls spilling from their flanks. *Was I finally having that heart attack? Were these mountains the last thing I'd see?* But never: *What, exactly, was I doing to myself?* I snuck off to pop an Ativan, as I'd learn to do all too covertly and well, returned, and tied back in, setting off up another climb, now feeling a druggie's indifference toward my shaky hands and erratic heartbeat.

When the semester ended so, too, did the Ativan, but I didn't think much of it. I'd never felt any cravings back in Boulder, but then again, I'd never had 120 milligrams of Ativan on hand either, nor taken the pills so regularly. Luisa had final examinations at *liceo* (prepara-tory school), so I booked a two-week solo trip to the Greek island of Corfu to give her space. I left Torino that night by train, in a sleep-ing car on the fourteen-hour voyage south to Brindisi, from where I'd ferry across to Greece. I hadn't taken an Ativan in a few days, but brought along a final pill I'd set aside "just in case." (This straggler had turned to dust by the time I left Europe a month later, bounced around by my travels.) Growing ever more "off" as the train jostled south, I felt a febrile and altogether foreign agitation peak some-where around the middle of the Boot. It was an acute restlessness, my toes clenching and legs twitchy, thoughts racing, a tight band across my forehead and itchiness over my skin, and a close, sweaty feeling of doom: a longing for something lost that I'd not known I had—GABA-ergic dampening of the brain's excitatory neurotrans-mitters. I couldn't place my anguish; it was something new to me. I'd chain-smoked Marlboro Reds my first two months in Italy, trying to fit in with Luisa and her hipster friends, but found that they made it hard to breathe while climbing. However, twenty cigarettes a day don't just let go of you, and I'd gone through a week of spacey, light-headed, dissociated nicotine withdrawal, which had felt physically similar—yet less calamitous. When the train pulled in, I stumbled around Brindisi in a fog, killing time, waiting for the overnight ferry to Greece, wary of the street thieves said to haunt the port alley-ways.

On Corfu during the next two weeks, I'd return from snorkeling in the Ionian and lie on the sand, feeling surges of palpitations and a heavy fatigue I chalked up to too much sun. But this didn't explain why I felt so edgy in a place that was tranquility itself, or kept having nightmares haunted by gray, gnashing-mouthed ghosts—if I slept at all. Only the cider I swilled each night with a group of traveling Texans brought fleeting calm: alcohol, the cross-tolerant downer, affording temporary relief to down-regulated GABA receptors. Random clouds of depression darkened my days. One evening, I'd become stranded far south of my hotel when my moped went kaput on a rough dirt track. I wheeled it to a *taverna* and asked the owner for assistance, and then ordered a Greek salad while I waited. I sat alone at an outdoor table under a trellis cloaked in grape vines, bathed in golden Mediterranean light, eating fresh, homegrown vegetables and feta cheese, pouring olive oil harvested from the surrounding grove onto dark artisanal bread, listening as the *taverna* owner made phone calls to track down the moped-rental guy to come make the necessary repairs. I'd just spent the day on a pristine, empty beach under gauzy June skies, reading trash fiction and snorkeling. Nothing should have been the matter; I should have been perfectly content, taking a pensive island repast like some character in a Henry James novel. But instead I felt a vast emptiness, as if everyone I loved had just been machine-gunned in front of me. Off under an olive tree, ducks milled about in a wire cage. A Greek family stood over them as their toddler son fed bread crumbs through the holes. The ducks darted about pecking at the crumbs, trapped in their cage going nowhere while the kid giggled and pointed and his parents applauded the spectacle.

The dumb, stupid, useless ducks, I thought, taking another bite of cucumber. *That goddamned idiot kid and his asshole peasant parents.*

We're all doomed.

It felt like some dark, hope-gobbling demon had taken up residence in my skull. The ducks were trapped in their cage, the kid was trapped in his infantile ignorance, his parents were trapped in blind love for their idiot child, and only I could see the truth of these matters. Unbeknownst to me, I was in the throes of classic benzo withdrawal, with all the symptoms: anxiety, tremors, sleeplessness, nightmares, agitation, hypersensitivity, depression. The darkness was not my own—normally, I'd be happy to watch a kid feeding ducks; I used to do the same at a pond with my grandparents in Virginia. And likewise unknown to me, by getting hooked and stopping abruptly—a cold turkey that jacked with my GABA receptors—I'd set the stage for potentially more severe withdrawals down the road. It was like the first ripple above a suboceanic earthquake: at first glance a nonentity, but as other ripples press behind it and the wavelets speed toward shore, they merge to form a dark, killing water wall, the sum having become more than its parts. That June in Corfu, I was coming off five months of seminightly Ativan use, and the symptoms did not improve for weeks.

I should have stayed away, but I didn't. That's the thing with drugs: You know that they're bad, you know that you shouldn't get in too deep and that they never, over the long run, make your life better, but you can't overcome your urges with reason. The pills and I, we came to love each other too much. It would be this way for years, getting worse and worse and worse. During my senior year in college, a climbing buddy brought me in on a "thing": A guy he knew was getting blue ten-milligram Roche Valium brought up from Mexico by the trash bag. Only $2 a pill. The first time I bought ten, mostly out of curiosity. I knew Valium by reputation only, and decided to give it a try. The Valium was sludgier than Ativan in that I couldn't do much more than veg in front of the TV after taking one; however, on those nights I fell asleep without a lick of anxious preoccupation, climbing muscles taut and tired turned to carefree jelly. Then I bought twenty, or maybe it was fifty, or perhaps one hundred, or perhaps twenty then fifty then one hundred. With the backward thinking that ensnares so many pillheads, I rationalized that a medically sanctioned, FDA-approved, factory-produced chemical had to be much less dangerous than street drugs like cocaine and ecstasy, which I'd always been too timid to try. Hell, you could even see the milligram count printed on the pill, and meter your dose accordingly. I'd found the secret loophole! I had the golden ticket! These pills were fun! As fall semester wound down, I noticed that one pill no longer cut it, so I'd take two or three or four on weekend nights, usually alone. Pill abuse is funny that way—it's much more antisocial than other drugs. There is no tribal ritual, no sneaking off to do rails in a bathroom stall with your buddies or passing the communal bong. It's just you and your vial and a glass of water, and whatever hermetic stupor that follows. I liked to slide Vivaldi's *The Four Seasons* into my Walkman, stretch back on my futon, wash down the Valium with white wine, and drift into dreamless sleep as the concertos rolled over me. I'd skitch through the week taking just one or one-half pill every night, to round the edges off. A few other climber friends got in on it, and we took to calling the pills "Blue Notes." One buddy kept them in a wooden bowl like Halloween candy, up on his countertop for anyone to sample.

It didn't seem like a big deal.

I visited Luisa in Italy over Christmas break 1995, smuggling thirty Valium in an Ativan bottle. By the end of the first week, I was down to ten pills, wondering just where they'd gotten to. Meanwhile, the Valium had begun to have a curious, unpredictable, paradoxical effect: The more I took, the more crazed I'd sometimes feel, spiked by an uncomfortable mania and then creeping dread as the Valium ebbed away. Benzos can have this so-called paradoxical stimulant effect, which includes symptoms like hallucinations, nightmares, insomnia, irritability, and aggression. Attacks, including assault and even homicide, have been documented, perhaps due to the "release or inhibition of behavioural tendencies normally suppressed by social restraints," theorizes Dr. Ashton.[1] That is, you're both disinhibited by the pills, like an alcoholic after his tenth shot of Jack, and pressurized by the adverse reaction. One morning amidst this chemical typhoon, Luisa dragged me to Balôn, a gritty bazaar near Porta Palazzo in Torino's baroque city center. I loathe crowds, so dropped four Valium before we went, thinking it would help. A half-hour in, moving from stall to stall as Luisa hunted for the secondhand clothing she and another friend would resell, I began to shudder. Tics and spasms coursed along my neck and shoulders. Our breath steamed into the smog, thick with the aroma of roasted chestnuts from the many street vendors.

"What's the matter with you?" she asked. "Are you okay?"

"I think so."

"You're shaking all over. Are you cold, *amore*?"

"I . . . I think it's this Valium," I said. Luisa knew what I was into—I'd slip her a pill here and there if she asked—but she didn't know how deep. I had thought these frissons somewhat chic back in Boulder, almost a druggie merit badge (Valium has myorelaxant properties, so it's not surprising that its withdrawal creates these tics), but now in front of my Italian girlfriend I realized I look like a sad, creepy spastic.

"Well, you need to stop," she said. "I know people here. You're acting very weird, Matt."

"I know. I—I'm just so fucking anxious. Hold on . . ."

I excused myself to find a restroom, ducking into a café in the Moroccan quarter at the edge of the market. Inside, amongst men in fezzes clustered around little granite tables sipping *tazze* of black espresso, I ordered a tea, thinking it might calm me. The barista asked if I wanted milk or lemon.

"*Si-si-si-si-si!*" I said distractedly. *Yes-yes-yes, whatever.*

"*Tutte e due?*" she asked. *You want both?*

"*Si-si-si-si-si!*"

"*Va bene. Come vuole.*" She gave me a look, just as my arms flapped upward in a breakdancer wave and my head gave a quivering wobble. Standing at the counter, I poured the milk into the tea and squeezed the lemon over it. As the citrus hit the liquid, the milk curdled into unappetizing globules: a bad chemical reaction. I looked down, saw the barista watching me with her eyebrows raised, and then drank the tea down in a single slurp. I paid up and left. I rejoined Luisa on the cobblestones and didn't take another pill for the rest of that day.

The Valium ran out midway through the third week, at a snowbound *rifugio* high in the Dolomites. Luisa and I would snowboard all day, take a SnoCat back to the *rifugio* at night, eat a gourmet dinner, and then collapse into bed, warm beneath a heavy duvet. Then suddenly, one evening I wasn't sleeping. I rolled over in bed and looked out the window. An ancient fear emanated from the limestone spires that towered in the night, black daggers etched against the starry firmament. The next day I told Luisa I felt like "everything was all wrong" but I could not for the life of me figure out why.

"Maybe we haven't had enough fruit or vegetables," she said. "Vitamins or something. We've been eating only pasta and cheese. . . ."

It was possible. I ordered extra orange juice with breakfast, but up on the slopes the doom sensation came right back. We ducked into a lodge—another orange juice—but the world still shimmered with menace. The fear felt externalized, cosmic, alien—a sinister cloud that both surrounded and targeted *only me*, that no one else could see or appreciate. The other skiers looked pinch-faced and hostile, their polyglot chatter too harsh and brittle, the sun too bright, the slopes too steep, too blindingly white, the air too thin. By the time we drove back to Torino a day later, I had to keep the car window open on the *autostrada* to let in fresh air despite Luisa's protestations. The next day I was so visibly anxious at the Milan airport, making frequent trips to the bathroom, that an undercover security specialist pulled me aside for questioning. I took my final half-pill on the flight back to America, tumbling in and out of troubled mini-naps as the plane bopped over the Atlantic. I'd cached fifty "welcome home" Valium under my bathroom sink back in Boulder. If I could just make it there, everything would be alright again. That night at the condo, I gobbled five pills, drew a bath, and dove back into the sewer. Vivaldi's *The Four Seasons* sounded even sweeter for my reunion with the Blue Notes.

A month later I'd reached nine pills (ninety milligrams) a night on weekends, with maintenance doses in the twenty- or thirty-milligram range during the week. A few close friends were into clubbing, into raves, and I joined them in a shared nihilistic pre-graduation maelstrom. While they took party drugs, I'd down Valium upon Valium until I felt disinhibited enough to dance, loose-limbed, freaky, and high. At concentrated doses, benzos get you off, and drug addicts have been known to shoot them, combine them with other pills such as opiates to enhance a euphoriant effect, and/or use them to come down from other substances. (In a 1995 paper, Ashton estimated that between 30 and 90 percent of polydrug abusers also abuse benzos.[2]) At these megadoses, I'd become as chummy as the raver kids rolling on E, bopping about hugging each other with their pacifiers, stuffed-animal backpacks, and glow sticks. The Valium also gave me the trots, and I'd spend as much time in the bathroom as dancing, which was probably just as well. "You dance like an animal," Luisa told me one night at a Denver nightclub. She'd come to Boulder for a few months and here I was gobbling Valium like Tic-Tacs, half-soiling myself as I flailed around the dance floor like a coyote in a snare.

Brilliant. I was starting to hate myself. My climbing fitness had lapsed into disrepair (I felt like a slug on the rock), I was half-assing my studies, I spent most of my time either partying or sleeping it off, and I'd begun to lose precious muscle weight—I had the slack skinniness of a drug addict. One night that March, I went over to visit friends at their town house in Boulder, where they kept the Valium out in a bowl. I'd taken a few pills at home and more when I got there. Seventy milligrams, eighty, ninety, one hundred? Who knew . . . Nuked out of my skull, I smoked half of one friend's bag of pot to prove to him that I could worship Jah like Bob Marley. But my buddy soon tired of my antics and went to bed, taking his weed. Another friend and I stayed up slugging wine, and then I spotted a half-dozen napkin rings on the counter by the Valium—black, red, orange, yellow toucan napkin rings in a cute little row. They spoke to me; I had to have them . . . in the biblical sense.

"Hey, Bucko," I said. "Watch this! I'm gonna screw me some jungle bird."

I fetched three rings, sat on the couch, unzipped my corduroys, took out my unit, and started racking the toucans along it. I recall standing up and somehow dancing about with the birds impaled like a child's stacking ring toy.

"*Mrrrpphh, grrrgle, grrrgle, garg*," I kept saying. "I'm a respectable toucan, and you must take that out of my mouth right now! I insist! How dare you?!"

And: "My name's Toucan Sam and I'm a filthy, feathered slut-boy."

And: "Hey, my beak hurts!"

And so on.

"Jesus, Bela," my buddy kept saying, using one of my nicknames. "You're out of your fucking gourd!"

We doubled over, tears of laughter running unchecked down our faces. Nothing had ever been as funny; nothing ever would be again. Finally, when we could stand straight and breathe, I zipped up and replaced the napkin rings on the counter, back where they belonged. I woke up the next day on my friends' couch soaked in drool, clearing away sleep sand and peering toward the kitchen. I could see them up on the counter, those toucans looking back at me with wide, accusatory eyes.

Oh, no. Had I really . . . ?

Yes, apparently I had.

I leapt up, filled the kitchen sink with soapy water, and threw in all the toucans, unsure with which three I'd consorted. I scrubbed and scrubbed, and then scrubbed some more with a bristle brush. People put fancy cloth napkins in these things, napkins that they then held to their lips, and I'd had them *on my cock?* What kind of deranged druggie pervert was I? Just as I was setting the rings to dry on a dishcloth, my friend M walked in to make coffee.

"Hey, Matt, what are you doing with those napkin rings?" she asked. "My mom gave me those for Christmas."

I had no ready answer. And then it hit me: The drugs had to stop. That very day, I quit cold turkey. As with climbing, as with starvation, as with everything I've ever done, it had to be all or nothing—in fact, from all *to* nothing in one fell swoop to create the biggest seismic ripple yet.

Have you been pursued across the galaxy by creatures called Reploids? Have you felt the earth rush, with the mass of each atom, up through the soles of your feet until it feels like your phalanges have been pulverized inside your shoes? Have you felt the ground turn into Jell-O, so that each step feels like pulling your foot from a molasses swamp? Have you had the world come at you in cubes, frames, and impossible Lovecraftian geometries, all objects both living and inanimate become square edged like in the old Max Headroom cartoon? Have you been sure that no matter where you stood it was a psychic North Pole, the globe dropping away and the planet poised to spit you into space? Have you had everything you say and hear spoken sound, echoingly, like it was piped through a culvert? Have you not slept for days? Had tremendous difficulty eating or swallowing? Heard your name called from random spots in the sky? Felt glassy arthritis shards coursing through your arteries? Had your hands and feet go cold, as if frostbitten, and tingle numbly with parathesia? Seen the veins shrink into your arms like earthworms drying on a hot summer sidewalk? Been confused as to where you are and precisely which day it is?

I pray that you haven't, nothing of the sort. Because that would mean that you've endured benzo-withdrawal psychosis, which hit me like a shovel to the face after going cold turkey off Valium. I went clinically loco only two months shy of college graduation—precisely because, as Dr. Ashton wrote in one paper, "Toxicity and Adverse Consequences of Benzodiazepine Use," "Abrupt withdrawal from high doses [of benzodiazepines] can cause a severe reaction, including convulsions and psychotic episodes."[3] The insanity climaxed the second day after stopping. Luisa lay asleep in the bedroom while I jittered on the living room couch, parsing the box for a Mega Man X video game as if this might hold the key to my deteriorating mental state. It had come on quickly, like food poisoning. The night before, Luisa and a friend and I were supposed to attend a punk show in Denver, but I kept waffling about going until finally I'd decided I was too agitated to leave the condo. I felt like I had influenza of the soul. I'd stayed up all night as my thoughts became more pressurized, spitting about the room like deflating balloons. I looked down at the box again. Mega Man, it seemed, had to battle rogue robots called Reploids before they destroyed all things decent in the universe. I couldn't stay here in my dim condo with this video-game box spawning Reploids. I had to go for my morning run.

I laced up my shoes and headed out the door along the Boulder Creek Path, the main bike trail through town. I jogged east toward a vast wetlands, and then hooked south into a neighborhood along an offshoot called the Skunk Creek Path. Like climbing, running had long been a balm against anxiety. I would run at night, in the snow, in the rain, in the wind until my eyes stung and endorphins wrote over any angst. I even ran in Torino where the air was filthy with pollution and diesel exhaust, and you'd get odd looks on the sidewalks as if you were a felon fleeing some crime. This morning it wasn't working: The farther I ran the more convinced I became that the Reploids lurked within the next pedestrian underpass. My feet hurt—terribly—as if my bones were made of fine china, and I could feel the thunder of each footfall clear up to my femurs. Reploids. Too much white sun, buds on the trees, no leafy screen of shade. Reploids. The concrete like a soupy tar pulling at my Nikes. Reploids. Then, from the ether, my name called out: "Matt!" "Matt!" "Matt!" Reploids, careering through space in a crystalline satellite or here already, phasers humming, set to "Kill Matt." Reploids. "Matt!" "Matt!" "Matt!" Thoughts become gluey and tangible, every last syllable (Rep.Loids) and letter (R.E.P.L.O.I.D.S) fat on my tongue as I whispered them into the day. Was I an insect? A dying mantis curled in on itself, vulnerable, sun-blanched, missing a leg—Reploid fodder ripe for the harvest? "Matt!" "Matt!" "Matt!" I'd run a little, take off my sunglasses, put them back on, rub my brow to wipe away Reploids, walk, run, walk, run, sunglasses, Reploids, insects, Reploids, turn around go home NOW ask for help *YOU'RE NOT THINKING CLEARLY SOMETHING IS WRONG WITH YOUR BRAIN.*

Reploids. Back at the condo. *Reploids.* I couldn't bring myself to look at the Mega Man X box, there on the coffee table. *What if they saw me looking? What if they knew?*

"Luisa, baby, I— I— Something is . . . I can't think like I've gone crazy like you've all gone crazy. I can't see very well my head hurts so bad we need to I—"

"Slow down, Matt, slow down." She was making coffee in the kitchen, barefoot in her shift, plunging a French press and looking at me quizzically. So beautiful, like a ghost clad in white, brown tresses spilling over her gown but also slipping away behind a separate frame that radiated from her person.

"I don't know what's wrong. I tried to run. I . . . I'm hearing voices."

"What? You are? What's going on?"

"I didn't sleep and I came out and tried to go for a run to calm down. But it's not working. This is like a bad acid trip or something. Worse, though—*WORSE!* Fuck, I'm all fucking jacked up. I feel like I've been poisoned!" I'd had LSD, which I've taken probably ten times, backfire twice on me in high school, but this felt way worse—somehow more permanent.

"We need to get you to your therapist," Luisa said. "I can't fix this."

I let her lead me to the phone, where I called Jack. I was to see him at 1:00 P.M. up on campus. For some reason, I remember the exact hour of our rendezvous.

"What's going on, Matt?" was the first thing Jack asked. We sat in a third-floor room in a building on campus, more albino March sun streaming in. Too much of it, so thick I could smell it.

"Something seems wrong, Jack. Like everything's coming at me in frames or like I'm going crazy or something. I—I keep hearing my name called out, too, but then nobody's there." I described more symptoms and noted that they had been mounting over the past day. The voices had been haranguing me as I shuffled up Colorado Boulevard to the appointment: "Matt!" *"Matt!"* *"MATT!"*

"It couldn't be Luisa, could it?" he asked. "This sounds almost like a psychotic episode."

"Wait, what? Luisa could make me go psycho?"

"People can have a strong effect on each other sometimes," he said. "But this sounds like something else."

I considered that: a psychotic episode. Naïve then to the real meaning of the word *psychosis*, I immediately conflated *psychopathic* (suffering from an antisocial personality disorder) with *psychotic* (deranged in thought, out of contact with reality).

"You mean, like I'm going to run out and kill people?" I asked. I pictured myself as some sort of Norman Bates, thought of the kitchen knives back home, shuddered, imagined running a butcher's blade into the soft flesh of Luisa's stomach, a blood amoeba seeping across her shift as she clutched at the wound.

"No, no, not at all. That your thinking is distorted, and it sounds like you're having hallucinations. We need to figure out why."

I thought some more, or tried to. I was ashamed of all the Valium I'd been taking, but perhaps it was time to confess on the off chance there was some connection.

"Look, Jack, okay, one thing, just one more thing. I—I was taking lots of Valium over the winter, but I stopped a few days ago because I wanted to clean up. I just wanted to think straight again, to get back into climbing and graduate. So I stopped the pills. But that's over now, so I'm not sure it even matters."

Jack looked at me. He knew something.

"Valium? How much Valium, Matt? Where were you getting it?"

"Just some guy had it . . . a friend. Sometimes up to nine pills, usually three or four. Between four and nine pills a night."

"What size pills?"

"The blue ones."

"The ten-milligram pills?"

"Yeah."

"And you just stopped? Cold turkey? You didn't taper them off?"

"Yeah. I just wanted to be done with it. I was disgusted with my-self."

Jack gave a long, slow exhale.

"Matt, we need to get you to the hospital right away," he said. "Look, you can't just do that. You will have psychosis like what you're feeling now, or have seizures and die. This is extremely dangerous."

"Really?"

"Yes, really."

With Jack's explanation, the Reploids finally retreated: The madness had a source.

By 5:00 P.M. I was in a ward of a psychiatric unit for the second time in my life, behind locked doors, diagnosed and observed. The taxi ride to the hospital, a two-mile straight shot down Ninth Street, had been fraught with chaos and confusion, as if Boulder had become a giant tunnel or sepia inversion of itself. I sat in the backseat kneading my fingers together, trying to keep up with the cabby's banter, sputtering out nonsense like "Your job must be hard"; I could still hear my name being called from side streets. At the ER they checked my vitals—all okay—and then committed me to the Mapleton Center beneath Mount Sanitas. This hospital, this mountain and its sandstone spine, and the neighborhood surrounding would become important again in 2005. Living at Fifth and Alpine just blocks from the Mapleton Center, I would go into a benzo-withdrawal fugue a final time and be committed back on the unit.

I wish I could regale you with lurid tales of depravity at Mapleton, of hissing pipes and peeling paint and steel bars on the windows, of rubber rooms and wild-eyed patients hurling feces at Nurse Ratched, of the lights flickering when they ran the electro-shock machine down in the basement. But the truth is that Mapleton, like most psychiatric wards, was a holding pen, as bland and purgatorial as an airport terminal, with rotating staff too brusque, indifferent, or harried to remember your name. It was a place intended only to stabilize you before your final destination, be it home, jail, a halfway house, or the state mental institution. (These days, insurance companies don't much like to pay beyond three days for psych-ward stays, so the pressure's on to de- or re-medicate you quickly and shove you out the door.) I remained five days at Mapleton, coming out of my fog a little on each. On the bad nights they gave me 0.5 mg of alprazolam—Xanax—so I could sleep, but otherwise they just observed. My brain remained hypersensitive; it recoiled from all stimuli. I wept openly during the inevitable confessional phone call to my father and when Luisa came, sad-eyed and silent, to visit, but otherwise tried to avoid feeling anything. When they brought in some felonious street tough, bloodied and reeking of gin, who'd tussled with a cop, I avoided the newcomer. When a manic, motor-mouthed gnome-man began shouting into the patient telephone that his lawyer was "Gerry Fucking Spence and he knows I'm not crazy and he's going to fucking well get me out of here!" I crossed the ward and shut myself in my room. When a kindly grandfather type, who'd committed himself because he had anxiety issues over his failing health, confessed his fears during group therapy, I had to excuse myself. I couldn't have these impressions entering my mind, where they'd linger and take form like golems.

Two other CU students were in there, C and J. C was over-the-top manic, and would walk around reciting grandiose business plans. He'd developed an obsession with opposites, and wanted to create a line of computers called "Drool Bottoms" to compete with laptops. He had shaved his head, and had a video of the process that I couldn't bring myself to watch. C also had a VHS cassette of old *Schoolhouse Rock!* videos, the educational animated shorts that ran on ABC in the 1970s and '80s. "Conjunction junction, what's your function?" played in the dayroom, the music tinny on the institutional TV/VCR combo. I could almost taste each note, and flinched from the dough-faced train conductor linking "conjunction" cars on the cartoon tracks. The jingle, simple and repetitive with Louie Armstrong–style crooning, sounded unnaturally slowed; it filled me with revulsion, as if it were slime in my eardrums.

In time, there was nothing to do but release me. A social worker sat with me in the discharge room, reviewing my file.

"Look, Matt, you're clearly a sharp guy," he said. He spoke plainly and openly, unlike the cold, arrogant Dr. Whateverthehell who'd vetted me a half-hour earlier with his "Um-hmms" and "I sees" and his fancy pen and reductive symptomology checklist.

"CU student, As and Bs, journalism major, Italian girlfriend, a climber. You've got lots of good stuff going on," the social worker continued.

"I guess."

I held a slim book in my hand, Camus' ruminations on the absurdity of life and its connection to suicide, *The Myth of Sisyphus*. I'd been struggling to read the book on the ward, my concentration diffracted by withdrawal. I'd reached the part where Camus dismisses suicide as an option, and then given up.

"Good book," he said. "I read it a long time ago."

"Yeah, I—"

"You're not thinking of killing yourself, are you?"

"No, no. Not at all."

"Okay, good. We just need to make sure of that. But with these drugs, with this Valium, you know you were doing exactly that, don't you?"

I considered this, said nothing.

"It says here on your chart that you've had some problems with prostatitis this spring—why do you think that is?" he asked.

"I dunno. Drug stress, maybe. The Valium." I'd gone through a period of burning, syrupy micturition—I was practically urinating salt crystals, the pain so sharp it made my eyes tear up as I swayed over the toilet. Antibiotics had followed, coupled with more self-prescribed Valium.

"I would say so. Think of what those things are doing to your body. All that partying, all those pills. You were killing yourself slowly, man, whether you admit it or not."

"To be honest, I never really saw it that way," I said. "I didn't know you could get addicted. I was just taking them because it was fun, because they killed my anxiety for a while."

"Until you're hooked," he said.

"Until you're hooked . . ." I agreed.

"Look, Matt. I'd like you to go to NA—Narcotics Anonymous. If you don't, I promise you I'll be seeing you back here in five years. And neither of us wants that."

"No, no. We don't."

"I mean it."

"I know. I don't want to come back either."

"Will you sign this paper agreeing to go to a meeting, and then we'll let you go?"

"Okay. Fair enough."

I signed; I complied. Then I packed my overnight bag and had them buzz me out of the ward. I bounded down the stairs and out onto Mapleton Avenue, into a gauzy spring afternoon with cotton-candy clouds and Cezanne blue skies. So enamored was I with my newfound freedom that I walked the entire three miles through town and surprised Luisa back at the condo with a big, wet kiss. And I did, as promised, attend that NA meeting. But despite showing up at the time and place listed in the newspaper, I found myself sitting in an empty room up at Wardenburg Health Center on campus. "Hi, my name's Matt and I'm an addict," just doesn't have the same ring when there's no one to hear you. I'd been in this room before, two years earlier, in my hopeless-virgin period for a "Meeting and Dating on Campus" seminar in which, save the instructor, I'd been the only attendee. I hated this room. Fuck this room. I could see the Flatirons outside tilting above Boulder, calling me to climb. I sat there for fifteen minutes and then got up and left.

Fuck this shit and fuck NA, I thought. *I'm going home.*

CHAPTER 8

Thudd-idd-bupp.

Luisa can't sit still either. It's late March 1996, spring break, two weeks after the Mapleton Center and we're at the City of Rocks, a backwater state park near Silver City, New Mexico. She's agitated, biting her fingernails, smoking cigarette after cigarette in the Golf's passenger seat beside me. Luisa is anxious, she tells me, nearly as anxious as myself, drumming my fingers on the steering wheel. We have a CD in, the Jesus and Mary Chain, unfurling slow and electric into the cool desert night. We've come here via Albuquerque, where we stopped for my father's fiftieth birthday party. When he began to mention me in a toast, I frowned and waved at him to stop: *No one needs to hear about your druggie asshole son.* Luisa and I headed south, spent two days climbing outside Socorro on the dark andesite of the Box Canyon. When I pushed myself on a 5.12+ top rope, I felt a sharp ache radiating from my weary prostate, a watery acid-flashback feeling, leaping jitters, spastic muscles that made my movements staccato and chaotic. This will go on for months, almost every time I touch the rock; calm remains elusive. GABA receptors de-invert but slowly.

A full moon rises to paint liquid chrome over the stone gargoyles that surround our campsite, welded-tuff penitentes beetling from the desert like fern buds, a rock "city" replete with corridors and plazas and boroughs and suburbs, a maze with its thousands of boulder problems. The problems have neither names nor ratings, chalk from the few passing climbers carried off by the winds that have sculpted the blobs. I took magic mushrooms here once when I was nineteen; a buddy and I wandered around giggling and bouldering. As the psilocybin reached its peak, I'd been trying to summit a freestanding globe of rock. I had my hands on razor crimps in the Northwest Territories, but couldn't elevate my hips past the equator—I had no idea what my feet were doing down in Patagonia. I fell and fell again until I found a tiny sliver of rock to paste my right foot on out near the Cape Verde Islands. My spine and knees were young then, malleable and strong. My friend spotted distractedly, laughing away at God-only-knows-what. There were other times like this, other drugs, other rocks. It was all part of the culture.

"I never told you this," Luisa says, "but I didn't flush away that Valium like you asked me to from the hospital."

"What?"

"I just couldn't, you know?" She lights another Marlboro.

"You couldn't? I told you to, baby." I didn't want the temptation when I returned home, and furthermore had grown paranoid about having illegally obtained drugs in the house. Too many people, from my therapist on down, knew. Luisa would take a Valium here and there, and she knew which dresser drawer I'd hidden the pills in. But had she really . . . ?

"Look, amore, I was taking more than you thought."

"Why, Luisa? Why? You saw what I was going through. Why would you do that?"

"*Non lo so.* It was just so awful having you in the hospital with those stupid people locking you up, and I couldn't sleep. I was all alone in this *fottuto* condominium in *fottuto* boring Boulder . . ." One evening when Luisa had visited the ward, fellow CU student C was bantering with a psych nurse, trying to explain to her who Vladimir

Lenin was apropos of some political rant. The nurse, a ruddy, dead-behind-the-eyes blonde, just kept repeating, "I've never heard of that one, but I know John from the Beatles!" Luisa's face fell as she overheard this tableau, as she turned to me and whispered, "We need to get you away from these people. They're crazy—the staff, I mean."

"How many?"

"Two or three a night."

"For how long?"

"At least that whole week. Okay, two weeks, *magari tre . . .*"

"Jesus, Luisa. I wish you hadn't." I take her hand; I know exactly what she's feeling.

In time we go to the tent. I'd like to think it's the full moon that keeps us up that night, but the following evening—the new moon, under the Milky Way and a brilliant glaze of stars—we're no less wired, even after a long day wrestling gargoyles.

Thudd-idd-bupp.

"Matt, Luisa viene su a Torino con Sandrina. Arrivano fra poco."

It's Luisa's father, Luigi, calling from their country home outside Bagnolo Piemonte, a mountain hamlet southwest of Torino. His baritone booms across the line. Luigi is six foot five, 300 pounds, a man to be taken seriously. I'm living in a working-class slum on Torino's western edge, renting a one-room apartment up four flights of marble-gloss stairs. I've come here after graduation to be with Luisa, to make a go of living in Italy; Luigi has given me a job translating his magazine's Web site into English. It's June 1996, and the Web is taking off. I commute to work on a bright-orange mountain bike, dodging Fiats, Lanzas, Mercedes sedans, trolley cars, Moroccan windshield-washer kids with squeegees and buckets, the deep-ebony African women, prostituted by the mafia, who haunt the paths of vast Parco Pellerina; inhaling clouds of diesel exhaust; getting drenched by Italy's frequent downpours; showing up to work sweaty and disheveled, so unlike my fashionista coworkers. On the nights I can't sleep—and there are many—I stand on my front balcony overlooking my street. The block across the way is prewar construction, two-story villas with classical red tile roofs in stark juxtaposition to the nondescript box in which I'm living.

"Tutto bene, Luigi? Non c'é problema?"

He pauses, sighs. I don't like this.

"Si, si. Tutto bene, Matt."

"Luisa sta bene? Cos'é successo?" Luisa's okay? What's happened?

"Ti spiega tutto appena arriva."

"Okay." *She will explain everything once she arrives.* Some minutes later Luisa sounds the buzzer.

"It's me," Luisa says, just those two words, flat and emotionless.

I buzz her in and unlock the apartment door. Footfalls echo up the stairs and then she stands before me in well-worn jeans and her favorite white blouse, proffering a red leather puppy's collar and a matching leash, tears sliding down her cheeks. That collar shouldn't be empty—there should be a wee, wiry-haired black Spinone in it.

"Lolita died," Luisa says, and just like that I take her in my arms and we're sobbing into each other. At some point I'm on the bed, punching the wall, screaming, *"No No No No NO!"*

Lolita is a pound dog only two months old, a squeaky ball of unadulterated sweetness. We've had her two weeks, brought her home and washed the pound funk off her in the kitchen sink, had our happiest day in months with her at a cliff near Bagnolo. As we climbed on rough gray gneiss above a roaring streamlet, Lolita wandered about sniffing wildflowers, recoiling as honeybees buzz-bombed her black gorilla nose. *"Le api, Lolita! Le api!"* Luisa said. *"Stai attenta a le api!"* and Lolita looked up, her brown eyes bright. She knew her name after only two days. I climbed a 5.12d onsight that afternoon, moving well for the first time in the post-Valium washout, and Luisa fared nicely on an overhanging 5.11. I felt poised, able to puzzle through sequences before my fingers gave out, moving smoothly from hold to hold as if I'd grabbed them all my life. Gilt late-afternoon sun sliced in across the Alps, and you could taste honeysuckle on the air. I'd shaken all my psychiatric meds, including the Serzone and BuSpar the shrink had tried me on after the Valium debacle. The former, an antidepressant, made me spacey and "Ser-zoned"; it has been pulled from various international markets amid allegations of liver damage that included deaths. The latter, a non-benzo anxiety drug, did precisely nothing; warm milk would have been more effective. I'd been glad to leave the orange bottles behind when I left the United States. It felt like starting a whole new life, one free of chemicals.

Lolita was not so lucky. In Bagnolo that evening, as Luisa prepared to empty a can of wet dog food into a bowl, Lolita sniffed out a similar bowl of insecticide gel on the kitchen floor and mistook it for her meal. By the time Luisa noticed what was happening, Lolita had taken a few bites.

"It was so bad, amore, so so so so bad," Luisa is telling me. "Papá and I loaded her on the moped and rushed down to the veterinarian. Her eyes had rolled up and she was shitting everywhere and foam was coming from her mouth, and it was so bad oh so b-b-b-. . . ." Luisa is sobbing again; so am I. Nothing will fix this.

"The vet got her on the table and she was still alive, still breathing. . . ."

I can picture little Lolita on the steel examination table, her chest madly inflating and deflating like a bellows, her pink cow belly rising and falling too quickly, and then not at all.

"But it was too late," Luisa says. "It was too late to save her. She'd eaten too much poison."

Thudd-idd-bupp.

We're in downtown Ljubljana, Slovenia's green, charming, hilly capital, and the camper van—Luisa's grandfather's diesel Ford *furgone*—is parked somewhere far away. We're walking along the emerald curl of the Ljubljanica River, looking for video-game stores. I'm obsessed with finding Doom II for my laptop. "It" is on me again, a terrorized searing, an interior chemical simmering that has spread to without, and I'm hoping the distraction of the game will help. I don't say anything to Luisa other than that I'm feeling woozy from the heat, from low blood sugar, from the previous week's climbing frenzy at the limestone horseshoe of Misja Pec near the Croatian border. We've come to Slovenia to escape Torino at peak summer heat and to forget the pain of losing Lolita. On a rest day from climbing we ventured to the coast in Croatia, fresh off the Balkan War. We found a rock beach with shelves of black limestone stair-stepping down to the Adriatic, its flat slate-blue plain spreading to the horizon. Fences warning of land mines and unexploded artillery beyond enclosed us on either side: SWIM ONLY HERE. The Croatians seemed jumpy, their pain like the raw nerves of an exposed tooth. We passed bombed-out skeleton towns en route to the sea, the rubble heaped in barrows beside the road.

Luisa and I duck into a department store and buy Chupa Chups lollipops. We take the suckers to a park bench and something—either the pacifier effect or the sugar—brings me down. For a moment. Then the menace returns: As we walk, I can feel it radiate from each sweat-glossed brick in Ljubljana's medieval labyrinth. We drive south that evening toward another climbing area in the Jovian Alps. We stop at a village café for cappuccino. Inside, the locals have flowing beards, long teeth, and names like Drago. They eyeball us, say something about "*due Italiani*," and I think that they want to kill me and rape Luisa. I go to the bathroom and splash water on my face. I'm completely out there, fucked up and paranoid.

I'm not sure why the Valium withdrawal has returned, and so fiercely. It just has. We had a little fun the first week at Misja Pec: Luisa "borrowed" a vial of liquid Tavor—Italian lorazepam—from her parents' medicine cabinet and we'd sip it at night in the van. If I'd been thinking, I might have realized that even a few days taking lorazepam would zero out the withdrawal clock. But I am a pillhead—I probably wouldn't have cared. You should know that about me: For years and years, if I saw something in your medicine cabinet and knew it would get me off, I'd "borrow" it. If I saw the droopy-eye icon, any prescription ending in -pam or -cet or -din or -done, if I saw that admonishment not to mix the medicine with alcohol, to drive, or operate heavy machinery, I would "borrow" a few pills or perhaps more if I thought my crime would go undetected. And if I knew you'd just broken a leg or an ankle but didn't really like those "pain pills that give me a bad stomachache," I'd hound you for leftovers until you forked over the bottle. This is how pill junkies operate. Never mind that I usually had pills of my own: Yours were always better.

Thudd-idd-bupp.

Here's a surprising thing about Italy: For all its Kafkaesque bureaucracy and old-world stodginess, they have lax pharmacies. The doctor issues a prescription and specifies the dosage, then you take that slip of paper to the pharmacist, he stamps it, fetches your pills, and then hands back the prescription. So, unless the doctor has specified, say, "No more than two refills," you can take that same paper to as many different pharmacies as you like—unless and until the day a pharmacist takes a closer look and sees a telltale proliferation of stamps, and reclaims the scrip. At which point, of course, you just return to the doctor for a "refill." Luisa's aunt is a general practitioner, and I mention one night when we visit their apartment that I'm having trouble sleeping. It's October; I've been in Italy since June.

"*Prenditi questi,*" she says, handing me a prescription. "*Sono un po debole, pero ti aiutano ad adormentarti.*"

Take these. They're a bit weak, but they will help you get to sleep. I look down: Ativan, one milligram, box of twenty pills, refills not specified. *Bingo!* Because I have Slavic features—thick stubble and a hard Russian jaw—and because Torino is overrun with barely tolerated Eastern European immigrants, I send Luisa to the pharmacy for me. How many times? Three, four, five, six? At some point, they reclaim the prescription, but by then it's February and I've decided to leave anyway. I'm out of money, my entry visa is expiring, it's clear that my job is thanks mainly to Luigi's generosity, and I miss Colorado. I've spent the last two months holed up at Bagnolo, renting the studio apartment downstairs from Luisa's family's place. I'm living in a converted livestock-feeding area: a *mangatoia*. It's frigid up there, hard against the Alps, but kerosene for the heater is expensive. It's cheaper to buy jug wine, roll up in a blanket, and swill—and take Ativan. I'm ruddy-cheeked, depressed, and fat, and Luisa has taken to calling me *biscottino* ("little biscuit") when she comes up to visit and sees me festering, sloshed in my bedroll. We have another black Spinone now, Magó, and I take him on runs past the eleventh-century castle up the road and on into the foothills, along winding tracks sheathed in frost and littered with fallen chestnuts. My legs are heavy, clumsy, slow; I wheeze with effort. Three days a week I drive to Torino in a beater Peugeot, arriving late after the best parking near the office is taken. I'll often park on a side street, a dirt strip without streetlights that's used come night by *i tossici* (junkies), by *le troie* and their johns. Dirty hypodermics and thousands of frozen condoms full of rotting jism crackle underfoot. There's no avoiding them. *Crunch-crunch-crunch*, I slog toward work. Everyone, apparently, has his vice.

Thudd-idd-bupp.

Rifle, Colorado, spring 1997. I've ended up on Colorado's Western Slope, house-sitting for a climber couple, two friends who've traveled to Australia. One has gifted me twenty Valium, leftovers from a trip to Thailand. The pills are gone in a week; I need melatonin to sleep. Luisa comes out for a month and we take a walk down to the

Colorado River one afternoon, down by the "Dumpster Barbecue" rest area. I feel crazed, scared, nervous about being out and about in a town full of what I perceive to be predatory rednecks, even though the hoariest locals roaring by in jacked-up F-250s don't, I'm sure, spare us a second glance. I'm paranoid is what I am—benzo paranoid. In time it dissolves.

That July I climb my first consensus 5.14, a route that all climbers who have redpointed it consider to be inarguably of that grade. I've met my lifetime goal; all the starving and striving and training have paid off. It's a hundred-foot route called *Zulu* in a giant upside-down bowl named the Wicked Cave. The climb takes its name from two spectacular back-to-back "dynos," or dynamic leaps, between volleyball-sized holes. You need to be as tall, strong, and dynamic as a Zulu to execute the moves, is the idea. I climb it on my fourth afternoon when a cold front comes through. On my second day of effort, I made it two-thirds of the way up but was too pumped—my forearms flush with blood and lactic acid—to stop and clip the bolts. And so I gunned it for thirty feet, sprinting from hold to hold hoping to reach a better stance. I wanted so badly to climb 5.14, I was willing to take that risk. Groaning with fear and exhaustion, my elbows chicken-winging skyward with imminent muscular failure, I finally fell, dropping sixty feet into the trees, snapping branches. So much force was generated that I burned the sheath of my rope as it zipped through the carabiners.

Nothing changed; being a "5.14 climber" changes nothing. I still feel exactly the same inside. I still want more. I'm not taking drugs and I enjoy being clean, but I *still want more.* Two days after *Zulu* I'm already sniffing around for the next project, the next redpoint campaign, the next big rating. When you set out to look over the horizon, you find only more horizon—it's no different with drugs, no different with rock climbing, no different with anything. If you don't immerse yourself in the process, you will never stop craving.

Then something happens: A tick bites me, perhaps at the organic tomato farm where I work, planting and tending to a one-acre field. I'm living hand to mouth, uninsured, dirtbagging, and so let days elapse, a week, until a rash covers my belly and the headaches are so fierce I can't peel myself off the floor. I lie facedown on an area rug by the TV, moaning, until my buddy Charley, out visiting, says, "Man, we need to get you to the doctor." At the clinic they find a tick-borne malady and put me on Cipro, a strong floroquinolone antibiotic. It quickly kills the infection, though I'll suffer joint pain and hot aches for months. I'm back to climbing within days, but what I don't know is this: "Quinolone antibiotics . . . displace benzodiazepines from their binding sites and should not be taken by patients on, or recently on, benzodiazepines,"[1] as Dr. Ashton has written. And I have no idea, as per the collective benzo wisdom I'll find on one Web site later, that "Floroquinolones are probably the worst type of medication to be taken during withdrawal or recovery and should be avoided at all costs," as they have a "very strong antagonistic effect" on GABA receptors and can cause adverse reactions.[2] I have unwittingly sabotaged myself.

The anxiety and the depression return with a vengeance. As autumn thickens into a marrowless, necrotic gel, I feel a black screen creep over my eyes, develop a nervous stomach, take to running the country lanes around Rifle to pound back the fear footfall by footfall. I mourn the separation of each leaf from the cottonwoods lining the roads: the absence of spirit as each yellow-brown folio shivers to earth, there to dissolve. I move back to Boulder to find work, look up my therapist Jack, and ask for a psychiatric referral. Just Paxil at first, ten milligrams to help with the depression—I tell this new doctor, "Dr. Porridge," my Valium story and we both agree that benzos should be a last resort. I begin landscaping for a climber friend, a bon vivant with no "off" switch, like me. He's always holding, and after an eight-year hiatus I start to smoke cannabis again. Just a little at first, to help with aching muscles and job-site tedium: moving rocks, stacking them, unstacking them, restacking them, digging holes, filling holes back in. But I'm soon puffing with gusto when my old friend Ativan returns to dull the weed paranoia. I've talked it over with the psychiatrist, and we reach an agreement that since Ativan is a different benzo than Valium, and since I've never technically *abused* Ativan, it's worth a cautious try. Just twenty or thirty a month to help with anxiety. No big deal.

Have the doctor and I been totally honest with each other? I can't answer, even now. We both know my history. On my end, I should have been open enough with myself (and him) not to request benzos, ever. I should have taken this opportunity and walked away from tranquilizers for good. When he agrees to prescribe them I do feel a little dirty, as if I've put him in a spot. Yet he, the medical professional, might have known better as well, and when I try to quit the pills eight years later I will wonder if his insistence that the benzos have stopped working because of comorbid substance abuse and that the mortal terror I feel as I taper is a rebounding panic disorder—and, later, a diagnosis of bipolar disorder—has more to do with him covering his ass than with any clinical certainty.

In June 1998, the twenty or thirty Ativan a month become sixty-two: two per day, every day. I take a single one-milligram pill in the morning, and the second at night: two white blips barely larger than pinheads, what the doctor calls "prophylactic treatment" or "benzodiazepine therapy." The idea is that panic attacks are prevented before they can start. This is precisely how patients often find themselves trapped: A doctor prescribes "anxiety medicine" on a daily, long-term basis, until down-regulation and tolerance withdrawal set in. Then to offset the tolerance withdrawal, often misdiagnosed as a worsening of the underlying anxiety condition, the dose—and attendant problems, from worsening anxiety and depression, to "emotional anesthesia" or emotional blunting, to gastrointestinal issues, to bizarre neurological issues like tinnitus, parasthesia, and perceptual disturbances—begins to climb.[3] This is what happens to me: Despite my past history of Valium abuse, I will not horde or recreationally abuse the benzos I'm prescribed during this period. Just like a good patient, I will take them only as directed (with only a rare few exceptions—out climbing) like so many others who, despite no prior history of or concurrent substance abuse, find themselves hooked. Take a study group of fifty consecutive patients (ten men, forty women) referred to a National

Health Service clinic Dr. Ashton oversaw from 1982 to 1994. Located in the Wolfson Unit of Clinical Pharmacology (part of the University of Newcastle upon Tyne) and run as part of the Royal Victoria Infirmary, Newcastle upon Tyne, Ashton's clinic was originally called the Clinical Pharmacology Clinic but later simply became the Benzodiazepine Clinic. More than three hundred "brave and long-suffering men and women," as Ashton writes, passed through during those twelve years; most were outpatients, and about 90 percent successfully came off the pills while working with Dr. Ashton on tapering schedules that she and each patient had customized. The patients had been referred by their general practitioners, mostly upon requesting referral help with prescribed-benzodiazepine problems that they themselves had noticed. Dr. Ashton was the clinic's sole physician and worked with each individual on a week-by-week (and sometimes day-by-day) basis, with the aid of supporting nursing staff.

In Ashton's study group, all the subjects had been on benzodiazepine therapy for one to twenty-two years, none were drug or alcohol abusers, and all presented with symptoms so troubling that they wished to be rid of the pills. Their issues were not mere chimeras of hypochondriasis: While on benzos, ten had taken drug overdoses requiring hospitalization, yet only two of these had a history of depression prior to benzos; after several years, ten had developed "incapacitating" agoraphobia; nine had had exams for GI complaints ultimately chalked up to irritable bowel diverticulitis or hernia; three had been diagnosed with multiple sclerosis, a diagnosis not later confirmed; most complained of parathesiae in conjunction with panic attacks; and two had "constant severe burning pain" in their hands and feet.[4] Yet in general, after these patients freed themselves from tranquilizers, the symptoms abated over time—a clear indication of the source of their woes.[5]

I'm neck deep within a month, though I must confess that benzodiazepine therapy rather suits me. My little orange bottle makes me feel special, simultaneously confers something that not everyone gets to have—a psychiatric diagnosis: anxiety—and a "cure" I happen to find chemically agreeable. Like each weekend's project rock climb or prospective alpine adventure, so, too, do I use the pills as enticements, as carrots-on-a-stick to get through the day. At work landscaping, I start each morning with Ativan and a "hippie speedball" (espresso and kind bud) with my boss, smoke all day in the work truck or at the rocks, come home, take my second Ativan and drink Malbec, and just keep that buzzed, glowy feeling burning like a well-stoked ember. I come by my addictions honestly—it's almost a family tradition. On my father's side, his older sister drank herself to death by her mid-sixties; she'd struggled with panic attacks, including periods of benzo addiction, all her life. On my mother's side, she'd had the eating disorder, her mother was an alcoholic, and my uncle died of a heroin overdose in his mid-thirties after years in and out of jail.

Everyone, apparently, has his vice.

Thudd-idd-bupp.

After six years of the long-distance dance, Luisa and I end it. She's a city girl and wants to be in Torino or New York, and I'm a misanthropic urban-agoraphobe. We still love each other dearly, but it will never work. I put her on the bus to Denver International Airport; it seems simpler this way, no hour-long drive full of "what-ifs" and "I'm so sorry, amore." The pain is startling, a suture clear to my heart. I've taken a job as an HTML coder, sipping Theraflu at my desk for a sneaky office-drone high, strapping on earphones, trying to tune out the thirty-odd telemarketers with whom I share space in a big, open office in downtown Boulder, trying not to cry when thoughts of Luisa come crowding in. The end of your first love: It's a grief like no other. I've started coming back to my climbing roots, the so-called "traditional" climbs in which the leader places removable protection—nuts, cams, and so on. In sport climbing, the only mental battle lies in psyching yourself up to try the same climb repeatedly, because every fall is at essence safe—onto a preplaced bolt guaranteed to hold thousands of pounds of force. But in trad climbing, the *head*, the *nerves*, are everything: You have only yourself to rely on to protect a lead and in cases where you must "run it out"—climb great distances between available points of protection. You also need to develop technical proficiency at quickly sizing up and placing the gear, which hangs in a "rack" off a padded shouder sling, and at hanging out in strenuous stances—sometimes by the fingertips of one hand—to tinker with placements. Even then protection can fail; the rock can break or the gear can skate, or you can have neglected to put a long sling on a piece around a sharp arête and your rope might sever in a fall. There are so many variables. It's like chess mated with Russian roulette: skill and savvy + a dash of dumb luck. For this reason, I know 5.14 sport climbers who refuse to lead 5.11 traditional climbs. I take up with trad friends, aficionados of Eldorado Canyon, the local sandstone bastion known for its death routes—climbs with legendary runouts. Something about the calculated nihilism these climbs require appeals to me, of panting twenty feet above micro nuts smaller than pinky nails, committing to a shaky reach off some embedded crystal as I plead with my belayer to "Watch me!" I lead climbs like *Night* and *Inner Space* and *Clear the Deck*, barely protected 5.11 horror routes that might go years without an ascent, collecting dust and bird droppings. Other friends and I get into highball bouldering, trying difficult problems twenty feet or taller over a nest of crash pads, flying to earth when we fail, pounding the cartilage out of our knees. I'm smoking weed nonstop, speeding down Boulder's thoroughfares without a seat belt, cruising home from friends' houses fucked up, downing three glasses of red wine a night, not giving a whit about personal longevity.

And I'm free soloing. I'm taking Ativan, smoking dope, and free-climbing without a rope.

Free soloing is climbing at its purest and most fatal: Alone, without a cord, you free-climb the rock, risking a fall to the ground should anything go wrong—should you get pumped and slip,

miscalculate a move, or break a hand or foothold; should a rainstorm slicken the rock, or a pigeon fly from a crack and thump you
in the chest, causing a startled release. Climbers die soloing, even
the best. Most ardent soloists will at some point either quit, realizing that they can't continue to tempt fate; have a soloing accident
but survive only to dial it back; or perish in the act. Soloing polar-
izes climbers like no other discipline, with some celebrating it as
the highest form of vertical poetry and others reviling it as pointless, juvenile, selfish, and suicidal. I once had a woman, packing up
to leave below a 5.8 crack I'd been waiting to solo, tell me, "Hold on,
I want to get my backpack out of here before you splatter blood all
over it." It's impossible to watch someone soloing and not have a
reaction: The act is so *naked*. I'd dabbled with soloing as a teenager, in that vulnerable period in any young climber's career when
experience has not yet taught you that you're mortal. I quit my senior year in high school after witnessing a friend, Pete, nearly fall
what would have been 150 feet beside me in the Sandia foothills.

In 1998 and 1999 in Boulder, I took to it again, mainly in Eldo and
the Flatirons in a disinhibited demi-deathwish frenzy. Many of the
solos were onsight—sans prior knowledge of the climbs' particular
nuances and sequences. In other words, unlike the "safer" brand of
soloing in which you first practice a climb on a rope, I'd go for it with
limited foreknowledge, heading up after a cursory glance at the
guidebook. I had an oversized gray chalk bag with a bottom zipper
pouch for holding sundries like car keys. In here I'd also shove my
Ativan bottle and a one-hitter. If anything went wrong, went the
reasoning, I could swallow a pill or find a ledge and get high(er).
The drugs were my "belay." I never did anything world-class—my
solos were in the 5.9 to 5.11 range, though often on slippery, licheny,
pigeon-droppings-covered friable rock. I never catalogued or documented any of them; I don't keep a route journal like some climbers.
This commando approach often landed me in trouble.

In spring of 1999 I set out to free-solo a 5.10 called *The Serpent*,
which meanders along a hanging arch on Redgarden Wall, which,
at eight hundred feet, is Boulder's highest cliff. *The Serpent* is a

two-pitch route, but I'd only ever done the first pitch, the 5.10 crux, which made a series of undercling moves along the belly of the arch, your feet dancing across tiny rugosities below. The guidebook confirmed that the second pitch was "only" 5.9, so I paid little attention to where it went. Screw it—I could sort it out when I got there. I climbed through the first pitch to a ledge separating the two ropelengths, regrouped, then set off along a layback crack that dead-ended at a blocky overhang—a "roof." From the crack, I could extend up to a poor, downward-sloping hold over the roof's apex, but saw nothing above, only blank lime-green sandstone. I moved up repeatedly, matched hands on the sloper, stabbed my right foot onto a crumbly red sugar cube of rock, and groped blindly for hidden grips. Nothing. I was starting to get tired, my forearms tight, alone one hundred feet above a tilted ramp that sloped down to a three-hundred-foot plunge to the base of Redgarden Wall. Climbers die this way, in stupid situations like this, and then mountain rescue has to come along later and piece together what happened from the chalk prints and bloodstains. I soon steeped in a hot rush of fear, what climbers call "getting gripped." When fight-or-flight hits and you're unroped, you become keenly aware of your surroundings. You leave the "bubble" of concentration you've so far cultivated as a buffer against your naked peril. Time slows, and you must let the moment pass before continuing. I call this the "sea of rock" effect—a sudden realization that you're trapped on this unnatural vertical plane, surrounded in all directions by nothing but cold, hard, unforgiving stone; a tabula rasa forged eons ago beneath the planet that could care less if it sees your limbs ragdolled and brains spilled across its flanks. The shadows deepen, the calls of darting swallows echo on into infinity, lichens grow more vibrant, vertigo spins the ground ever farther away, and you can *feel* each air molecule around the cliff, the cooler, emptier ethers climbers associate with exposure—with the drop-offs we fear just as instinctually as everyone else. Then come the thoughts: *Man does not belong here. You're walking on the moon without oxygen. Get down NOW!* But you must shove them into the background and move into autopilot to find a quick exit, be it up, down, or sideways.

Up-down, up-down, up-down, up-down: I grew ever more gripped, suddenly, painfully, cognizant of the cruel red slabs, lightless maroon corners, and bottomless black huecos all around that mocked my plight, *Ha ha ha ha ha! Die die die die die! Die, loser, die!* This seemed *way* harder than 5.9; maybe I was missing a hold. I shook out each forearm, chalked up, and reached to the lip a final time. As I came halfway over my right foot, my quadriceps started to quiver with "Elvis Leg." *No, no, no, no, no.* I had no right to be here, threshold-soloing like this; I was going to crater and die *right here right now.* I reversed from the roof in a chattering frenzy, and sprinted down to the ledge like a rat fleeing floodwaters. Perching my buttocks on the sloping platform, I sat, took off my rock shoes, and popped an Ativan, letting it dissolve on my tongue. The pill tasted sweet, like a Smarties candy. I must have rested that way for fifteen minutes, an owl on a tree branch. In time, I spotted an escape left onto an easier climb, a 5.8, and moved across until I could reverse to terra firma. I asked around later and learned that *The Serpent's* second pitch went hard right, and that the roof I'd been trying was unclimbed, a possible 5.12. I wish I could say this was the only time like this, but there were others—like the day I came *millimeters* from falling fifty feet to my death alone in the Flatirons, barely catching a fingertip slot as I, quivering and off-balance, began to "barn-door" (swing) off on an unfamiliar 5.11c I had sequenced poorly due to fear-fueled haste.

Thudd-idd-bupp. Thudd-idd-bupp. Thudd-idd-bupp. Thudd-idd-bupp. Your heart can only handle so much adrenaline.

Two questions you probably want to ask are, "Were benzos performance enhancers? Did they let you try climbs you otherwise never would have tackled?" The answer is complex: It's both "yes" and "no." "Yes" in the sense that, like marijuana, Ativan can be disinhibiting: It removed certain barriers to self-destruction that might have otherwise remained in place. And "yes" also in the sense that, in these early months of daily benzo use, the drug—at least the first dose of the day, which always came on stronger—had enough of a sedating, anxiolytic effect that it did dampen fear . . . at least until early afternoon when the pill wore off and I felt panicky with interdose withdrawal. And "yes" also in that there were a select few climbs for which I took extra benzos, knowing how much fear I needed to face. In 1998 for example, at Hueco Tanks, a few of us crossed into Juarez and purchased ninety Valium directly from a crooked pharmacist. I burned through my allotted thirty pills by the second week, when we found an untapped labyrinth of caves and boulders atop West Mountain, Hueco's tallest mound. We called this area The Realm, both for its surreal, otherworldly feel and for the mentally foggy "realm" of substance abuse in which we dwelled. All day at the boulders it was pills, homegrown crippler and hashish, and Carlo Rossi jug wine. We climbed boulder "problems" that were fifty-foot miniroutes over black, yawning chasms, over lightless caves that spilled off cliff edges, over tilted, ankle-shattering slabs and punji-stick dead trees. I believe that two of the first ascents I made, difficult "super-highball" problems called *Chewbacca* and *Big Right*, remain unrepeated. The former climb is a thirty-foot flat brown face cooked into terra-cotta plates, your only holds the minuscule razor-crimps at the joints. The landing is a canted rock ramp, and once past the overhang you must steel yourself for a thirty-foot 5.10 slab, dancing from declivity to declivity, the void at your back. I'd been so out-of-body gripped as I lunged for an incut flake near the end of the difficulties, at twenty-five feet, that I'd had to scream at myself—"C'mon, Matt!"—as if in the third person. The latter problem, *Big Right*, navigates an overhanging slot from which the landing drops catastrophically, with the hardest moves—dynos to flat, bricklike holds—coming over the worst possible fall. Both problems were done drunk, stoned, and pasted on Valium, in a fearless fog so thick I had to jump-start each morning with a "crappuccino"—a one-liter Nalgene bottle filled with four tablespoons of instant coffee, four tablespoons of nondairy creamer, and four tablespoons of sugar. My friends thought I was nuts.

I wrote an article—the basis for this book—that appeared in the June 2010 issue of *Outside*. In it I asked rhetorically, "Can an acme be a nadir?" in particular reference to *Primate*, a 5.13 death route I established in the Flatirons in 2000. Because *Primate* climbs a crackless, overhanging wall that's off-limits to bolting, I did the climb in a style called "headpointing": top-rope rehearsal in antici-pation of a dangerous lead, with the idea that you must not fall. (The word is a hybrid of "heady" and "redpointing.") With my friend Steve, a crusty, old-school Wisconsinite carpenter who abhorred sport climbing and would even go around removing bolts he disap-proved of, I spent three days rehearsing the line, then led it while Steve belayed and my then girlfriend, Haven, took photos. *Primate* follows a black water streak splitting rainbow-hued rock, and the crux, a series of tenuous moves on fragile crystals and crimp-ers, comes sixty feet above a VW-sized boulder we jokingly chris-tened "the Pillow." Your fate rests entirely on an expanding tube chock called a Big Bro (think giant, spring-loaded toilet-paper tube) jammed diagonally against a small overlap. Should the Big Bro skate out at the crux, you will land on the Pillow and ram your legs through your skull. Before I set off to lead *Primate*, I snuck off into the Ponderosa and took four Ativan—twice my usual daily dose—returned, took a slug off Steve's ubiquitous hip flask of whiskey, and then donned rock shoes. That was just how it went in those years.

But the answer is also "no," the benzos didn't aid me as a climber, because I surely would have gone through this risky period any-way, being a nihilistic twenty-something male recovering from heartbreak. (There is a longstanding tradition in the climbing world of young men pulling off crazy, often solo feats after failed relationships.) And "no" also in the sense that with each passing month, as I built tolerance to the Ativan, it began to elevate my overall anxiety level such that I had to take the pills just to feel *normal*—that is, primarily to stave off withdrawal symptoms. Which is certainly consistent with Dr. Ashton's finding that tolerance to benzos' anxiolytic action can develop over just a few months, with clinical observations showing that "long-term use does little to control, and may even aggravate" the condition."[6] And finally "no" in the sense that, as the years wore on, the pills in their ever-escalating doses made me uncoordinated, slow-minded, fat, and increasingly fearful. By 2003, on three milligrams of Klonopin a day, I'd become a full-on liability at the cliffs. It was that summer that a partner, the late Michael Reardon, caught me pill-popping— at the Needles, California, an eerie beetling of granite spires high over the Kern River Canyon in the Sierra foothills. I was there with Michael, a Hollywood producer, notable free soloist, and onetime glam-rocker with a proud blond mane, to sample the area's legendary trad climbs. Halfway through the trip we tried *Don Juan Wall*, a beeline of thin cracks and bald corners on the cleaved southern edge of the Sorcerer Needle, the Kern River spinning in the mix a mile below. The third pitch, a blank stemming problem with micro protection, was my lead, but locked in mid-afternoon tolerance hell I remember being loath to commit. I dithered at the crux until my legs quivered and my hands threatened to slosh off. I downclimbed twenty feet back to Michael's ledge in a panic, tugging out the gear as I went, and said the thing you never want to hear your partner say on a perfect, bluebird climbing day: "Man, I don't think I can go any farther." I slunk off to the edge of the ledge, took the bottle from my windbreaker, popped a Klonopin, and then saw Michael looking at me.

"What are those?" he asked. "Some sort of medicine?"

"Anxiety, man. Anxiety." It was our first of many trips together, and we were just getting to know each other.

"Really? You're popping anxiety pills up on the rock?"

I told him that I had to, that I took the medicine daily for a panic disorder and that my doctor had said I'd need them my whole life. Later, as Michael stayed in touch during my struggle to quit, he told me, "I had to wonder how that worked, you being a climber and all."

Around the turn of the century, I had a Flatirons training circuit
I'd do at least once a week, a mixture of free soloing and bouldering on the First, Second, and Third Flatirons that comprised miles
of hiking and thousands of feet of climbing. I loved flogging myself
this way, alone and in constant motion for hours, sweat stinging my
eyes, red planes of sandstone flying by, the Ponderosa dropping
away to become a lush green carpet and the city a distant roar beyond. In general on the Flatirons' east faces the rock is tilted only
at a forty-five- or fifty-degree angle, and you can usually find good
ledges to chill out on—it's almost a hybrid between rock climbing
and scrambling. I nearly always felt comfortable soloing up there
(it's a Boulder rite of passage), but as 1998 became 1999 I started to
feel erratic, unpredictable bursts of fear. One afternoon, I had a terrible panic attack alone on a foot-wide ledge one hundred feet up
the East Face of the First Flatiron. I eventually calmed down, took
an Ativan, and reversed back to the ground, but the experience had
so shocked me that I felt panic flares whenever I climbed past that
spot again. I never quite knew when or why the attacks would hit—
was it from not eating enough, overexertion, mood swings? Or maybe
those little white pills?

I actually tried to quit the pills twice, in 1999, my first semester as
a creative-writing major in CU's master's program. That September,
I made it down to 0.5 mg of Ativan over a few weeks but became so
shaky, sweaty, and agitated that I quickly upped my dose. Out at
the rocks, I'd felt myself go from fit and focused to paranoid and irrational. Exposure—drop-offs—filled me with horror; every hold
looked loose, as if it might explode and precipitate a fatal fall; and
I could barely bear to watch friends climbing, fearing I'd witness a
terrible accident. When I broached the subject of my mounting fear
with the psychiatrist he never implicated benzos, even when I
asked if he thought I'd been on the pills too long. Instead he suggested another medication, "alprazolam, which also has some great
antidepressant properties." As I recall, he neglected to mention that
alprazolam is generic Xanax, a benzo with high potency, rapid on-
set of action, and a short half-life (six to twelve hours, to Ativan's ten

to eighteen[7]) that essentially makes it "benzo crack," with the potential for profound interdose withdrawal. In fact, I don't recall him telling me that Xanax was a benzodiazepine at all. On alprazolam, the anxiety worsened immediately. One week in, up on CU campus as I rode an elevator to meet a friend at the biology lab where he worked, I had a perfectly pointless panic attack—elevators had never bothered me before. "Whatever these pills are, they aren't doing me any favors," I thought as I huffed into the hallway in a tizzy. I asked the doctor to switch me back to Ativan, tried to quit again that December, and hit the same wall at 0.5 mg, going straight back to two milligrams a day. I had neared the threshold both times, unaware that each dosage reduction was going to be tougher than the last. I would later realize I'd given up because of rebound anxiety, a flare-up in anxiety symptoms caused by tapering too rapidly, mistaking it for my baseline state. The psychiatrist never suggested otherwise. "It's your panic disorder coming back, Matt," was the party line. I tended to believe his assertion that this panic disorder was a lifelong condition we could never again leave untreated. The evidence was right there before me: Each time I tried to quit my pills, the panic came back worse than ever. In fact, this same sort of "relapse" can happen with all the psych meds thanks to the changes they inflict on neurotransmitter systems, trapping people into becoming patients for life.

By 2002, I'd completed my master's degree and moved to Carbondale, to work as an associate editor at *Climbing*. I calculate this as the last year I knew peace, before the pills dulled my edge as an athlete, before tolerance withdrawal made the anxiety so pervasive that I could no longer rely on climbing skills I'd spent sixteen years honing. By 2003, the anxiety had in fact become so bad that I started seeing a therapist again, a woman down in Glenwood Springs. I'd also taken a job as senior editor for *Climbing*'s main competitor, *Rock and Ice*, right across the street. My therapist knew about my taking benzos, but not the wine and weed. "We have to get you off these nightmare drugs," she told me one day during session. "They're not doing you any favors."

With the therapist, I worked my way through a somewhat dated series of tapes, exercises, and readings on panic anxiety. The tapes featured two Southern women bantering idly with a psychologist. ("Ah do declare, Beulah Mae, I saw a bare-chested Negro upon my front lawn and felt mah heart go all aflutter.") I couldn't relate to their dialogue—their quaint antebellum agoraphobia treated little with my own—but I did use the relaxation tape to get to sleep at night. It felt like a huge step backward to have to work another panic program after I'd already successfully done so in my early twenties. Why this again, why now? Why the need for therapy again? Hadn't I already grappled with the life events, childhood trauma, and poor dietary choices that initially drove the panic? I knew exactly what panic attacks were and what caused them, and yet I kept having them anyway—on the rocks, in traffic, in movie theaters, at the office. More and more often, the attacks amassing to tower ever higher like monsoon thunderheads until life became all but unbearable.

In late 2003, bored, curious, and a bit desperate for outside chemical intervention, I began ordering the muscle relaxant Soma over the Internet. I remember justifying it with, *Well, hell, I'm already on these two pills, Paxil and Ativan, so what's another?* Soma soon turned to Vicodin, for which I'd long had an affinity, though on the come-down, they only made my anxiety worse. I'd sit there on my deck each morning, shivering with paranoia as the sun failed to thaw my soul. I hid it all from my friends, from my coworkers, from my then girlfriend, Katie, a strong climber, fit blonde, and wise soul who'd moved to Carbondale from Boulder. Alone in my efficiency on nights Katie didn't stay over, I'd tuck into the wine, weed, and pills. And if she did stay over, I made sure I was well medicated before her arrival. In some sick way, I loved it, despite the fear. Or maybe I liked this sick fear, liked seeing how far I could push it. Years of practice had made me an ace at masking both panic and drugging; I have a good poker face. Later, during a mental-status evaluation in 2005, at my absolute sickest with withdrawal terror, a psychiatrist at the Mapleton Center would write, "In discussing the patient with the staff prior to meeting with him, they stated that from their perspective he reported a high degree of subjective anxiety but did not appear outwardly anxious. . . ." Neither did the doctor detect any anxiety in person: "[Matt] was not fidgety, did not have a facial expression reflective of anxiety, and did not have a tendency to create anxiety in me which I often experience . . . in the presence of someone manifesting the outward signs of anxiety or panic." Perhaps being a climber, where you learn to mask your fear lest it contaminate your partner, had helped with this.

The biggest, longest-lasting panic attacks came when I smoked marijuana, not surprising given the high THC concentration of modern strains and their profound psychotropic effect. The fits roared in as thunderous as freight trains in those vulnerable periods of inter-dose withdrawal, leaving me sweaty and enervated, my right eye frozen half-closed as if I'd had a minor stroke. Still, I kept smoking. And God forbid I get separated from my pill bottle—then it would be even worse, with nothing on hand to "save" me, like an asthmatic fumbling for his inhaler. I took to stashing pills everywhere: the master bottle at home, miniature travel bottles for work, trail running, or the cliffs, one in my car, another in my climbing pack, one in a windbreaker pocket. So many squirrel caches all over I could barely keep track of them. There was no doubt that I was now an addict.

Finally, looking for a solution—any solution to the anxiety—I quit smoking pot. It helped for a spell, until it didn't.

Whether the Vicodin and Soma had triggered a final, catastrophic slide into chronic tolerance withdrawal is to my mind immaterial. I certainly would have or already had arrived there anyway: Benzos were the engine driving this train. (My psychiatrist would later attribute my increased anxiety to Vicodin and marijuana abuse, but never to benzos.) By Christmas 2003 the Ativan had jumped to three milligrams a day, and then four. I'd feel better for a little while with each dose increase—maybe a few weeks—then begin anew experiencing dread, insomnia, spates of attacks, and trouble breathing due to what had become chronic low-grade hyperventilation. It just got worse and worse, a classic downward spiral. By spring 2004 the psychiatrist, with whom I'd consult by phone back in Boulder, suggested we switch to a longer-acting benzo, Klonopin, three milligrams a day, which seemed like a step in the right direction: a seeming "dose reduction," stabilizing the anxiety with an eye toward eventually tapering off once I'd "treated" the panic disorder with this new medicine. What I didn't know—but should have suspected from the way that first Klonopin knocked me on my butt—was that in terms of equivalency, one milligram of Klonopin roughly equates to two milligrams of Ativan. That is, I'd gone from four milligrams of Ativan a day to six.

Ironically, in order to escape my fear, I was hurtling toward the abyss. As a climber, I should have known that you can't run from fear but must instead turn to face it or it will kill you. I'd learned then promptly forgot this lesson as a teenager in the Sandias, when my friend John and I set off one midsummer day to climb a 5.9+ called *Aviary Ort Overhangs*, a right-leaning arch/dihedral on the dark, somber north face of a spire called the Thumb. The route follows a big crack along the arch, the right wall a blank pane of red rock, the left a series of stair-stepping roofs. I took the first lead but, as I came closer and closer to running out of rope (and gear), I couldn't find a satisfactory ledge to stop on and belay. Only two years into lead climbing, I'd not yet learned that it's better to stop short of the end of the rope and build an anchor should you find a stance. In my inexperience, I'd climbed right past the first belay.

Small, shadowy depressions in the right wall, which looked like ledges from below, tempted me ever upward. I yelled down to John that I was going to push on, but each "ledge" turned out to be a sloping, crackless ramp. Soon John, tattooed, muscle-bound, his head shaved to the quick and wearing a big, awkward backpack jammed with our water, running shoes, and rain jackets, had to climb with me—"simul-climbing." Simul-climbing is hairball even with loads of gear between the climbers, but I was having to run it out, going twenty feet between pieces; we couldn't chance a fall. Finally, I came to the end of the arch where the crack closed shut two hundred feet off the talus. I could go no farther—I only had two pieces left, a small nut and a TCU. I fashioned a belay as best I could, then braced into a stem on two footholds and belayed John up. "Try not to fall, dude," is what I told him, but fall indeed he did as he reached my stance and led off into the crux. Ungainly backpack on, eyes bugging with tension, scrabbling to stay in balance on a delicate traverse, John was saved only by a drooping, downward-pointing piton he'd clipped off the belay and by me taking the force of the fall in my legs, before it came onto and in all likelihood tore our miserly anchor.

Be it on the cliff or in a fresh bottle of pills, you can't just continue along blindly, uninformed, unthinking, hoping for the best. You'll only get in deeper. By summer 2004, the tolerance withdrawal had become so pervasive that I was consistently failing on climbing goals. That August, I demurred on a ridge traverse of the Sierra's many Minarets peaks before a friend and I even tagged the second summit. I'd been training all summer, but psychologically I could not continue. Come autumn I had to stop climbing at 2:00 P.M. each day and could only sit back and watch friends, baffled that they weren't feeling this terror and could keep trying, keep taking falls with impunity. I'd watch them as one might watch footage of astronauts on the moon, doing something so dangerous and alien as to be nearly unrelatable. Even though I'd always been a climber, and this is *exactly* what I do, I found myself benched. It felt permanent.

Despairing, not caring, I ordered more Vicodin. If I couldn't climb hard, I could at least *drug* hard. I'd range through the day on benzos and Vicodin, pounding Dr Pepper so I could stay awake at my desk; I started to get fat from all the sugar. I wasn't so good at my job in this loopy state: I'd often, without consideration, write incendiary articles ("America's 10 Best and Worst Bouldering Areas") or *Onion*-style parodies of facets of the climbing world. But climbers have their sacred cows—as rowdy as we can be, most of us don't like to be made fun of, which garnered me negative attention on climbing forums. So I'd use aliases to snipe back at my critics, logging in as Sally Cummings, Rick Spoot, L'Innominato, Dongi Bzaznyk, and Hentai Bukkake, the latter of whom sent a series of e-mails to the editor of a competing magazine posing as a Yakuza gangster seeking to buy a famous female professional climber. I was drugged up, out of it, crazy in the worst way. I'm not proud of any of this. The flame wars only made my anxiety worse, entangled me in petty, hand-wringing battles over something I'd once loved—climbing—that had gone dark for my sad twilight as an athlete. Come night, I'd come home, silo more Vicodin, pour out wine, and plop down in front of the TV playing Halo until I passed out on my futon, my fluffy black cat Spike on my belly. I had the big Vicodin, the ten milligram ones, and was taking up to ninety milligrams a day. I was a nasty piece of work, all edgy and paranoid, no filter on my mouth. This was not the me I'd set out to be or that anyone would want me to be: Drugs take that from you. They ruin your personality. They make you angry.

The pills had made me slow, portly, irascible, and unpredictable, yet somehow this was not evident to the person who most needed to see it. I continued climbing halfheartedly, even as I grew weaker, plumper, and more logy. In photos from that epoch my facial features appear blurry and diffuse, eyes dull like a drunkard's, the edges softened by chemicals. I'd always used the climb *Sprayathon* at Rifle as a fitness benchmark: If I could redpoint this 5.13c, I was in fighting form. *Sprayathon* has a leap move down low that I never missed, but in summer 2004 I could only stick the jump one time in four. My timing was off, my commitment was nil, and the black hand of fear pressed me hard back toward earth. I redpointed *Sprayathon* only once that year, and by a hair's breadth at that. All the years of pushing myself on the rock and all the pills and drugging had burned out both body and brain. I'd lived too long in extremity.

Finally, predictably, came injury. In September 2004, my then girlfriend Kasey and I drove up to Independence Pass, a series of granite crags and boulders along a winding mountain byway east of Aspen. Kasey is a tall, pretty, sandy blonde, with an incisive wit; a volleyball player and strong climber who used to routinely upstage me at the bouldering gym. She has talon fingers that clamp down on holds I can barely see. This day we started at a twenty-five-foot fin along the Roaring Fork River called the Jaws Boulder, a highball face by the parking lot. I'd done its primary route before, a 5.11 called *Jaws*, and warmed up on it. At the crux twenty feet off the ground, as I reached with my right hand for an incut edge, my left hand rocketed off a tiny crimp. The smooth granite was covered in morning dew, the moisture having caused me to lose purchase. I gave a brief, surprised whimper and then launched sideways and out, trying to twist midair and get my feet under me, but the fall was too violent. I missed the one crashpad and landed sideways in a bowl of rock and roots exposed by the river. I lay there panting and sputtering as Kasey rushed over. Before I'd started up *Jaws*, she'd asked me if I wanted a spot, but I'd been too arrogant to accede. I'd been highballing for years, done problems orders of magnitude more difficult. *Bosh—why would I need a spot now?* I paid for my hubris: I had to crawl to the car, lamed by a cracked tibial head and damaged IT (iliotibial) bands on both legs. I remember a nurse weighing me on a follow-up visit to the doctor's a month later, as she asked if I was on any medication. ("Um, ten milligrams of Paxil and three milligrams of Klonopin a day.") I weighed 196 pounds. I'm only five-six. She gave me a look. I knew that look—it was the same one the pharmacists reserved for me when I came in a few days early to refill my benzo prescription, if I needed it before a trip. It's like they're looking right through you, seeing some truth you've obscured from yourself.

I was no longer a climber. I was a junkie. I was the excrement of society. Sometimes, however, you need to get dipped head to toe in feces before you break down and shower.

That November in 2004, I clogged my literal bowels up with Vicodin. It embarrasses me to write about this incident, but this shame, this low point, is what made me turn my life around. A friend, Luke, and I had gone to the midnight release of *Halo 2*, down at the Sam

Goody store in Glenwood, but I began to feel queasy as we waited in line with a slew of hyper twelve-year-olds and their mothers. I'm not sure how many Vicodin I'd taken that evening, but probably at least five. My gut had torqued into knots; something pressed on my bladder, causing a constant feeling of a need to pee. Then I couldn't pee at all. Back in Carbondale, alone in my efficiency at 1:00 A.M., my bladder had swollen but I couldn't make myself go, no matter how long I stood over the toilet. I ran the water in the sink, hoping it would send a subliminal message—*trickle, trickle, tinkle, tinkle.* Nothing. The pain grew sharper, a lancing spear. Growing desperate, fearing my bladder might burst, I called the hospital in Glenwood. The ER nurse said it might be a kidney stone, but that she couldn't diagnose me over the phone and that I should come on in. No way, forget it, too embarrassing. I'd sort this out myself. I had to pee so badly, the fluid was now bubbling around within my belly. Then I remembered an old summer-camp prank: the hand-in-the-warm-water trick you'd pull on sleeping kids to get them to urinate in their bedrolls. I stripped down, stood in the shower, and turned the water on as hot as I could stand, letting it run over my fat body, trying to think "fluid" thoughts. A little pee trickled out, then a little more, then a small, steady stream of yellow spinning down the drain. But my bladder still sent bolts of pain through my viscera.

If this all sounds ridiculous, it's because it is. But this is how drugs reduce you; they turn you into a buffoon.

Then—*WHOOM*—I doubled over with peristaltic spasms. I had to move my bowels, and *now*, but that felt blocked up, too. I made it to the toilet just as more spasms convulsed me, but whatever had lodged up there wasn't budging. Having no other choice, I reached behind, stuck two fingers up my backside, and pulled myself apart as another spasm rocketed through my guts. With a horrible ripping noise and caustic burning all through my rectum, something the size of a geode dropped into the toilet: a fecolith, a ball of hardened shit. And behind that, a torrent of urine. Now, if you've ever had your hand up your own ass, pulling it apart to pass a huge, stinking, calcified ball of excrement, then you have known rock bottom. Even if you never tell another soul, a crime has been committed. Nobody was doing rails off my erect penis and neither did I have a gun to someone's head demanding money for crack—the only victim was myself. But that barely matters *because there was still a victim*. No matter how much I washed my hands that night, I could still smell the abasement—stale, brown, heavy with indole, a grim reminder of my vile labor. That's the real definition of drug addiction: giving birth to a shit baby, over and over and over again. Only you're too high, self-destructive, and feckless to care for the baby, so you abandon it on the doorstep at your coworkers' or parents' or friends' house to take care of until their fingers and hands and arms turn brown with shit, too.

I had better things to do than birth shit babies. I had better things to do than root through the chaos of my closet, beneath the ropes, cams, bolts, and rock shoes I'd so carelessly scattered in disorganized druggie heaps. To snort around like a truffle hound for the big Vicodin bottle, which I'd hide from myself each night while buzzed in the hopes that I'd not find it the next evening. To stand abashedly in line at the City Market pharmacy once a month and shell out ninety dollars for Klonopin and another fifty for Paxil. To have wasted all those hours chasing down weed, driving to a friend of a friend of a friend's house and having to patiently abide the labyrinthine ramblings of whatever shady dealer lurked therein, eyes black-rimmed and glassy, while he weighed your glassine bag on a little scale. I had better things to do than to be so dependent. Climbers are strong, free-willed people, and climbing is a sport that fosters those traits. But I'd let myself become the opposite. This had to change.

It took time to start cleaning up. I'd been at it way too long. I reduced but wasn't able to totally quit Vicodin for another couple of months; meanwhile, my benzo dose continued to climb: four milligrams of Klonopin every day. That winter, a thick slab of dread descended with each snowflake that landed outside my windows, a terror so palpable I was the first, before Lee, to shovel the walkways, driveway, and sidewalk after each snowstorm, as if the white, fluffy powder had brought pure evil with it. I often wondered if I might not just up and die of this bizarre, mounting fear. Around Thanksgiving, the Klonopin stopped working and the psychiatrist switched me to a new pill, Xanax XR, a time-release form that looked like a swollen blueberry: four milligrams a day, working on subreceptors unaffected by Klonopin and buying another month of temporary relief. Because I hate swallowing big pills, I'd often chew the Xanax and end up inadvertently flooding myself with benzodiazepine, dropping into a stuporous evening nap then resurfacing icy cold and shaky. Some nights, when the Xanax and Vicodin narcosis wore off, I'd wake up screaming; the cat would jump off my chest and run under the futon. I'd later read on the Web that mixing benzos and opiates gives a heroin-like high, and my head was often on my chest before the Xbox, a junkie on the nod.

Enough was enough. This had to be rectified. I was only thirty-three. I could not do this any longer. The drugs had to go—the benzos, too.

Four milligrams of Xanax didn't sound like much. I'd been taking ninety milligrams of Valium in 1996 and survived a cold turkey off what I mathematically surmised to be twenty-two times more of the drug. I wonder how optimistic I might have felt had someone pointed out my fuzzy math. I wonder what my reaction would have been had they pointed out that a single milligram of Xanax equates to *twenty milligrams* of Valium and that I was on the equivalent of eighty milligrams of Valium a day, every day, and had been for some time.

PART THREE

THE LAST MILLIGRAM

CHAPTER 9

Four milligrams a day, Xanax, January 2005:

Y ou're *chewing*?" It's my psychiatrist on the phone. I stand beneath the Highway 82 bridge over the Colorado River in downtown Glenwood Springs, in a redbrick pedestrian zone lined with tourist bakeries, bars, and boutiques. It's a dishwater-gray Saturday and my father has ducked into a bookstore for *The New York Times*. Cars and semis rumble past overhead, kicking slush over the guardrail where it slops to earth, forming raw, sooty ridges. My dad flew out from Baltimore one day earlier, after I'd confessed everything to him and my therapist, unable to take the anxiety and the drugging anymore. I also called Kasey, in Boulder. She's finishing up a graduate degree in journalism and now, perhaps, has a lens through which to understand my cracked behavior.

That Friday, my father and I visited the Glenwood ER, where the doctor offered a prescription for the opiate antagonist Naltrexone to wean me off Vicodin. I sat in the waiting area afterward spacing out on a bright-blue aquarium full of exotic fish, holding the prescription, weighing the pros and cons of taking yet another drug as the creatures brushed against the glass. At only two pills (twenty milligrams) of Vicodin a day, it seemed simpler just to taper, but first I needed to tell my psychiatrist everything because I wanted his help quitting benzodiazepines, too.

"Not to get buzzed, no . . . I—I have trouble swallowing, Dr. Porridge, especially later in the day when I'm more anxious, so sometimes I chew the Xanax just to get it down," I say. I know this sounds a little lame, but it's the truth.

"And you were abusing Vicodin, too," he says flatly. "Look, Matt, I could get into a lot of trouble over this. I'm supposed to be seeing you in my office, not just consulting over the telephone." He's on his speakerphone; his voice has a metallic echo to it. Because I've lived on the West Slope for the past three years, most of our check-ins have been via telephone, with the occasional sit-down in Boulder. He pauses as I collect my thoughts; he's jotting notes.

"Why? You weren't prescribing the Vicodin. And I never abused the benzos you gave me."

"I'm not sure I'm able to believe you right now. . . ." His voice has a hard edge.

"Well, it's true, Dr. Porridge. I'll admit it—I did smoke pot for many of those years, and was taking Vicodin the last two winters. But I haven't smoked pot in a year, and the Ativan, the Klonopin: I took exactly what you prescribed. Nothing more, nothing less."

"I always wondered why your anxiety kept getting worse, why the pills stopped working. Look, Matt, you lied to me."

I pause to let this sink in. Technically, he's right—it was a crime of omission.

"Yeah, I know. I am sorry. I really am, Dr. Porridge, but I'm telling you the truth now. And I don't know if the other drugs caused all this anxiety anyway, at least, not totally." My voice wavers. "I feel like it's something else . . . something we missed. I— And I really *did* take the benzos as prescribed. I don't know how else to say it."

"Look, Matt, it's highly likely that you were abusing the benzos," he insists. "They would still be working otherwise."

The doctor feels that I've violated his trust. His voice is strained, angrier now.

"I didn't," I say. "I don't know what else to say. I abused the other drugs, but not the Xanax. I really do have trouble swallowing big pills. I—I didn't know you can't chew them up."

Then it hits me: Would he go so far as to fire me as a patient? I think back to 1996 and the Valium psychosis. I can't go through that again. He can't just cut me loose.

"You're not going to stop prescribing are you?"

"Not now, Matt, I'm not. But I might need to refer you to another psychiatrist who can see you in person."

Not good. What if the next doctor refuses to prescribe benzos, knowing my history? Then what? Another cold turkey? Left to have seizures, dementia, to languish in a mental hospital half-psychotic like Barbara Gordon in *I'm Dancing as Fast as I Can*?

"But what if that doctor won't help?"

"I'm not sure, Matt. That will be for you and him to figure it out."

Dr. Porridge is going to fire me, to leave me to die insane on the streets. The Greyhound bus depot is here beneath the overpass. I picture myself bivouacking there at night, wandering the bricks by day plagued by Reploids, bearded, natty, piss-stained, badger-eyed, shouting gibberish and panhandling tourists.

"I— You can't do that, Dr. Porridge. I'm totally hooked on these pills."

"Well, Matt. I'm really angry. . . ."

"Look, Dr. Porridge, I'm *sorry* I didn't tell you everything, but you have to believe me now that I want to get clean. And that I didn't abuse the benzos—they just stopped working on their own. I'll come out to Boulder for an appointment and we can talk about it face-to-face."

He pauses. Then:

"Okay, Matt. Okay . . . well, we can't have you chewing Xanax anymore. I'm going to switch you back to Klonopin, and I want you to start going to NA or some sort of substance-abuse therapy."

"I'll try that. And yes, I'll go to a meeting." Relief . . . He'll help me. NA seems like a small price to pay.

"Let's see . . . at four milligrams a day of Xanax, that's . . . Okay.

Four milligrams of Klonopin, starting tomorrow. I'll call it in to your pharmacy. Would you like the name brand or the generic?"

"Generic is fine. And I'll find an NA meeting and let you know that I'm going."

"You do that. And we'll check back in next week. I'll have my assistant set it up."

"Good-bye, Dr. Porridge."

"Good-bye, Matt." He sighs, hangs up.

My father comes out of the bookstore, the *Times* tucked under his arm. He seems out of his element, with a bewildered owl look in his eyes that's only enhanced by his bifocals. I'm his only child and he's never been around drugs, has in fact devoted his life to researching the deleterious effects of cigarette smoke on the heart and the lungs, and on the health of others through secondhand exposure. He keeps calling the Vicodin "Hycodan," and I can tell that it troubles him—a hyperintelligent man used to dissecting, comprehending, and then resolving complex problems—to feel so powerless. His son, a drug addict, is in pain and will be for some time, and there's nothing he can do. Until now, he's had no idea how many pills I'm taking or of what variety. The fear, the concern, are written in his eyes; they mirror my own misgivings. *When will I feel normal again?* And: *How much longer must I withstand this terror?*

Years, it will turn out. It will take me years to heal from the greatest damage, that caused by the benzodiazepines. Each benzo has its specific action on GABA subreceptors, and the abrupt, one-day changeover from Xanax to Klonopin comes as an exquisite torture, a new level of terror in the frozen heart of winter. Carbondale turns white under its blanket of snow; the world screams at me, as if all objects are audibly decomposing, hissing, steaming, streaming into comet tails of oblivion and I evaporating along with them, sleeping only a few hours a night and suppressing my panic at work through sheer force of will. I contract the stomach flu somewhere in there and, febrile and fragile, spend an hour on the phone with Kasey, sobbing because I don't want to die by age thirty-four like my uncle the heroin addict. I take walks with Lee or short, faltering jogs, my feet crunching in the snow, wind howling, blue-white spindrift and strange arctic halos coming off Mount Sopris. As tired as I feel, it's impossible to sit still. I've been surviving on turkey burgers, grilling them up in a panini press, but the grill's remnant odor of old, cold grease permeates the efficiency and turns my stomach. I picture a slab of dead, flaccid flesh when I walk through the door, and soon the sight of the grill alone is enough to trigger a panic attack. Next door, Lee practices "Moonlight Sonata" on the piano; I can hear it through the wall. He's good, very good, but Beethoven's elegiac notes coupled with the turkey-grease smell conjure nothing but entropy.

Four milligrams a day, Klonopin, March 2005:

I've stopped taking Vicodin. I cut slowly over a month, five milligrams a week until the final week when, using a sharp, redwood-handled steak knife, I quartered the pills the final three days. Then nothing. Zero. It's gone, over; I barely miss the opiates and, other than a few weeks of agitation, I detect no lasting damage. Compared to benzos, opiates are dead-easy to quit. Weed is dead-easy to quit. Alcohol, the same. I feel happier, lighter, less sludgy, and am even climbing again. Still I move tentatively, afraid to push myself, succumbing to odd waves of vertigo and a hopeless, shaky feeling at cruxes. Down in Glenwood I attend weekly, therapist-led meetings with other addicts, most of them grizzled Western Colorado alcoholics. There's a girl in there, eighteen, tall, beautiful, brunette, coming off crystal meth. She sobs one day during group, telling us her dentist said she might need dentures because all her teeth are rotted out.

"Eighteen is way [sob] too [sob] young [sob, sob, sob] for dentures," she's saying. "I wish I'd never touched that stuff. My teeth are all fucked up and I ain't even twenty."

Optimistic given my own rapid progress, I tell her that it will all work out and that she's young enough to turn it around. I'm thirty-three, I say, and I've pissed away almost more years drugging than she's been alive, but I still feel hopeful about the future.

"Yeah, well, age ain't nothing but a number," the girl says, blowing her nose. "Eighteen years starts to sound like a lot when you've been smoking meth the last five of them."

Kasey and I drive to California over spring break. We make it to Ibex, Utah, the first night, out in salt pans in the West Desert along U.S. Route 50. I've climbed here twice before, in this vast no-man's-land of scrubby mountains, endless basins, and milk-blue skies. Ibex is known for its varnished, wind-hollowed red and brown quartzite boulders, the best ones a tumble of blocks—some large as office buildings—beneath a three-hundred-foot cliff that lords over a dry white lake bed. It's a harsh, isolated, elemental place, like so many of the great climbing areas. Ibex's wind is ripping, driving silt into the tent, howling around the scoops, whorls, and bevels that it's carved into the biggest boulder, the Red Monster, above us. I unroll my sleeping pad and an orange bottle falls out: Vicodin, one of the mini-stashes I'd hidden from myself back in Carbondale.

"Hey, babe, look at this," I tell Kasey. "Vicodin."

Her face goes blank. "I thought you quit, nuggins," she says.

"I did," I say. "I really did. I must have had these stashed away— stowaways, it looks like. Umm, whoops?" Her face falls again; Kasey is not psyched.

It makes me nervous having these semi-licitly-obtained pills in the car. And besides, for all intents and purposes I'm clean—the psychiatrist has applauded my recovery efforts and finally conceded that the benzos are drugs of "use, not abuse." Great news! I look forward to a similarly smooth transition off Klonopin. I've informed my doctor that I'll cut a half to a quarter milligram every two weeks, which means I'll be free of the benzos by October. He agrees that that's a solid plan. By headlamp in the bluish gloom, I peel off the Vicodin label, take a piece of athletic tape from my climbing pack, write on it, and slap it on the bottle. As Kasey and I leave for Bishop the next afternoon, I cache the bottle in the Red Monster, inside a chalk-lined crack that climbers thrust their hands into where I know someone will find it.

"Vicodin painkillers," is what the label says. Then: "Help yourself, as I no longer have any need for them."

Three and a half milligrams a day, Klonopin, late March 2005:

The first cut is the biggest and establishes the pattern: Two days after each reduction begins one week of worsened symptoms, including curious spates of hyperventilation, drowsiness, and toxic naps from which I wake up hypothermic. Then a return to "normal"—i.e., the standard benzo roller coaster, like an old acquaintance whom you publicly tolerate but have secretly always loathed. Kasey and I are in the lower Owens Valley, at a dystopian desert junction where Route 395 from Bishop meets Route 58 to Barstow. Power lines swing low as a windstorm builds. Trash and dust blow around as we pull into a convenience store to gas up and make a left toward Joshua Tree, where we'll meet Michael Reardon. I've been panting the whole way from Bishop where, two nights earlier at Kasey's grandfather's trailer, I first took a half pill instead of a whole one at bedtime. I know that I'm overbreathing and I know that it makes me anxious, but I'm powerless to stop. Breathing exercises don't even dent the pattern. Harley bikers are about, gangbangers creeping in boomcars, sun-dried methheads in greasy flannels and with hammerhead-shark eyes. I've never liked California—the aridity, the random nutjobs, the *Road Warrior* vibe—even as I appreciate its wealth of superb granite cliffs. We're in Kasey's Elantra, "Lani," a brown plastic triceratops our mascot on the dashboard. I play with the toy as I wait for her to return from the restroom, its black eyes staring back, revealing nothing.

Three milligrams a day, Klonopin, April 2005:

I've made another big jump, a half-milligram cut, feeling positive, bolstered by a new SSRI antidepressant, Lexapro, which has helped temporarily with the breathing, letting my body assume a natural rhythm. The benzos are down to three times a day—morning, noon, and night—and after a rough first week, I actually feel better than I did at higher doses. Could it be that each cut will be easier, as I come closer to zero? I have no reason not to think so, and my psychiatrist still feels that I'm tapering at a reasonable rate.

I've flown out to meet Michael Reardon in LA, and then we're off to Joshua Tree National Park again, an otherworldly, wind-swept plateau of the eponymous dream-trees, of endless tan domes and gritty boulders popping from springtime tracts of yellow and purple wildflowers. We barely rope up except for longer climbs. Michael runs through his multiple-route free-solo circuits, which he does as comfortably as laps at the pool, while I join him when I'm feeling it, one of us sometimes climbing right above the other, cracking dirty jokes, feeding off each other's raucous energy. I notice that I solo better before noon, after the first Klonopin or the second, but that I need to ease back later. One afternoon, just past this window, we head to *Clean and Jerk*, a sixty-foot 5.10 on a formation called Sports Challenge Rock. Two guys rest below the shady north face; they wear giant Everest-climber backpacks, an overkill of equipment for this puny cliff, helmets on though they haven't yet roped up. Safety nuts, in other words. Michael pulls out the video camera as I start unroped up *Clean and Jerk*, as we both shout "Cali extreme!" and make ironic shaka-brah hand gestures. I realize that I'm shaky and that it's a little late in the day—and I've only done this climb once, two years earlier—but I free-solo anyway. Halfway up, the crack esses through a smooth bulge, forcing awkward body positions. I quiver, slowing as I fuss with fist jams and foot smears, as Michael continues filming. "You doing okay, brotha?" he asks at one point. "Sure, sure," I say, but as I look down thirty, then forty, then fifty feet to the ground, I can see that the other two climbers have packed up and left, unwilling or perhaps unable to witness whatever finale.

Two and three-quarters milligrams a day, Klonopin, May 2005:

I've given notice at work, having stepped down from editor to senior editor as I prepare to detach from the publishing world. It feels like the right decision, one that should ameliorate stress and anxiety, and as soon as my tenure is up I'll move in with Kasey back in Boulder and work as a freelancer—a quieter, simpler life.

Kasey is interning at Boulder's newspaper and is sent to do a human-interest piece on the Humane Society of Boulder Valley shelter. She sends me an e-mail entitled only, "Can we get him?" with a link to a photo. It's of Clyde, one of two brown brindled puppies (his sister is Bonnie), rescued siblings listed as "Labrador/pitbull mix." There he is, a tiger-striped, two-month-old furball with a fat pink belly, a white blaze on his chest, wide brown eyes, and velvety ears. A hundred fifty bucks, including shots and neutering. I don't even think, just type *"Yes!"* and with that we have Clyde. When Kasey brings him out to Carbondale the next weekend, I have to carry him through the talus below the cliffs, as he keeps slipping between the rocks and tripping over his pedestal paws. He whines when we're up off the ground until he figures out he can crane up and see us. After which Clyde scoops out a hole, curls into a ball, and takes a long puppy siesta.

Two and a quarter milligrams a day, Klonopin, June 2005:

To stick to my self-imposed schedule I must make this cut, even on holiday on Kalymnos, a mountainous Greek isle covered in perfect bands of gray, orange, white, and beige limestone. Things have started to become, well, *difficult*, an intimation of some storm brewing over the horizon. I'm moving at the same pace, keeping my chin up and focused on the end goal, but I'm beginning to think that quitting benzos this final time might be harder than I'd originally thought. (As I'll learn later, from anecdotal experiences shared on a Yahoo group, each taper is often more difficult than the one/s prior.) Back in Boulder, Kasey has found us a place, one half of a duplex at Fifth Street and Alpine in far west Boulder, the last tumbledown rental on a block of redos and scrape-offs beneath Mount Sanitas. It has two bedrooms, a big picture window in the living room that reveals the First Flatiron in profile—a thin plane of sandstone slicing the horizon. There is even a backyard for Clyde, though the fence is low and we have to electrify it. I like where the house is, so close to trails and the rocks, and how the thin slits of window in the two bedrooms give east past the city onto the Great Plains. But something about it also feels ominous, like bad things have happened or might someday happen here.

Now in Mediterranean climber paradise, I need to cut again, even as I know it will leave me jelly-limbed and noncombative on the harder climbs, less able to enjoy Kalymnos' amazing three-dimensional routes on stalactites and "tufas" (extruded vertical dikes) overlooking the glaucous Aegean. I've given up coffee and chocolate, as they're too stimulating, and have to leave Kasey to do the shopping in the narrow-aisled grocery stores in Kalymnos' port, Pothia. The crowds are too much; I'm too edgy. The Greek sounds like bursts from a machine gun. I feel infinite sadness.

Depression becomes despair one hot afternoon at a cliff called Kasteli, where Byzantine castle walls sit crumbling atop an exposed spit of maritime limestone. Kasey wants to try a few climbs here, but too tired to climb myself I come out merely to belay. You can hardly see civilization, tucked into a nook on the back of the hump, overlooking a deep-blue channel and the neighboring isle of Telendos, which broke off from Kalymnos in an ancient earthquake. I say little, holding the rope, lowering Kasey after each climb, sweating behind my sunglasses. By now she knows how anxious I get, but also, frustratingly, that she cannot help. We leave as the sun drops behind Telendos, casting orange light over the weathered crags of white stone. As we pass the neck of the spit, from where you can scramble up to the castle, I consider having a look. I've always done things like this, loved exploring. But this evening I can't bring myself to walk the extra hundred feet to the ruins.

Who is this person? I wonder, and: *When did I stop being curious about the world?*

And then it hits me: It's not me; it's the pills. I have them in my climbing pack, the whole goddamned bottle. *What might happen*, I ask myself, *if I simply hurled these fucking things into the ocean? Will I wake up tomorrow back to my old self again?*

How lovely that would be. How linear and tidy. How convenient. But then something stops me, an interior voice saying, "You *don't* want to do that. You don't want a repeat of 1996. You cannot afford to go crazy again. You really aren't that strong."

Two milligrams a day, Klonopin, Carbondale, Boulder, mid-June 2005:

I'm not sure if it's the hammer *through* the countertop or my fist *not through* the wall that will end up costing me more, though both happen in the same few cursed seconds. Kasey and I have returned to Carbondale to pick up Clyde at Lee's and pack up my things, and I've just finished a frustrating phone call. I'm starting to have no brakes on my emotions, feeling more suffocated, both physically and emotionally, by the day.

"You should see your dog," Lee told me when I phoned from the Front Range a day earlier. "It's crazy, but he looks totally different, like his legs got longer and his face has changed. I'm not sure he's a pit bull. Man, you gotta see Clyde—it's hilarious!"

And Lee's right—in just the three weeks that we've been gone, Clyde has gone from a fat little dumpling to a stilt-legged adolescent with a werewolf snout. He still has his floppy ears and soft brindle coat, and his feet are still huge, but it's clear that Clyde is some other breed. Clyde is out in the yard playing with Lee's

Australian shepherds when I go berzerker, so he doesn't have to witness my apoplexy like Kasey. I've just called the local motorcycle shop to see if they've been able to repair a Chinese motor scooter I bought some months earlier. The scooter is silver, cagey, plastic bodied, more often than not broken, and I've been embroiled in an ongoing saga of ordering parts from the scooter company, taking them down to the shop where the scooter has become derelict-in-residence, and trying to get the thing running again. I've spent $300 already trying to maintain a $1,000 scooter, and now it's still broken and not yet ready to move to Boulder. This trifle triggers a wrath attack well beyond any normal proportion.

I hurl the phone against the kitchen floor but that doesn't break it. I'm screaming it—"Fuck, fuck, *Fuck!*"—as I fetch a hammer we've been using to pull picture hangers from the walls. Kasey stands to the side mutely, wondering where this is leading. I place the phone on the countertop and rail down hammer blow after hammer blow, but I'm too frantic to aim properly and strike it only after a few attempts. Meanwhile, I've punched a ragged hole in the countertop—on move-out day. This infuriates me all the more, and I turn around and punch the wall, right on the stud, which resounds with a dull crunching noise as something gives in my hand.

I can't breathe, I'm anxious all the time, everything is broken, and I must punch this wall again. Then Kasey is behind me, clutching my arm as I recoil for a second blow, yelling, "*No, Matt, no, no, no, no, no!*"

I crumple to the floor, sobbing while Kasey holds me. She will tell me how frightened she was that day, as if I might have harmed her, and I will apologize profusely and tell her no, no, no, no, no, I will only ever hurt myself. The counter will cost $800 to replace, which I'll pay to Lee over two installments. My right pinkie finger, meanwhile, has sustained a spiral (boxer's) fracture. I don't get it looked at until two weeks later, by which time the bone has already healed crookedly. It dangles askew like a torn battle flag; to this day the finger aches whenever a storm front is coming.

One and three-quarters milligrams a day, Klonopin, Boulder, July 2005:

"I really think we should head up here, into this chimney," I tell my friend and climbing partner, Lizzy.

We stand below the north ridge of Spearhead, a 12,575-foot granite wedge in a tarn- and tundra-stippled alpine basin beneath Longs Peak in Rocky Mountain National Park. I've climbed some of Spearhead's more difficult east-face routes before, thin slabs of burnished knobs and wavy stone cut by fingertip seams. Because of the peak's altitude and pointy summit, you want to be up and off by noon, before the thunderstorms build. Today we've come to simul-climb a 5.6, the North Ridge, which I should be able to do even with my splinted right pinkie since the low-angled rock means you barely need your hands.

"I'm not sure. Look . . . here, the description says start in a 'left-facing corner' and head into a box feature, which to me looks like this crack out right," Lizzy says. Lizzy is a strong climber, an attentive listener, an intense and thoughtful writer with curly brown hair, often died henna red, who once worked birthday parties as "Frizzy the Clown." We've been friends for five years.

I'm not convinced. "I don't know—that's not much of a corner, and then how do we get back to the ridge?" I ask. "I'm pretty sure the upper pitches are right on the edge"—where the east face meets the north.

Lizzy looks down at a xeroxed guidebook page again, looks up at the wall, scratches her head. We walk back and forth a couple more times between the route I think we should take and Lizzy's selection. I had been hesitant about coming, worried about the breathing troubles and how they'd affect me on the approach hike, but it's July—*the* time to climb in the high country. And besides, my psychiatrist, concerned about my rising anxiety levels, has just added a "mood stabilizer," an expensive antiepilepsy medicine named Trileptal that has helped with my breathing, if only because it sedates me. The doctor is prescribing "off-label," exploiting a legal loophole through which doctors can prescribe a drug for conditions other than the one it's indicated for. I feel mixed emotions about adding another medication when all I want is to quit Klonopin, but Dr. Porridge insists that I need to approach the taper from a "place of strength." We've also reverted to Paxil from Lexapro, as the Lexapro stopped working—"pooped out," in the doctor's terminology, as psychiatric medicines are known to do. I'm on 12.5 milligrams a day of Paxil XR, a time-release version.

Because of my finger, Lizzy will take the lead position, placing the gear as she climbs and making the route-finding decisions. In the end I defer to her when she says she wants to start out right, where the climbing looks steeper and more interesting. We can, she points out, traverse left to the ridge once we're up a few hundred feet.

Lizzy starts up a thin crack midway along the north face, placing small cams; around eighty feet she slows to pass a black water seep oozing from a steep layback crack. She hollers down to be careful on the wet rock, and then continues. Soon Lizzy hits the end of the rope, tied in at my harness, and I start climbing. We move in unison: I adjust my pace to match Lizzy's so that no extra slack enters the line. I'm in approach shoes, a hybrid between a tennis shoe and rock boot with climbing-rubber soles. They slip a little on the water-washed granite. The climbing is harder than I'd bargained for—5.8 or even 5.9—but by relying on my left hand and staying over my feet, I skitch up the layback without falling. Four hundred feet up we enter an obtuse gully-like depression right of the ridge. I call up to Lizzy, 150 feet higher on a big ledge, to ask if she doesn't want to head to the ridge now, but she says we should climb higher first. We have only one piece between us, a wired nut thirty feet below Lizzy. She heads right on her ledge, the rope running along the lip.

Then:

"Rock!" Lizzy yells. *"Rock, rock, rock, rock, rock!!!"* This is the word no climber wants to hear, a warning of some inbound lithic projectile. I'm not wearing a helmet—a boneheaded move on a

mountain route—and my first thought is that I'm going to get brained. I look up, trying to anticipate the rock's trajectory, but see nothing. *Why is Lizzy yelling so much? I don't see a damn thing. . . .*

The horizon separates: One of the castellated points along the edge of the gully breaks free and is suddenly in motion. My mind tries to make sense of this—it seems impossible that such a big piece of mountain could come detached. Directly, the block comes crashing end over end into the bowl, a granite tombstone the size of a refrigerator.

Jesus CHRIST!

I'm on a sliver of ledge barely two feet wide that opens to four feet on my right. I'm about to leap that way and cower at the back when a voice pops into my head: *GO LEFT!* I obey, strafing left, still looking up, seeing the rock somersault in great leaps and crashes, the smell of ozone preceding it on the air it's displaced, a micro-burst of wind. The block bounces again, arcing high, gaining speed, then alights to fracture into a surging stone avalanche. Hundreds of pounds of rock thunder by on the right, at head and chest level where I would have been had I traversed in that direction. Simultaneously a briefcase-sized hunk nails me in the left leg, below the knee. The force of the blow whips me around 180 degrees and I teeter on the lip of the ledge, flapping my arms like a fat kid on the high dive, trying not to let momentum win. If I fall now, I'll pull Lizzy off and she'll drop at least sixty feet onto the lone piece that separates us. If the piece holds, maybe we'll live; if not, we'll both rocket straight to the tundra. The ground is a painting, distant and unreal, a flat mosaic of green tundra tufts and tan and gray boulders so far below. We're the only climbers up here. If I don't recover and *NOW*, we could crater in seconds. That's what separates life from death in the mountains: seconds, milliseconds. You're dead even before you have to time to consider your imminent demise. You make a decision and you live—or die—with it.

I recover my balance and take a halting step backward, doubling over as my left leg gives out. A grotesque lump has formed there, looking like a compound fracture.

"*Oh, Jesus*, are you okay, Matt?" Lizzy yells down.

"I—I—I think so. I'm alive. . . . I might have a compound fracture. *Fuck!*" I roar with the pain, the adrenaline.

"Thank God you're alive!" Then: "I'm so, so, so sorry," she says. "The rope—it hung up and when I went to free it, it cut that rock loose. It was just sitting there on the edge of the ledge and I didn't see it until . . ."

"I think you—should climb back—down here, Lizzy—and take a look," I tell her, my breath hitching. "I need to—sit down right—now."

I'm prone, groaning on the ledge when Lizzy reaches me, massaging a knot the size of an apricot on my upper left shin, the skin broken and bloody but no bone peeking through. I've taken an extra Klonopin to calm my nerves and built a small anchor with the extra gear on my harness; I sit there shocky, shaky, sipping water, wondering if I can stand. Lizzy beefs up the belay, ties herself in, and helps me slowly to my feet. By making Gollum-like crab-shuffle moves and weighting my good leg, I can get around. We're able to self-rescue over the next two hours by climbing up and right to escape the face. The hike out is endless, hot, excruciating, the knot on my shin turning bloodier, black and blue, swelling to the size of a softball. My leg is floppy and limp, able to sustain only 20 percent of my body weight. I'm in a pissy mood—if only I hadn't abused narcotics, I could take some Vicodin for the pain.

One and a half milligrams a day, Klonopin, Boulder, August 2005:

"Matt, I'm not sure what's going on with your anxiety, but I don't think we should rule out anything in terms of medication," the psychiatrist is telling me. We're in his office in town, in an upstairs suite with wraparound vistas. I had to limp up the stairs to get here: The rock that clobbered me on Spearhead caused compartment syndrome, internal pressure within the muscular compartment on the front of my shin. The swelling is very slowly going away.

"I'm not so sure, Dr. Porridge. I guess I—I just don't feel like taking another drug when all I want to do is get off the first one," I say.

"Well, I'm still not entirely certain that the Klonopin is the real problem here," he says. "It seems like something else could be going on, a mood-cycling disorder or a flare-up of your underlying depression and panic disorder."

Really? I've told the doctor more than once that each cut has been progressively harder and that I'm beginning to suspect the Klonopin, but never elicited more than a noncommittal "Huh . . ." or "Interesting . . ." I've even asked if other patients of his have gone off benzos, and what he saw of their experience. He's adamant that he's seen them all quit "without severe anxiety problems like you seem to be having," but also concedes that one, a Vietnam vet with PTSD, has unsuccessfully tried to taper a few times but always "ends up freaking out" below a certain dosage. For me it's become bad—evil bad, sad bad, unmanageable bad. Kasey now does all the grocery shopping, as I'm often too nervous to leave our duplex. I want an explanation for this fear so I can understand and confront it. I feel that I'm approaching the Klonopin taper slowly and deliberately, a fact the doctor readily confirms at least every other week—I've been checking in with him more often. So why am I so terribly anxious?

The pain in my leg has been intense, but I'm committed to not taking narcotics, so stave it off with Tylenol and ice packs. I'm so committed, in fact, that I've been attending NA meetings despite hating group-anything. I don't really like talking about myself, especially in front of strangers. I don't like being around people. I go to the meetings, plop down in my chair, and then nod off midway through because I'm nuked by Trileptal, garnering hateful glances from the other attendees who must think I'm still "using." I quickly realize I don't click with NA—it's cultish, weird, and doctrinaire, unquestioningly placing faith in rigid structure and some unseen and unknowable higher power instead of in personal responsibility, substituting hokey "days clean" chips and key tags for whatever drug you've been addicted to, succumbing to an absolutist world view instead of searching inside for the core malfunction. To me, it's simple: I've stopped abusing Vicodin, and I recognize my problem with benzos and am working hard to get off. As a climber used to realizing the fruits of my will, it couldn't be any clearer that once I've decided to quit, I will simply and finally do so. Meanwhile the psychiatrist, who has himself urged the meetings, warns that NA takes an "all or nothing" approach—that they frown on psychiatric medicine and might request that you quit your meds cold turkey, which I will not do. So I also feel conflicted, hypocritical, like I'm living a lie and have no choice during meetings but to sit back with the doctor's chemicals coursing through my bloodstream and clamp my mouth shut. Which begs the question, Why even go? One evening, I sit beside a flannel-n-jeans she-skeleton with zombie hair and tobacco teeth who proclaims, "I'm tweeking right now. OH FUCK OH SHIT I feel so bad I can't help it but I came to a FUCKING meeting FUCKING TWEEKING!" It's the last straw. NA and AA may work for many people, and that's great, but they're not for me. This sideshow only makes me feel more depressed, these hopeless meth-heads and key tag collectors and born-again exercise junkies with their doe-eyed prattle about "milestones" and "cravings." The used-up lifers who loiter outside whatever venue before the meetings chain-smoking, chatting each other up, giving the stink-eye to newcomers. The stale, coffee-soaked church basements and airless, humming-fluorescent addiction centers with names like "Hopeful Vistas" and "New Beginnings." Having to leave the house and be around these joiner-weirdos when it's the last thing I need. To hell with them and their lame-ass cult—these cats are as addicted as ever, to NA and to each other. Me, I'd rather *live*.

"Well, Matt, I know you've been resisting, but one drug I still think might help is Lamictal," the doctor continues. "It's a very effective mood stabilizer and antidepressant. I've seen it be a literal lifesaver."

Lamictal, eh? This again . . .

"Is that the one with the risk of—"

"Yes, Stevens-Johnson Syndrome."

Doctor Porridge has explained it before—he'd said there's a roughly one in one thousand chance that Lamictal will cause an adverse skin reaction, which in the worst case can end in the ICU with third-degree burns covering your entire body as your dermis sloughs off and you die of sepsis and/or shock. Thanks, but no thanks—if someone told me a climb horribly killed one in a thousand suitors, I'd find another climb.

"No thanks. I'm just too scared." And it's true.

"Well, then, I'd like you to think about adding Zyprexa. I'm going to give you a few samples to take home. It's a good 'freak-out' pill, to take when you're having a really bad day."

"Umm, okay, a bad day . . . I have a lot of those. What kind of medicine is it?"

"More or less a mood stabilizer. It's a new drug that's proving to be very effective, but again, it's nonaddictive and it has no street value."

The psychiatrist is quite proud of this tidbit; he smirks a little. That's been his new selling point lately—not that whatever new drug he's pushing doesn't come with the usual litany of oppressive, mind- and body-numbing side effects, but that it doesn't have any street value and hence can be taken "safely." His spiel has come to feel hollow, like a used-car salesman pushing a Ford Pinto onto unsuspecting buyers because it's "safer in front-end collisions"— safer, that is, than the rear-end collisions that blow the cars up. That's what I've begun to realize: For every condition that the pills allegedly "cure," you can pile on a half-dozen side effects orders of magnitude more depression-inducing and reality-obfuscating than the original condition itself, perhaps with more pills prescribed to temper *these* side effects like an endless hall of mirrors. (Seen an antidepressant commercial lately and heard the side effects, listed rapidly and at sotto voce over images of those weird, rubber-skinned, space-alien drug-commercial actors bouncing back to life upon ingesting said nostrum? "In certain cases, Koflaxalon has been known to cause complications not limited to worsening depression, suicidal ideation, green urine, a third eyeball sprouting from the back of your neck, Exploding Heart Syndrome, homicidal rage, and rubberization of your bone structure. Koflaxalon should not be taken by teenagers, the elderly, pregnant women, ladies, men, or children. Consult your doctor if any of these extremely rare side effects occur.")

I pocket the samples and leave the office. Outside in the parking lot, I pour a few Zyprexa into my hand—brown rabbit turds seemingly named for a Klingon serial rapist. I stash them in the side panel of my car and forget about them. I dislike the idea of blindly, unquestioningly taking another medication.

Zyprexa, it turns out, is not exactly a mood stabilizer like the doctor told me. It is rather, like its chemical cousins Seroquel and Risperdal, an atypical antipsychotic, a schizophrenia and bipolar disorder drug that's been linked to complications such as massive weight gain (Eli Lilly's largest pre-FDA-approval study of the drug found that on average Zyprexa packs on twenty-four pounds in year, while later clinical trials showed one in six patients gaining sixty-six-plus pounds total[1]), dizziness, hyperglycemia, and high cholesterol. It is a serious, heavy chemical. A stellar investigative article, "Bitter Pill" by Ben Wallace-Wells, in the February 5, 2009, issue of *Rolling Stone*, examines the blockbuster drug's troubled history: how such a potent molecule, due to its developer Eli Lilly's naked profit motive, found mainstream prescription through a campaign that illegally promoted off-label usage for unindicated conditions like dementia, anxiety, and garden-variety depression. (It is not illegal for doctors to prescribe drugs off label; it is, however, illegal for drug companies to market off-label prescription.) According to the article, Eli Lilly paid out $62 million to thirty-two states in October 2008 over its Zyprexa campaign, as well as $1.4 billion "to settle federal charges of illegal marketing" the following January.[2]

Let's examine how a drug like Zyprexa might find its way to an off-label patient like me, who's not psychotic, not bipolar, and certainly not schizophrenic. First, a drug company—a *for-profit* entity—might spend on average $4 billion developing a molecule.[3] It will thus do everything in its power to earn back its money and

ates, which show the benefits of a particular drug. In his book *Unhinged*, the psychiatrist Daniel J. Carlat estimates that there are two hundred thousand KOLs in America,[9] for whom teaming up with Big Pharma is a lucrative side business: During his year as a KOL for Wyeth Pharmaceuticals, touting its antidepressant Effexor to other psychiatrists, Carlat, for example, cleared $30,000, paid in $750 per lunch meeting with the doctors,[10] while former *New England Journal of Medicine* editor in chief Marcia Angell has estimated that one way or another U.S. drug companies provide tens of billions of dollars a year to physicians.[11] Meanwhile, sleek TV and magazine advertising conditions would-be consumers to "Ask your doctor if Koflaxalon is right for you." Other than New Zealand, no other country in the world allows this odious direct-to-consumer hucksterism, marketing money that's exploded from $1.3 billion spent in 1999 to $4.8 billion in 2008.[12] That's how off-label marketing campaigns arise like the one with Zyprexa: a spam blast on all possible fronts.

The system skews radically in favor of the companies and the doctors. As a patient, you can never quite know why your doctor recommends one particular medicine over another—is it because of the research, his clinical experience, or the far-reaching tentacles of the pharmaceutical industry?

On the political side, as with Wall Street's naked symbiosis with the SEC—you know, the cozy "oversight" that helped catalyze the current economic depression—the ties between business and regulators are murky, fluid, and byzantine, with drug-company execs routinely leaving to work as FDA regulators and vice-versa, and with untold examples of the KOL physician-academics who supervise the drug trials—again, most often funded by the drug companies and *not* an independent agency—themselves being well-paid consultants for said corporations. Now throw in a wolf pack of slavering lobbyists pushing Big Pharma's agenda within the Beltway, and you begin to see, if not exactly a conspiracy, at the minimum a cash cow in which the profiteers unite to protect their shared interests. Lest you think I'm a conspiracy nut, I'd urge you to pay particular attention to Big Pharma's well-documented, decades-long history of bringing toxic, ineffective, and even fatal agents to market even as they knew the risks: Thalidomide, Vioxx, Darvocet, Serzone, and so on. And consider the fact that we Americans, all too credulous in our institutions, tend to blindly trust any drug with FDA approval, assuming that must mean it's "safe" or without any perilous side effects. (An online survey of nearly three thousand Americans revealed that 39 percent believed that the FDA only approves drugs that are "extremely effective," while 25 percent held that the FDA only approves drugs without serious side effects.")[13]

And remember also that *we* asked for this, that we're voting with our wallets. Just as McDonald's quickly and cheaply fills our guts, so, too, do psychoactive pharmaceuticals slap Band-Aids over our souls. It's the same quick-fix thinking that keeps us all opening our wallets for the latest, greatest "cure"—anything to keep from feeling the pain of existence. But life is pain; life is death and decay and entropy. As a climber, I should have known this—I should have known better. We're all always but one breath—or handhold—from oblivion.

A few days after my appointment with Dr. Porridge, my leg finally feeling better, I almost perish climbing one hundred feet up the First Flatiron as I free-solo with my friend Rolando, a talented Argentinean alpinist and mountain guide. That afternoon, I lock up and freak out on the little ledge where I'd lost it before, and Rolo has to coax me out of trouble. He points out handholds as I steel my frazzled nerves and traverse hard right off the formation, to where it blends into the hillside. The minutes there, shaking, terrorized, exposed on the face, feel like hours. I'm inconsolable until back on terra firma, and no longer have any business climbing without a rope, or maybe at all. It's never been this bad before. Perhaps I should try this Zyprexa—at this point I'll try anything. The antipsychotic turns out to be about as calming as eight Benadryl and a pot of truck-stop coffee . . . on an empty stomach . . . during a meth binge. The first time I take one, Kasey and I are out to dinner with friends at The Hungry Toad, an unpretentious pub where climbers and families congregate in north Boulder. I have fond feelings for the Toad, having stopped in for a burger or cider after long days on the rocks. This night we're at a table in the rear, and I've hidden in the far back corner by the bathrooms. I swallowed the Zyprexa right before we came—the doctor said to try it with food. Now, glassy-eyed, with rubber lips and a paralyzed jaw, I sit silently and observe my friends talking as if through an aquarium. Someone asks me about a climb somewhere and I stammer an answer, slurring the syllables: "Umm-Err-Yarr-Zass-A-Gorrrd-Climb." I'm ten seconds behind, in a dead world being unwoven by devils. Lizzy is out with us and keeps asking if I'm okay—she'll later tell me that a friend of hers, similarly drugged up on psych meds, took his life in his early twenties. She is worried that I'll do the same.

The next night is little better. Kasey is out at the bars with friends until the wee hours—it's been like this lately: her going out, me staying in—and I can't sleep. I take a Zyprexa and lie atop the covers, buzzing and sweaty. The bedroom's two slat windows give east from on high, down past the back drive into Boulder. It's hot but clear, and the stars are out. I peer upside-down at them through the glass, muscles locked with mortis. I fumble into the next day, bristling with chemical rage. On night three, my final one on Zyprexa, I get no sleep at all. I feel like puking, perspiring freely out on the couch alone, thoughts coming in a frenetic, dissociated rush like derailing train cars, heart slamming, too dizzy to read or watch TV, counting drywall dots on the ceiling. This "freak-out" pill has not helped. Like the Risperdal, Seroquel, Ambien, Depakote, lithium, nortriptyline, Neurontin, and Sythroid soon to come, Zyprexa only makes me sicker. All neurotransmitter systems are complementary and interdependent, and when one is on fire—in my case the GABA system—pouring more chemicals onto other systems only fuels the original fire. Ask any firefighter: Pour gas on a fire—any part of the blaze—and the whole thing will grow.

One milligram a day, Klonopin, Baltimore, Maryland, September 2005:

This psychiatrist is wearing sock garters—*sock garters*—and he's sitting here trying to tell me that I'm crazy because I get up early during summer to climb mountains. Each time he crosses his legs his slacks ride up his pale, hairless shins and I can see the garters, like old-lady pantyhose, holding up his black dress socks.

"No. You don't get it. I said I was getting up at 2:00 A.M. to climb the peaks around Carbondale because I was training for a specific objective and—"

"But why so early? You said you weren't sleeping, right? That you sleep less in the summer."

"No. I was sleeping just fine; I'd set my alarm and get up. Like I said, I was heading out on a big trip to California and wanted to get in shape, so I'd get up before work and climb the Maroon Bells to train. Also, you have to be up and off the peaks early, before the thunderstorms, so I'd get an 'alpine start.' That's just how we do it in Colorado."

"So you're saying that you're getting up alone at 2:00 A.M. to head up alone free-climbing along the mountaintops. I'm sorry, but this sounds like mania to me," he says.

"No, no, no; you're not hearing me. You start early so as not to get caught above tree line—there's nowhere to hide and you're totally exposed if the weather moves in. Have you ever been in a mountain thunderstorm? It's scary."

"I'm sure that I haven't," the doctor says. "So I suppose I'll believe you."

He scribbles more notes, head down, caterpillar eyebrows waggling. This cat is freakishly thin, as in "picked-last-for-kickball" thin, and it occurs to me that he's probably never set foot in the mountains and that no matter how explicitly I explain whatever facet of climbing he'll find some way to misconstrue it as psychiatric illness—bipolar risk-taking, manic early awakenings, depressive slumps when I'm fatigued after a long day on the rock, cyclothymic mood swings as I ride out a roller-coaster redpoint campaign. We're sitting in a windowless room within the belly of the Johns Hopkins Meyer Building, across Wolfe Street from the School of Public Health, where my father has chaired the Epidemiology Department for the last ten years. Hopkins has a sprawling medical campus the size of a small city, teeming with steel-and-glass skyscrapers that loom over the hospital's original ornate brick buildings. The campus has its own subway stop and a network of underground tunnels; there are armed guards on each corner and in every parking garage to keep the hoodrats away. My father knows how bad my anxiety has become, so after much coaxing on his part I've flown out to consult a Hopkins psychiatrist. Given the hospital's sterling overall reputation, maybe they're smarter than the ones in Colorado. Or perhaps not: This guy still can't grok what I'm telling him, probably because his ears are plugged with free Abilify pens and Seroquel samples.

In the end, I can't help myself. I blurt it out: "It's not mania—it's *training*. It's called being smart," I say. "Everyone gets up early to climb the Fourteeners."

The doctor looks up, squints at me nonplussed as if I'm speaking Swahili, goes back to scribbling.

I think back to those predawn starts for the Maroon Bells and Pyramid Peak up by Aspen, some of Colorado's steepest, gnarliest Fourteeners, with wedding-cake striations of loose red and purple sandstone. I think back to all the ridge link-ups I did in the Rockies and Sierra Nevada, stringing together ten or more technical summits in sixteen-hour continuous solo pushes. I can picture my headlamp bobbing off cobbles in the trail as my airways tightened with cold predawn air, wondering if mountain lions lurked in the aspen glades. I remember the forty-odd songs on my MP3 player, which I came to know by heart by one season's end, and the time I lost the cairns on North Maroon and headed up the wrong gully in the dark, encountering smooth, fifth-class headwalls, pressing desperate mantels on wet, rounded ledges as I made for a stegosaurus skyline, as night spread into infinity behind me, the void velvet and hissing. I think of the venerable bighorn sheep I found atop North Maroon, starting to bloat with decay, having chosen this summit to lie down upon and die. I can smell skunky sky pilot wafting from fractures in the rock as I scrambled past stands of cheerful blue columbine and white tufts of alpine phlox. I recall watching the sun pierce the jagged pink horizon from fourteen thousand feet, of seeing rolling green-tundra and red-talus basins spread at my feet blazing yellow with dawn. I smell the screen-door ozone odor given off by rocks accidentally dislodged. I can barely, just barely, remember what it's like to be strong enough to treat peaks some might climb only once in a lifetime like a jog around the park. I miss the unfettered movement, the all-day spiritual buzz I'd get when soloing ridge link-ups, the man-on-the-moon energy of being alone all day in the mountains, the endorphin bath when I finally stopped back at the trailhead. Yes, I must be manic—must be unbalanced—to want to wake up early to experience something like this.

What other explanation is there?

The doctor will write it later in his eight-page evaluation, what $500 of my father's money purchases at the Johns Hopkins Hospital's Affective Disorders Consultation Clinic: "The patient does describe episodes that are suggestive of mild possible hypomania. He describes in the summertime lasting 3 or 4 months, having significantly more energy and sometimes getting up very early in the morning to rock climb, even at 2:00 A.M."

Two things: A) This clown can't tell rock climbing from mountain climbing. And B) Who doesn't have more energy in summer? It's always been this way: Of Russian and Irish extract, I get a little sadder, a little slower, a little sleepier in winter like a hibernating bear, and when summer comes I feel re-energized and become more mobile. This doesn't make me manic; it means I calibrate to the seasons the way that man always has until artificial constructs like psychiatry came along with labels like "Seasonal Affective Disorder." It means that I'm a climber and know the true length of the day, the natural rhythms of our planet.

"Well, we'll just have to agree to disagree on this point," the doctor says, closing the discussion.

We talk for a long time—an hour and three quarters—he taking my family, drug-use, and mental-health history, I answering dutifully in the defeated whisper that has become my speaking voice. At the end of the session we discuss diagnosis and treatment. The doctor delivers his verdict:

"What I think we're looking at is depression and anxiety worsened by taking too long to come off benzos," he says. "I look at it sort of like pulling off a Band-Aid: You need to just yank it off, or you'll only prolong the pain." In the evaluation's History of Present Illness section, the doctor will write, "Nowadays, panic attacks are present several times a day with much anticipatory anxiety."

"But I'm going pretty quickly," I say. "A quarter milligram every two weeks. I—I couldn't go much faster."

"It's actually really slow," he says. "I think you're just prolonging your agony."

I think about the two-day spike in symptoms, in fear, I've felt after each cut and how it now takes me the entire intervening two weeks to "stabilize" before my next cut—and how I can't stomach the thought of speeding things up. In my head, I can't picture a Band-Aid, but more like a pressure bandage applied to a gashed artery—rip it off too quickly and you'll bleed out. I have a copper battery taste in my mouth, one that's been there for weeks, my liver digesting itself. I smack my lips and swallow.

"I stopped Valium abruptly years ago, like I told you, and I basically went insane. I don't see how I could go through that again. . . ."

"Yes, but this time it's different," the doctor argues. "You haven't been abusing the Klonopin, though you have been on it for far longer than the Valium. So I think a rapid taper would be relatively safe, and of course we can monitor it. This benzo is really keeping you down."

"But how exactly is it making me more depressed, more anxious? I don't get it. No one has really explained this to me."

"Look, these tranquilizers are very dangerous. We see a lot of patients come in here on them, and we always take them off right away. Benzos can depress you, in particular Klonopin, and you've been on it for years, which is far too long."

"And so the depression gets worse, as well as the anxiety?"

"It could be, and it could be that with less and less benzodiazepine in your system, it's hitting you on the way off as well, making you more and more anxious," the doctor says. "I fear that if you continue to taper slowly, your problems will only go on and on . . . Regardless, you need to come off these pills, and I think we need to go ahead and get it over with."

At last, a doctor who acknowledges that the benzos might be my problem, who doesn't shovel the blame back onto me by telling me that my tough taper is some anomaly or insinuate that it's all my fault because I have a history of substance abuse. I feel a vast sense of relief. Maybe Hopkins can help.

"Okay, and how would you do that?"

"Well, I'd increase your Paxil dose to twenty-five or even fifty milligrams and take you very rapidly off this last milligram of Klonopin . . ."

Shit.

"That much Paxil? But I've never been able to take more than ten milligrams."

"That might be true—and you might attribute any increase in anxiety to the Paxil, but it would in all probability be because we're going rapidly off the Klonopin, and because it gets harder with each cut. Think of it this way: The last milligram is the toughest. It's like getting a heroin addict off methadone. It's most difficult when you go from that last increment to zero, to having no more of the drug in your system. You're going to have to feel much worse for a little while in order to feel better, Mr. Samet."

"Quickly?" I ask. "How quickly?" I'm trembling.

"A week, a few days . . . we'd just have to see. We go by blood pressure and heart rate—it's a medically safe taper."

"And I could do that staying here in Baltimore, like at my dad's, and coming to check in at the hospital?" I think of my father's place, a row house on Federal Hill, of how it might feel to weather the withdrawal there. I could sit out on his rooftop deck, watch boats chug into the Inner Harbor, do breathing exercises, count floors on the downtown skyscrapers, try to walk when I felt well enough.

"Oh no, you'd have to be an inpatient so we could supervise you." *What?*

I go stiff, feel ice in my belly at the notion of being locked up on a ward so far from Colorado and my life as a climber, so far from Kasey and from Clyde. I don't like other people dictating my decisions, controlling my fate. I remember this one thing from Mapleton: A "voluntary hold" doesn't mean you can check yourself out whenever you want, but that you've voluntarily checked *in* for X amount of time and that *they* can hold you for at least that duration. And that if during that period you refuse treatment or insist on leaving, they'll toss you in jail. If, like me, you just want help getting off drugs and the doctors decide, no, not good enough, he needs more drugs, declining the meds will see you, at your weakest, most crazed, vulnerable hour, thrown into county lockup.

"I'm not sure," I croak, "that I am willing to stay on your ward."

"I want you to consider it, Mr. Samet," the psychiatrist says. "I really think it's the only option. You are quite obviously in a bad way." I'll see it later on the evaluation, his professional impression: "[Matt] was obviously psychomotor slowed. He spoke slowly and there was latency to his answers. . . . He reported being depressed and looked depressed."

I'm sure that I did.

We are to meet with my father in two hours to discuss the evaluation. I shuffle back across Wolfe Street to my dad's office, running the gauntlet of security guards, sign-in sheets, and doctors and grad students clipping briskly along the hallways. Only the anointed come to Hopkins, and their crisp, erect carriage is designed to let you know this. I sit with my father in his office and relate the doctor's diagnosis. My dad wants me to check myself in, too, wants me to be here close to him to sort out this mess. He walks me through the School of Public Health, shows me a gym on one of the highest floors with a row of treadmills, with grad students sweating away before floor-to-ceiling windows facing grand city views. "See, you can even come over and work out when you're feeling anxious, Matthew," he says. "We could run together."

"Dad, I'm not well enough to run on a treadmill," I say. "It's all I can do to walk the dog. . . ."

"It can't be that bad," he says. "Exercise has always helped you."

I bite my tongue. I love my father dearly, but right now his cluelessness annoys me. I know that he's forcing optimism because he wants to see my pain end as much as I do, but I also know that he has no idea what I'm feeling subjectively, internally. No one does. No one wants to. We have lunch and return to the psychiatrist. My father sits and listens raptly to Dr. Sock Garters's spiel, but this time there's a new flourish:

"There's also some evidence," says the psychiatrist, "that electroconvulsive therapy helps with benzodiazepine withdrawal, so we might also try five or six rounds of that." He's almost giddy, like a car salesman who smells blood in the water and sneaks in another few hundred dollars for the factory coating—only ECT costs a thousand dollars a pop and I don't have health insurance. Moreover, it's barbaric: You're strapped to a table with a giant rubber band around your head, sedated and given succinylcholine, a paralyzing agent that prevents your vertebrae from cracking and limbs from snapping during the post-shock seizure, fitted with a tooth guard, and then electricity—up to hundreds of volts—is pumped through your temple, precipitating the "curative" epileptic fit (the believed mechanism of treatment, inducing, as it does, neuronal firing). Sound like fun? ECT stems back to the notion of "convulsive therapy," first deliberately applied in the 1930s by the Hungarian psychiatrist Ladislav von Meduna, who triggered seizures in his patients with camphor and, later, Metrazol, a cardiac stimulant (an Italian psychiatrist, Ugo Cerletti, began using electricity in 1938);[14] a typical course of ECT will involve multiple sessions—a few a week for up to a month.[15] While ECT fell into disfavor in the

1970s, it has made a resurgence, and estimates point to one hundred thousand Americans a year receiving it. ECT can cause memory problems, particularly with short-term memory and memories accrued during the treatment phase, brain-cell death and hemorrhage, and—as I'd later learn, talking to other patients upon my return to Hopkins—set you up for deep depressive backslides, necessitating more shock therapy ad infinitum. One description of ECT presented in *Unhinged* describes it as "resetting" your brain, like hitting control + alt + delete on a frozen computer. However, the human brain is not a $300 laptop. ECT only works, as Dr. Peter Breggin points out in *Toxic Psychiatry*, by "disabling the brain . . . by causing an organic brain syndrome, with memory loss, confusion, and disorientation, and by producing lobotomy effects."[16] The patient, bombarded by neurotransmitters, feels temporary euphoria masquerading as improvement, but over the long run, argues Breggin, becomes more apathetic and "makes fewer complaints"—a perfect subject for continued, profitable shocking.

I'm almost desperate enough to consider it.

"Electro-shock? Really?"

"Yes," says the doctor. "It would be your decision, but we have seen some benefit with benzo-withdrawal patients."

I look over at my father. The pathos is clear in his eyes, bright blue through his bifocals. What father wants to hear that his only child needs shock therapy?

"I'm not sure we want to do that," my father says, giving an uneasy chuckle. "But, Matthew, I do think that Dr. Garters is right, and that you do need to check yourself in."

"Yes . . . no. Well . . ." I stammer. "It's . . . ECT's not for me. And I don't really want to be an inpatient here." In one gushing soliloquy this doctor has mentioned megadoses of Paxil *and* ECT; I'm starting to feel less willing, if indeed I ever was, to trust him. The three of us talk it through some more, both of them working on me until a lump forms in my throat. I know that I'm scared, know that I'm depressed, know that it's not going well back in Boulder, but an interior voice is shouting that I should not do this. Call it intuition, but this is the same voice that told me to "Go left!" on Spearhead. It is the same voice I'll heed a year later when, despite the protestations of many friends and family members, I quit my final medicine.

Finally, I make a concession.

"Okay, I'm willing to try an inpatient stay," I tell them. "But I want to do it back home, close to my girlfriend and my dog. I'm sorry, but Colorado is where I live. Not here, not Baltimore, not Maryland: Colorado."

"But Hopkins is one of the best hospitals in America," my father says.

"Yes," chimes in the doctor. "Our affective-disorders unit is one of the oldest in the country."

I say nothing.

My father asks if Johns Hopkins has any satellite clinics or affiliations near Boulder, and the doctor says no. My dad places so much stock in Hopkins, having worked all his life to reach a chair at this storied institution. His and the psychiatrist's East Coast parochialism irks me, this attitude that anything out West is inadequate or hayseed. And besides, it's not their decision.

"I'll do this," I tell them. "I'll commit myself. But it will have to be back in Boulder."

Three quarters milligram a day, Klonopin, Boulder, Colorado, September 2005:

The only other time I saw my father cry was after his mother died, in her early seventies, from heart disease caused by cigarettes. Even when his marriage went south, he never shed a tear in my presence. Now we slouch in the lobby of a psychiatric hospital outside Boulder, he, Kasey, and I, all three of us moist-eyed and mute in the face of the reality that I am committing myself. A staff member spots our trio, comes over, starts asking questions. She's African American, middle-aged, matronly, kind in a way that cannot be faked. Whoopi Goldberg would play her in a movie. She asks me why I've come, and I tell her it's to get off benzos.

"It's hard, honey," she says. "Benzo withdrawal is really, really hard. But you're strong—you can do it. You're a healthy young man and you want your life back. I'm not going to say it's not going to be difficult, but we'll be here to help you. We have good doctors, and they've seen this sort of thing before. They will help you—I promise you that, honey."

Something in me relaxes. *They're going to fix this.*

"Thank you," I say. "Thank you so . . . very, very much." I cry some more, not caring who sees me. That's become the norm lately: sobbing fits, triggered by the merest trifle—a sparrow on a branch, a dead squirrel in the road, a gutter curl of red autumn leaf. And weeping: wordless weeping. Decay, dissolution, self-pity, salty tears.

I hug my father good-bye, kiss Kasey, and let a nurse lead me back to the ward, to the intake room. This intake room is just like all the others—they never have windows. The hospital doesn't want you to see the outside world, to get too torn up over what you're leaving behind. And the lobbies are always nicer, too, more calming and feng shui than the wards themselves. It's a ruse, a trick to placate would-be patients and the family members guiltily dropping them off like dogs at the kennel. Potted plants, terra cotta floors, soft-lit golden lamps, and leather chairs give way to banged-up laminate cabinets with outdated board games and dog-eared puzzles. To TV/VCR combos with flickery low-resolution screens, white linoleum hallways, institutional bench-and-table dining sets, black-plastic toilet seats and leaky shower heads, blurry metal mirrors, and fungible plastic chairs that can be quickly wiped clean and stacked against the walls. To the odor of bleach and the starchy, spoiled-milk-and-baby-food stench of cafeteria fodder. To med stations where nurses call names off a sheet and bark orders at the patients, making them stand there and swallow every last pill. To impersonal, fluorescent-lit group rooms with scuffed tabletops and blackboards covered in fading chalk hieroglyphics—years upon years and layers upon layers of psychobabble nonsense.

The nurse takes my history; I recount my story automatically and then hand her the Hopkins evaluation to relay to the psychiatrist who will take my case. I've been told that he'll either see me this evening or early the next day—in either case within twenty-four hours of admission. This nurse says that she had to come off Valium three decades earlier and that she knows what I'm going through. I'm encouraged when she squeezes my forearm and says that I can do it. She's middle-aged, her hair pulled back in a salt-and-pepper ponytail, brusque but with a kind smile. I'm led to my room, told to strip to my boxers, and patted down by two orderlies, fresh-faced Baby Hueys barely out of high school. They go through my bag, distributing the contents on the bed with surprising daintiness. I have a stuffed animal with me, a green frog, Smeech. My father and Kasey return with new boxer shorts and an electric razor. They've been to Target, they say, *out in the world.* We bid each other another rough, sad good-bye, and then I sit on my bed. It's night now, a sudden and total autumn darkness. I have a roommate who shows up some time after dinner, nods at me, grunts, and lies sidelong in his bed facing the window, looking out into the central courtyard. He's in his mid-thirties with jaundiced skin, a billygoat beard, and the "fuck-off" air of an ex-convict. I'll learn the next day in group that he is months shy of liver failure, that his name is on a transplant list but that alcoholics don't get precedence. I try not to let him hear me crying. Lately, I've been experiencing a torturous transition into sleep, hallucinating that my pillow is a gnashing mouth, swallowing me up like the ghosts in Pac-Man. I clutch the mouth face-to-face, grasping it as I collapse through the mattress and into hell.

The next day it's breakfast before meds, and I sit at a dining table at 7:30 A.M. trying to choke down a mealy heap of scrambled eggs. Mornings are bad—I wake up in a toxic funk, sleep fog quickly giving way to anxiety shivers before the first Klonopin, my breath accelerating as soon as my eyes shutter open.

"Meds aren't until nine," says my tablemate when I ask.

I couldn't tell you his name; only that he's come for a med

checkup, says he's bipolar, and is a repeat visitor. A friendly guy, indistinct, bland as a manager at Applebee's. He suggests a game of gin rummy, and he and I and a mute, dark-haired woman who can barely make eye contact play a few rounds. I glance up at the clock every five minutes, willing the time to pass. Soon it's 9:00 A.M., and I queue up for my pills: Klonopin 0.5mg, Paxil-CR 12.5mg, Trileptal 150mg. I know from experience that the warm, sedated "it's all going to be okay" glow the pills impart will vanish by 11:00 A.M., at which point I'll feel even worse. But I ride it out for now. This particular hospital leans heavily on group therapy: Every other hour you pack like sardines into a meeting room and discuss this or that topic while a social worker or nurse steers the conversation. I'm not sure what they're on about in the groups—as the pills wear off, it's harder and harder to concentrate. I snap out of it long enough to listen to a burly young guy at the end of the table recount how, on a bender, he drove his truck through a wall and is now withdrawing from painkillers. After group, I overhear him tell a social worker that he cried and cried the first few days, but that now he feels better. The social worker tells him that it was chemical, a result of narcotic withdrawal causing low dopamine in the brain, and that it will pass quickly.

Lucky him. Me: I'm constantly on the cusp of fight-or-flight. I squirm atop my bed between groups, jolt up agitated, the cheap, windrowed blue bedspread itchy and tactile along my back. I scan the hallways, looking for exits; I spy a battered exercise bicycle down one hall and take tepid consolation in the fact that perhaps I can jump on that and ride myself into exhaustion if need be. I'm like a wolf in a trap, ready to gnaw off its own leg. The doctor has yet to see me, but I need to see this doctor. This doctor will fix me. That's what doctors do: They heal. They fix people—they've even taken a Hippocratic oath to do so.

By the third group I stake my claim on the seat closest to the door, so I can escape (but to where?). The social worker in charge, Tom, a reformed ex-biker judging by his denim ensemble and handlebar mustache, takes me aside afterward and asks if everything is okay. He says he could feel the fear radiating off me like no one else in the room.

"It's anxiety," I tell him. "Fight or flight. I need to be by the door."

"What are you scared of, man?" asks Tom.

"Klonopin withdrawal."

"Oh . . . yeah, that's a hard one. We don't, uh, see it very often."

"What should I do, man? What should I do?"

"I guess I don't know," Tom says. "You'll have to ask the doctor. . . ." The guy drifts away.

After lunch I wander out in the courtyard with the other patients. They stand around in packs smoking on the lawn—it's all very high school. They have the world-weary air of combat veterans. The doctors shocked the catatonically depressed woman with whom I played cards this morning. Now she prances about like a child hunting Easter eggs, pointing out the rabbits that occasionally emerge from a warren beneath the grass and proclaiming, "Bunnies! Look, *bunnies!*" Her happiness looks put on to me, like a kid feigning elation at receiving dress socks for Christmas. Maybe this woman thinks the doctors are watching. Or maybe she needs to believe in this because, really, what choice is there?

It's a clear, perfect, autumn day, and I can see a corner of Longs Peak over the fence, the tip of the Diamond in fact, a great alpine wall topping out at fourteen thousand feet where I've had incredible adventures. I feel like pointing it out to somebody, telling them that I've climbed it at least ten times, but then realize I'll only sound grandiose, like I'm fabricating fictions. I swallow my words and look up at the rock, black at this distance, an artifact from another man's life. It's warm enough in the flatlands that climbers could be up there today, making a late-season ascent, donning a third layer of clothing for warmth as the sun slips behind the massif and the meltwater lining the vertical cracks freezes into verglas.

By the fourth group I'm in such a tizzy that I practically hover over my chair. I situate myself again by the door, beside a plumpish, curly-haired woman who was there alone when I came in. She sat spraddle-legged, skirt hiked up, grinning into space, a small boombox blaring tinnily on the seat beside her. I wondered why she had her legs open, glanced over, caught a wink of panties, saw something curious about her eyes like they had sand in them, looked away to spare her any embarrassment. Other patients filed in and the group commenced, more talk about feelings and med compliance and chemical imbalances. I was not and am not listening. I cannot listen. Then:

"Sally, why don't you tell everyone why you're here today?" the nurse prods the woman with the boombox.

"I, uh . . . Oh really, do I have to?" Sally says. Her face falls a little, the Cheshire cat grin vanishing.

"You don't have to, Sally, no. But I think it would really help everybody."

"You do? I can't imagine how."

"Well, you do have quite a story. . . ." the nurse says.

Sally pauses, then says, "Okay, well, then—it's depression. I've had depression for a long time. Most of my life, I suppose."

"Depression is tough, isn't it, Sally? That's why you've come here again this week, so we can help you with your depression. . . ."

"Yes, I'm hoping to feel a little better so I can go home again and be with my family."

"But this isn't your first time here, is it, Sally?" says the nurse.

"Well, no."

"And why did you come the first time?"

The woman pauses, inhales, speaks.

"Do I have to?"

"Well, Sally, I'd love it if you did," the nurse says.

"Okay, it's because I blinded myself," Sally blurts out. "I took my fingernails in my eyes and scratched them until I couldn't see anymore."

The room goes silent. I glance over, and sure enough she has the offset gaze of the sightless, her sclera black and sparkling, the irises scarred and furrowed—the "sand" I'd noticed earlier.

"And Sally, why would you so something so terrible?" the nurse asks after a few beats.

"I was having trouble breathing," says Sally. "Just . . . trouble breathing all the time, like I couldn't get a full breath."

"But it wasn't asthma?"

"No. They couldn't find anything wrong with me. . . . They looked and they never did. To be honest, I was sick of being a soccer mom. I felt so bored and empty and . . . just depressed, just driving my kids around, driving from one place to the next. Just driving and driving them around until there was no more 'me' anymore, just this chauffeur. A chauffeur for my kids. One night I looked at myself in the mirror and hated what I saw. And then I started with my fingers."

"And you blinded yourself," says the nurse.

"Yes, I blinded myself."

"And then you came here."

"Yes, that first time . . ." says Sally. "They sent me here after the emergency room, after the hospital."

"Thank you, Sally," says the nurse.

"That's okay," says Sally. As soon as she stops talking, Sally's grin comes back over her face. She aims it at nowhere and at nobody in particular.

Then: "See," says the nurse, "what can happen if we don't treat our depression?"

Nobody says a word. I feel that I might throw up—I have this same trouble breathing. *Was Sally on benzos?* After group ends I almost stop to ask her but then lose my nerve, fearing what she might say. And besides, really, it's Sally's business and no one but hers; she seems almost happier in a world in which she cannot see and in which her only charge is a portable plastic stereo.

Night comes again, dinnertime, a black crashing wave—I'm growing increasingly more confused and agitated around dusk, like my grandfather when he was fading with Alzheimer's. They call this "sundowner's syndrome," only I'm thirty-three and he was eighty-seven. The anxiety rages like a fever, and I emerge from my room to ask the nurses once, twice, three times when the doctor will see me. This expert shrink will surely, upon, reading the Hopkins evaluation, wave a magic wand and make everything better. He will see me quickly and safely off the final three-quarters of a milligram. They call us for dinner, and I vibrate at the table, wondering how I'm going to choke down a gray slab of dog's-ass meatloaf with a side of spinach entrails when a nurse takes my elbow.

"Okay, Mr. Samet. Dr. Jabba is ready to see you," she says.

I follow her to a windowless room, go inside, and sit down across from the doctor. He's a fat, jowly, bearded troll with Dick Cheney lizard eyes and all the warmth of an Antarctic ice shelf. He does not extend his hand nor introduce himself.

"It says here, Mr. Samet," he launches in, leafing through my file, "that you want help getting off Klonopin. Is that correct?"

"I—I—Yes! Yes, I do," I say. "Please, please, Dr. Jabba. You've got to help. The anxiety is so bad . . . so, so bad. Oh God, oh please, I need your help. . . ." I'm openly sobbing before this man, a man I've never met in my life. It's something I would never ordinarily do—in fact, before this period and especially after it, I'm often accused of being too reserved, too silent and emotionally standoffish around family and friends.

"And how long have you been on it?"

"Years. I—I was on Ativan for five or six years, then Klonopin for the last year or two."

"And you want to stop?" His words are clipped, emotionless.

"Yes, please, please, please help me quit, Dr. Jabba. I—I—I—just want to get my life back. To be with my girlfriend and my dog." I reach for some tissue, dab my eyes, blow my nose. "I . . . I'm a climber."

"And you live here in Colorado?"

Something is wrong. Why is he asking questions he could have easily answered himself by reading my file?

"I do. Boulder. But I thought you—"

He cuts me off: "Look, Mr. Samet. You have chronic anxiety. Why would you want to stop your pills?"

My spirit sinks like the proverbial man who wakes up in a coffin, realizing that he's been buried alive.

"Because I think the pills are making the anxiety worse, Dr. Jabba. Because I—I . . . This is what I came here to do. The woman out front, she said you guys could help me get off benzos. That's the *only reason* I'm here." I stutter and stammer as he stares at me with all the compassion a black widow might feel for a fly: "It's . . . it's what I came here to do. All the way back to Colorado . . . Didn't you read my evaluation from Johns Hopkins? They said I needed to stop the Klonopin, too."

"No."

"No?!"

"No. I haven't had time."

What? It has been twenty-seven hours since my admission, three hours beyond the timeframe in which, legally, a doctor must evaluate his patient, and he hasn't even cracked my fucking file? What kind of cunted-up three-ring shitshow is this place?

"But you need to read it to understand what—"

He cuts me off again: "Klonopin *treats* anxiety, Mr. Samet. And I see you sitting in front of me sobbing and clearly severely anxious and wanting to go off, but you need to be on it. The proof is your extreme anxiety. The proof is right here in front of me—*you* yourself are the proof. In fact, Mr. Samet, you need to be on Klonopin for the rest of your life. It is a safe, reliable anxiety treatment, and I can't see why you would want to stop. I'd even suggest that we increase your dose tonight."

How can this doctor, knowing me for all of two minutes, make the snap judgment that I need to be on benzos forever? This is "health care"? I'm waiting for Allen Funt to emerge from behind the door and say, "Hey, great one, Matt. Well-played, but you're on *Candid Camera*!" What a fine joke that would be.

"But, Dr. Jabba, I'm not here because I want to *keep* taking Klonopin," I protest. "In fact it's the opposite. I keep trying to tell you that."

He inhales deeply, rubbery man-teats rippling beneath his cardigan, drawing air down into his panniculus, this shabby, obese, dead-eyed motherfucker who could not even crawl up the cattle trail on mountains I've climbed by their toughest routes. This "doctor" pauses, scribbles a note in my file, and then sighs, loudly, the-atrically, exhaling sour smoker's air. This is who I've flown back to Colorado to see: Jabba the Fucking Psychiatrist Hutt.

"Fine, then," he mutters. "We'll switch you to Seroquel, see how that goes tonight."

"But—but how long will I be here?" I ask.

"I don't know," he says. "We'll just have to see. I'll call it in to the med station." And with that the psychiatrist waves one flabby paw and dismisses me. I shamble out of the room, too dazed even to be anxious anymore. I forgot to ask how Seroquel works, but it hardly seems to matter. I know that it's an antipsychotic. Still stunned, I head for the med station and queue up next to a small, grandmo-therly woman who asks my name. I tell her it's Matt, and her eyes light up. She says that Jesus had asked a "Matt" to relay a message to her. Thinking of no better option, I hug her and tell her that every-thing will be okay. The woman looks into my eyes, mumbles some-thing, and takes my hand to thank me, saying God bless you God bless you God bless you God bless you. She swallows her pills and wanders off. I take the meds they proffer in a tiny Dixie cup, like the sample cups at an ice-cream shop: Trileptal and a dose of Seroquel. I swallow them and return to the dinner table. There someone tells me that the grandmotherly woman's son died and that she has not been the same since, that she is lost in a way no one can fix. I try to eat but within ten minutes can barely move, as if my entire body has been shot full of Novocain. When I stand the room yaws like the deck of an Alaskan trawler, so I shuffle unsteadily to a couch and plop down poleaxed, gripping the armrest and staring at patterns in the lino-leum floor. I space out on scuffs and scratches and puke-colored flecks. My thoughts are like blood clots: lodged in there somewhere but dark and obscure, obstructing the proper flow of information.

I couldn't tell you how long I'm on the couch. Minutes? An hour? Days? I feel an arm around me and it's my father. I turn to the other side: Kasey.

"Dash, yoov harsh tor gar meen aortarrr har," I say. "Kasey, theev garve me a barn pile and eesh . . . marfing me snicter."

"What, Matthew? What?" my dad is asking. "Are you okay? Did you see the doctor?"

"Arsh dard I dinnint tell nawr."

"He didn't see you until now? What—What did they give you?"

"Zhairerquill." My eyes are glassy, fixed.

"Oh, nuggins," Kasey says. "What have they done to you? What did they give you? You're not yourself."

"Auntie shycaustic."

"Antipsychotic?" my dad asks. "But why?"

"Strawp klonnerpenn . . . preesh, I wanter go harm."

"I think maybe you *should* go home," my dad says. "Did the doctor even read your file from Hopkins?"

"No."

A flicker of anger crosses his eyes; this is a man who's accustomed, in the medical milieu, to seeing things done immediately upon his request.

"They can't do that," he says. "They have to see you in twenty-four hours, and we paid a lot of money for that evaluation. I can't believe this."

Kasey takes my hand and holds it, kneading it in her lap. My mitts are smoother than they've been in decades—office-worker hands, not those of a climber. I'm crying again, but silently, tears gliding over my cheeks, the face muscles frozen. I just want to go home and finish this taper on my own. My dad stands up and says he's going to find the hospital administrator. When he returns with the man—to his credit, profusely apologetic—they agree to release me, and my father pushes the point that in addition to a full refund the facility note that I did *not* leave "against medical advice," as it might prejudice future practitioners against me. The administrator agrees to everything and has me sign discharge papers. I trail my hand across the page, willing my fingers to close around the pen. We collect my clothes, my new boxer shorts, my new razor, Smeech the frog, a self-help paperback on chronic hyperventilation that I've been reading. I'm starting to unfreeze simply by moving around while my father steadies me. I look back into the room a final time as we go and my roommate's still lying there, looking into the night and awaiting a liver that might never come.

One half milligram a day, Klonopin, Boulder, Colorado, late September/early October 2005:

Autumn—not "fall," which is a dirty word to climbers—is a sacred time for Colorado rock jocks. We call September "Sendtember" for its cool, dry conditions, and October can be even better. The cliffs, etched against azure skies, ripen to their full beauty, dark smudges of stone emerging from red, sienna, and golden stands; underfoot ferns turn yellow then dry, flaky brown, and even noxious plants like poison ivy glow vibrant crimson. Unlike late spring, with the whole climbing season before you, in autumn you feel the clock ticking—it's time to finish up any outstanding projects before the snow starts to fly.

Too bad I have to sit this one out. Tragic, really—it would tear at any climber's heart. You get only so many autumns in a lifetime.

Before my father left, we devised a plan to see me through my taper. He wanted me to return to Hopkins, but I just couldn't. I agreed to start seeing a therapist in addition to working with Dr. Porridge. This therapist came highly recommended, an anxiety expert who'd mentored the woman I used to see back in Glenwood Springs. I approach it all with fresh optimism, at least for the first week or two, happy for my nominal freedom. The therapist isn't cheap—she works from her stately Victorian home—but my father is paying and seems fine with doing so. I feel guilty, a broke and uninsured thirtysomething leech, until he tells me he just wants me to get better.

This therapist: It's complicated. She is a well-meaning woman who did come to care for me, who once came and plucked me from my house when I'd stopped answering phone calls and become semisuicidal. She helped me to leash-train Clyde by showing me how to use a Gentle Leader and how to bribe him with bits of frozen hot dog. She visited at Mapleton when I ended up back there as an inpatient. And she would have me come over for an oatmeal-and-blueberries breakfast, and then take me walking around the Pearl Street Mall, downtown's pedestrian area, to show me how to be out in the world again. But she is also distinctly overbearing and takes a narrow "tough-love" cognitive-behavioral approach, which means she operates only within certain paradigms. She really does not know the first thing about supporting benzo withdrawal, a fact borne out by her confession to me, after I returned from Hopkins, that not one of her patients had ever successfully tapered without hospitalization. Things could have been framed so much better, so much differently.

Early on, this therapist gives me solid tools: a bag of birdseed in a pillowcase that I heat in the microwave and then place on my belly for breathing exercises. The heat, weight, and pressure are reassuring, and it's nice to have something I can reach for other than pills at sundown. And she refers me to a healer and yoga teacher, Steven, who leads therapeutic-yoga classes in Boulder and does private sessions at home. With Steven, I work on chi breathing exercises, stretches, and "bottle work"—using the neck of a plastic bottle to massage my belly as I visualize breathing through it, drawing the air down deep using the diaphragm instead of taking nervous upper-chest breaths. Steven has a theory that by using the bottle until your guts soften and burble, you're stimulating the enteric nervous system to promote calm. I begin carrying a Perrier or Vitamin Water bottle with me—it will become a talisman, my only solace on nights of unending agony.

I also start visiting a massage therapist, a beauty with a South American accent and miracle hands. I have a secret crush on her, so it's no problem battling my way across town for an appointment, and I always leave feeling better . . . at least for a half hour. Between the psychiatrist, the therapist, Steven, and the massages, I have at least one appointment every day: all the king's men, trying to piece Humpty Dumpty back together again. These visits provide the only structure to my days—a raison d'etre when the ones that matter most, climbing and work, have been stripped away. I've taken to lifting weights at home, using chi exercises between sets to temper my breathing. I will keep to the weights religiously for the next two years because it's often the only exercise I can do.

The therapist promises that if I can "withstand some strong sensations" she will get me off benzos. I'm encouraged. We start with a benzo-tapering workbook. It's written by two psychiatrists who, given their breezy, clinical tone, have clearly never undergone withdrawal. It's on loan to me, the pages coming loose from the binding, the glue old and cracked. I take the book home, start reading, dutifully tracing the withdrawal timetables onto paper of my own so I can track my progress. According to these experts, I should be done in four to six weeks—not so long at all. I can't wait! I have it in my head that once I'm off, the anxiety will, lacking fuel, smolder and die out. I just need to be shut off this last half milligram. Then I see it: an equivalency table. It reveals that my "tiny" dose of four milligrams of Klonopin a day actually translated to eighty milligrams of Valium, as much as I was abusing in 1996. Right now, at a half-milligram of Klonopin a day, I'm still on essentially ten milligrams of Valium: an entire Roche Blue Note. I flip the page, landing on a random paragraph: "There is some evidence that the higher the dose and the longer the duration of use, the more symptomatic will be the withdrawal process, though the patient should not let this fear impede his or her progress off the drug."

I don't like this book so much anymore. I also don't like a couple things the therapist lets drop, careless tidbits discouraging in timbre, things not to say to someone as fragile as I've become: Namely, that she can't be certain that Vicodin abuse hasn't left me permanently panicky, like a musician client of hers she mentions who fried his circuits with cocaine, and that I have the absolute worst anxiety of anyone she's seen. When you've lost all sense of yourself in a crisis and your brain has been chemically rendered so malleable, ideas like these congeal like footprints in wet cement. They're dangerous. They extinguish hope. As she tells a roomful of fellow panic sufferers one night during weekly group therapy, "This is Matt, who's joining us for the first time. And can you believe that his anxiety was so bad that his doctor had to put him on *four milligrams* of Klonopin a day?"—the implication of course being that the problem is intrinsic to me and not entangled with these addictive pills.

Bullshit—I'm a climber. I deal with more fear in a year than most people will in their lifetimes, wasting away before the idiot box second by brain-dead second.

Remember, we go to health-care practitioners for, if not perfect wisdom, at the minimum an infusion of hope to empower us to keep fighting. *Primum non nocere*—"First, do no harm"—is the guiding principle of modern health care. This should also extend to the way one's condition is verbally framed by a caregiver, especially if the patient is psychically vulnerable.

Housebound and hopeless, I've lost all sense of myself, all discernment when making decisions, especially when it comes to my health. I'm able to work a little, on freelance transcription and copyediting projects for a local publishing house, but besides my various appointments this work is my only contact with the outside world. I dwell in a thickening twilight, a fear-fog teeming with winged bugaboos, howling banshees, and fanged demons. There are no longer any boundaries between the anxiety and me: I've *become* anxiety, though a better word really is *terror*. It is existential terror—not a fear of any particular thing, but a bottomless horror at simply existing so lancing it precludes rational thought. As my father would later put it, "You certainly didn't have control over your thinking." My brain is like a sponge, but not in the good way, like a toddler soaking up language. It's more like a cinder-block wall on which any gangbanger can spray-paint his tag because the ego boundaries that make me *me*, my assembled years of opinions, emotions, thoughts, and experiences, have been obliterated by benzodiazepine withdrawal.

Little wonder then that I continue to drink the Kool-Aid when Dr. Porridge reiterates that this taper must be approached from a "place of strength" and that "not having other meds on board could be very dangerous." I still trust and believe him that there mustn't be any "gaps in treatment." I am the empty, shocky vessel into which he can pour his steaming elixirs, a walking, talking human-test-tube experiment. I find myself at his office on a dim late-autumn afternoon, the sky snot hued and gauzy out the window, telling him how much trouble I've been having sleeping and focusing. I ask the doctor what he thinks about taking another month to get off Klonopin, and he says that I could easily cut a quarter milligram every three days, which would mean I'd be done in, well, a week.

Only a week?

"And you've seen other patients do this, Dr. Porridge?" I ask.

"Yes, certainly."

"Tapering this quickly, without any problems?"

"No. No problems—they were completely fine, with no spike in anxiety after a week or two. You might feel some flu-like symptoms for a few days, a headache, fever, and chills, but that's about it."

"And I'm done."

"Yes, you'd be done."

"Just like that?"

"Just like that."

Dr. Porridge writes a prescription for a few sleeping pills, Ambien, which he assures me won't interfere with my taper. What I don't know and what the doctor doesn't bother to relate is that Ambien, like Lunesta and Sonata, is one of the "Z drugs"—for their generic names zalpelon, zolpidem, zoplicone, and eszoplicone—which despite being labeled "nonbenzos" because of structural differences have a nearly identical chemical action. The drugs bind selectively at BZD receptor sites and can cause similar problems to benzos, among them rebound insomnia when you quit taking them. I shouldn't be on Ambien, especially not now. But he doesn't tell me that. He also gives me samples of Risperdal, an antipsychotic.

I have just one more question:

"Dr. Porridge, what do you think about doubling my dose of Paxil, like the doctor at Hopkins suggested?"

"Well, Matt, I think that's probably a very good idea. It might give you the foundation you need to get off benzos."

"Should—should I try it?"

"Yes, I think you could do that."

"Okay. I'll try it starting tomorrow and see what happens."

"Great. We'll see you back here on Friday. Let me know how it goes."

"Okay, then. Friday . . ."

The Paxil blows up my world. I become suicidal.

One old chestnut the psychiatry establishment likes to trot out to explain away any such adverse reaction to antidepressants is that the risk of suicide goes up your first few weeks on a new drug because the drug has "activated" you. (I heard this echoed again and again at the hospitals.) In other words, you, the poor, shambling, hapless depressive, newly recharged by said miracle potion, have finally found the energy to exact your undoing. It's a drive that you lacked earlier, being somehow too enervated to walk to the garage, turn the car on, and run a hose from the exhaust pipe into your window. To me it's a specious argument: Look at how many people commit suicide every day—32,637 in America alone in 2005, for example.[17] They *all*—sadly, horribly—found the energy to kill themselves, and it's highly unlikely that every last one of them was just starting antidepressant therapy. In fact, I'd hazard to guess that most of them were indeed massively depressed at the time.

The fact remains that if you want to kill yourself, you will find a way. Man always has and always will. What antidepressants can do—and what twenty-five milligrams a day of Paxil did to me—is foment an insidious condition called akathisia, which we might call "activation times one thousand." Dr. David Healey, a psychiatrist and author, in 2004 published a book called *Let Them Eat Prozac*, an unsparing look at the known dangers of SSRIs, including akathisia, and how they were nonetheless kept on the market. The word *akathisia* was coined by two German-speaking psychiatrists in 1955 and literally translates as the "inability to sit still," though it is best understood as "agitation" or "inner turmoil."[18] (The condition has been associated with the antipsychotics as well.) In 2004, the FDA directed manufacturers to put a "black-box label warning" on SSRIs for children and adolescents and proposed an extension extended up to age twenty-four in 2007, warning of the risk of suicide and suicidal thoughts early in treatment. But what drives this risk? Well, according to Healy, iatrogenic akathisia. As he summarizes, "Prozac and other SSRIs can . . . cause suicide in individuals who have no nervous conditions, primarily by inducing mental turmoil during the early stages of treatment."[19]

"Turmoil" is a nifty term—we use it to talk about the Middle East or that troubled uncle who never quite finished high school. But akathisia is something different; a better synonym would be "hades." For me, one day after increasing my Paxil, it begins with a manic, dissociated, rushing feeling, like I've taken too many truck-stop energy pills. By day two I experience heart flutters, random flurries of palpitations that trigger heart-slamming panic attacks. Very little fear accompanies the attacks, however, almost as if they are happening to someone else one body away; my psyche feels distant, shellacked in Pepto-Bismol. Kasey and I go to Target one evening and bump into Rolando and his wife; just seeing them there, the first time I've run into Rolo since the First Flatiron de-bacle, triggers the response. Rolo is a good friend and would never judge me, but just a moment's flashback to being trapped on that ledge with him sets me off.

The worst part is, I stop sleeping. It's not a quaint, Bohemian "trouble sleeping," with thirty minutes here and there adding up to a few hours each night; it's straight-up not sleeping. I'm too agi-tated to read or watch TV, out in the living room so Kasey can slumber in the bedroom, adjusting and readjusting my position on the couch in the hopes of tricking my body to shut off. I thrash, I sweat, I tremble; I watch paramecia whip around the corners of my vision. After two nights of this, the world takes on a white insub-stantiality as if being rendered into paste. Day and night become one vast, gray, unchanging crepuscularity, the hours and minutes like blank, effaced mile markers on some unending purgatorial high-way. I feel a high, hollow nausea like I've consumed too much cof-fee. My bones *itch*, like my skeleton wants to peel free and run away from my muscles. This is akathisia: inner turmoil. I can see why it might drive you to suicide.

On day three, I return to Dr. Porridge's office. I mention that the Paxil might not be working, but he urges me to give it a few more days. That night the myoclonic jerks start, those seizure-like spasms and plummeting sensations we all get just before falling asleep. But these "sleep starts" are so violent that they jolt me off the couch as if it were electrified. I float inches above the cushions before slamming back down, arms outstretched and hands fluttering like a skydiver's. This will go on for the next year. As soon as my eyes droop another myoclonus comes, my body kicks, and I wake up in fresh terror. My lower back is getting sore from the spasms, and often the jerks are accompanied by a sonic boom, as if a barrel of gasoline has exploded beside my head. Between that and the gnashing-pillow hallucinations, I develop a Pavlovian abhorrence of anything to do with sleep. A psychiatric evaluation done at Mapleton one week later will read: "[Matt] stated that sleep was especially problematic as he would doze off and then suddenly awaken in a panic and have vivid feelings, which he acknowledged were not literally true, that someone was in the bed with him threatening him."

At my behest, Kasey calls my parents to explain this dire turn of events. My mother drives up from Albuquerque. She takes charge, drives me to my various appointments, gets me and Clyde out on walks, but it's no use—I still can't sleep. One golden afternoon we hike up Sanitas Valley, a gradually inclined, bow-shaped cleft between Mount Sanitas' eastern slopes and the sandstone hogback, Dakota Ridge, that sequesters it from town. Piddling red-brown rocks protrude from the ridge, peeking between the Ponderosa that spill off the spine. I look over and see two people bouldering, a mother and her teenage son, moving crashpads about as they attempt traverse problems. That's how I got my start, asking my mother to take me to the rocks. Now, plying clifflets barely taller than VW vans, these two look like superheroes, remote and courageous in a way that I never will be again. I point them out to my mother, tell her how much I miss climbing. The anxiety has grown so all-pervasive that just *looking* at photographs of people climbing, seeing them high off the ground, gives me panic attacks.

I return to see Dr. Porridge first thing Monday. I creak and crack into his office, flop down in a chair, and tell him I now feel incredibly sick on the Paxil and describe the insomnia. I have not slept in five nights. I'm no longer sure if I'm alive or dead. The doctor takes notes, pauses, chews on the end of his pen, and looks up at some phantom point in the middle of the room. He pauses again. Then:

"You know, Matt," he says, "I think I've got it!"

"You . . . you do, Dr. Porridge?"

"Yes. I can't believe I didn't see it sooner."

"You—you know what's going on?" *A solution! Finally!*

"Yes. You're *bipolar*. It's been in front of me all along!" He's so happy with himself, so pleased to have cracked this great medical mystery—the man grins from ear to ear.

"I am? But I don't get manic, I mean—"

"You don't necessarily need to be a classic manic-depressive to be bipolar, Matt," the doctor continues. "You can be what we call bipolar type 2, which is more of a depression with episodes of milder mania called hypomania."

"You mean, like in summer when I've had more energy or—?"

"Exactly!"

"But why would I be bipolar now of all times? I mean, why didn't we see it sooner? I don't quite understand how . . ."

"We've been seeing more and more of this lately, Matt, which is a bad reaction to an SSRI that indicates some sort of bipolar or cyclothymic condition."

"Cyclothymic?"

"Sorry: mood cycling."

"But I mostly feel one way, Dr. Porridge, and that is 'scared-all-the-time.'"

"Yes, Matt, but we've also talked about the better periods you've had, the 'ups,' if you will, when you were climbing well and feeling good and had energy. These mood shifts can be very insidious, very subtle—I have one patient, a woman, who can cycle through different moods four or five times a day. And it just tortures her. Heck, she's even changed moods right here with me in the office!"

No comment.

I ponder that. For months the only two moods I've been cycling through have been despair and terror; no euphoria. There has been nothing to be euphoric about. Something doesn't quite add up, but I'm not thinking clearly enough to put my finger on it. What an ex-girlfriend, Katie, will later relate after discussing my situation with her mother, a psychotherapist, is that the "bipolar" diagnosis due to a bad SSRI reaction is currently all the rage, and should not be implicitly trusted. Later my own research will reveal that, in my chemically fragile state, I've had an understandable reaction to Paxil, a drug I never tolerated well at high doses anyway. I believe I suffered "serotonin syndrome," a toxic overload of serotonin that in cases can be fatal—this serotonin dump is what's fueling the akathisia. So much again harkens back to the interdependency of the neurotransmitter systems: With GABA receptors down-regulated, a rift in the armor that widens with each Klonopin cut, there is nothing to countervail the excitatory neurotransmitters, and on a higher dose of Paxil my brain catches fire like dry tinder sparked by lightning. Moreover, the benzos have for years been dampening the action of the excitatory neurotransmitters, so to suddenly, artificially increase the activity of one, serotonin, yields a double insult to unprepared neurons. As Dr. Ashton framed it in a scholarly paper, "As a consequence of the enhancement of GABA's inhibitory activity caused by benzodiazepines, the brain's output of excitatory neurotransmitters, including norephinephrine (adrenaline), serotonin, acetyl choline and dopamine, is reduced."[20] In other words, I have no business attempting to "cure" benzo withdrawal by artificially increasing serotonin activity—it just unbalances my brain even further.

"And how do you treat mood cycling?" I ask. "Or if I'm . . . I'm bipolar?"

"Well, we need to get you off the Paxil right away and try you on another mood stabilizer."

"Which one?"

"Depakote, for mania," the doctor says. "I'm sorry about the Paxil, but it will have to be tapered quickly, which is going to be unpleasant. But you can't stay on it now that you've had an adverse event."

I ask him why Paxil has affected me this way. The doctor speculates that it's triggered a "mixed state," a dastardly blend of depression and mania peculiar to the bipolar spectrum. Then he reiterates that Depakote will fix this.

I know about Depakote: A climbing buddy once spiraled into a depression after his beloved grandfather took his own life. A doctor told my friend he was bipolar; he then prescribed Depakote, or valproic acid, an anticonvulsant used for treating seizure disorder and bipolar mania. My buddy, in all the years that I'd known him, had never been the least bit manic. He took the pills anyway. After gaining twenty pounds in two months, and tired of being foggy-headed, my friend stopped, confronted his grief, and healed on his own. But me, I'm still spellbound by this doctor, as if he and he alone has the answer.

"Do you really think it will help, Dr. Porridge? Another . . . another pill?"

"Yes, Matt. I do. It's clear to me now that you're bipolar," he says. "I don't know how I missed it all those years, but it explains everything: your bouts with depression, your sensitivity to antidepressants, the weird way you metabolize benzos."

Weird way I metabolize benzos?

"I'm not sure I follow."

"What I mean is the fact that the benzos appeared to work for many years but then just stopped, or only worked erratically after that. That is another classic sign of bipolar disorder, as, Matt, was your substance abuse."

Voila! *The blame has been shifted firmly back to the patient: It is his individual failure to metabolize the drugs properly. It is he, the drug addict, who has unhinged his brain and no longer responds properly to a "safe, effective anxiety treatment." Of course it is not that the patient listens attentively to brain and body signals and has for years been on the roller coaster of tranquilizer addiction, but that he's a manic-depressive junkie in need of thorough, ongoing medical intervention.* Voila! Hallelujah! Eureka!

One more night without sleep is what does it. A great pressure has built inside like a swollen volcano. Kasey and I are having an out-and-out spat or perhaps just another dead-end kafuffle when I go into the kitchen, fetch the red-handled steak knife, and begin cutting myself, slicing gill-like slits along the outside of my thumbs where the hand-meat is thickest. Red blood drizzles onto the kitchen floor, onto the white-green linoleum tiles lifting at the edges where they're cracked by the laundry closet. This duplex is so old, so rickety, so battered and used up.

"Look at this!" I'm yelling at Kasey. She stands in the living room wide-eyed. "Look at this look at this look at this look at this! I can't fucking take it *anymore! I can't fucking take it!!!*"

I've cut myself to release the pressure, but also to show seriousness of intent. I don't know what else to do. I throw down the knife and make for the front door, trying to squeeze past Kasey. I'm not a cutter and never have been, but later, during my first year postwithdrawal in Carbondale, I'll often sport half-moon welts across my cheeks and brow: fingernail crescents, cicatrices of pain and self-hatred to vent inner torment. My plan—one I've been cogitating on for days—is to hurl myself off a cliff. There is an eighty-foot bluff at the southern toe of Mount Sanitas, with a tangle of stones, vines, and briars below it upon which to dash my brains. I've also fantasized about throwing myself off the Naked Edge, a cleaved sandstone arête in Eldorado Canyon. The Edge rounds off onto a great slab eight hundred feet above the silver tumble of South Boulder Creek. Romantically, I've pictured myself scrambling up the back of Redgarden Wall by moonlight, the air cold and crisp, the lights of south Boulder and Louisville twinkling in the distance. I walk out to the point, take a deep breath, and then swan dive, a final few seconds in freefall. But the route is iconic to climbers, and I don't want to sully it so. This cliff on Sanitas, however, has been closed for years due to nesting birds, so no one should care if I explode myself in the talus.

I've got one hand on the doorknob when Kasey stops me.

"What about me?" she's screaming. "And what about Clyde? *You can't just leave us like this!*"

Kasey is right. I fall to the floor, convulsed with sobs, wracked with guilt. This is some black, horrible shit I've laid on this poor girl. We've only been together a year and a half, and the last six months have been this nightmare. We're both crying and crying and clutching each other. I can't leave now when I really don't know what's going on, when my departure will forever scar Kasey, and my friends and family. So we cry and cry, there on the floor, until there are no more tears. Kasey leads me to the kitchen where the knife lies in its bloody Rorschach blot. She picks it up and drops it in the sink. Kasey runs my hands under cold water, bandages my thumbs, and calls my mother at her motel. A plan is made for the following morning.

One and a half milligrams a day, Klonopin, Boulder, Colorado, early October 2005:

You know those dreams in which you're back in high school and will never, ever graduate, no matter how many classes you take, and your despair when you realize your predicament? These are like that, only worse—seven years later I still have them, the dreams in which I, for whatever reason, am permanently stuck on the last milligram of benzodiazepine. Usually I'm with friends at the cliffs or in some public place—a rock gym, movie theater, or restaurant—when the hour comes for a pill. I take out the orange bottle, uncap it, and shake out an Ativan. "But didn't you quit, Matt?" someone will ask, to which I'll reply, "I did—well, almost. Okay, I tried, all but for this last milligram. It has been impossible to stop." And then I add: "The doctors say I need to be on it for the rest of my life."

I swallow the pill and the panic starts, percolating upward through my consciousness. Until I wake up thrashing in the sheets.

The seed for these nightmares is sown at the Mapleton Center where, locked on the ward for the second time in my life, they triple my Klonopin dose, moving the goalposts nearly off the field. This will be done against my will to "stabilize" me. This second time it's not a voluntary committal but instead a seventy-two-hour mental-health hold. I *will* take my meds or else. My mother has brought me to the emergency room. We wait together on black Naugahyde chairs in the lobby, me red-eyed and sniffling, until an intake coordinator leads me away to a hospital bed and starts recording my history. I can recite the story by rote, even in this zombie whisper. I'm like a lump of jelly, answering her questions through copious tears, passive and balled up on myself, cradling my belly like it's a colicky baby. No, I tell her, I don't have insurance. No, I tell her, I don't abuse drugs; I just take the ones that have been prescribed to me. Yes, I tell her, I have stopped drinking. No, I tell her, I have not slept in six nights. At all. Six nights. It is driving me batshit bonkers. Six nights. From here it will be a two-minute ambulance ride, lashed Hannibal Lecter–like to a gurney, to the Mapleton Center. Because I've shown suicidal tendencies I'm strapped in just like that. How humiliating, to be wheeled around like some freak. I will sob in the ambulance, and one of the EMTs, a girl really, pretty with deep-blue raccoon eye shadow, will tell me that she was in the suicide gurney herself only a few years earlier and that she wants me to hang on. She calls suicide a permanent solution to a temporary problem, and adds that she's glad she didn't succeed because life got better.

Good for her.

I spend three days at Mapleton, on an empty ward only two blocks up Fourth Street from my home. At first it is just me and one other patient, a woman. Kasey comes to visit, as do my mother and the therapist. They talk to me; I answer. Updosed on Klonopin, I sleep again—a little; the myoclonic jerks temporarily fade to aftershocks, the pillow fangs retract. I can glimpse Sanitas edgewise from my room—its eastern facet midway along the ridge, white-golden grass carpeting the steep slope beneath the backs of the boulders. These were the last rocks I'd been able to frequent, close to home as they were. I'd walk up alone, hands quivering and belly hollow, and do easy traverse moves close to the ground. The fins of smooth chocolate, red, and tan Dakota sandstone cant south and west above Sunshine Canyon, warmed by late-day sun dappling through the Ponderosa. The few times I mustered the courage to stand along their spines and gaze out over town, I'd succumb to vertigo and have to sit. I'd feel so isolated fifteen feet above the ground, light years from humanity. Such is the plight of the panic-attack sufferer: that there always be a lifeline on hand in case you "lose control"—access to a phone to call 911, proximity to a trusted doctor, family member, or emergency room . . . a bottle of benzos. Your mind tricks you into believing that such things equal safety. Even in better years I harbored a secret trepidation on multipitch climbs, especially at hanging belays (ledgeless stances in which you depend from the gear), where I'd feel pinned, exposed, and trapped, balefully alone as my partner climbed out of sight around some overhang. At Mapleton, I'm in a corner room by an elevator shaft, its brick ramparts and a spruce tree impeding the view up-hill. The window doesn't open, so I can't see the rock fully. But I know that I want to be there—even doing pathetic traverses on low boulders close to the ground sounds like heaven. Just to touch stone again would be divine. Just to feel its grit beneath my fingers, the warm, smoky smell of sunlit rock, the tang of pine and lichens.

Nothing is accomplished by this hospitalization. Not one thing. They increase Klonopin, step up Depakote, add Ambien, and halve the Paxil. The Depakote erases my short-term memory, puts me in an affectless mist in which I find myself fumbling for words. The first morning, a nurse acts like I'm junkie scum when I ask that they split my benzo dose three times across the day as I'm ac-customed to instead of two. The doctor has ordered the Klonopin only in the morning and night, but by 11:00 A.M. I'm twitching with interdose withdrawal. I approach the nurse's station to plead my case. We go back and forth, this slack-jowled, clown-whore-makeup apparatchik and me. Finally, she agrees to call the doctor. He will not budge: "I look at the brain as a bathtub," he tells me during consultation. "You can pour the meds in all at once and they're not going to drain out. It's perfectly fine to stagger your doses out morning and night. Your net intake will be 1.5 milligrams of Klonopin, which is where we will keep it."

"But I—"

"You should feel the antianxiety benefit of the medicine throughout the day, as it's designed to do."

"But you don't understand," I continue. "Two hours after every dose I get so—"

"And besides," he cuts me off, "I don't think it's good that you're used to taking the Klonopin three times a day—that's too many. We need to break you of the habit." This doctor, apparently, has studied neither interdose withdrawal nor the fact that different people metabolize benzos at the different rates. Two years later I'll bump into him and his wife leaving a Boulder restaurant and he'll look at me with puzzlement, as if seeing a ghost, as if marveling at the fact that I'm even still alive.

During the days I sit around watching TV and coloring for art therapy, chatting with the only other patient. Her name is Emily, a sharp young woman and a recovering heroin addict. We talk about her daughter and my dog, Clyde, while we trade crayons back and forth across the table. This is what goes on in psychiatric wards: People like us, high-functioning adults, are given coloring books, key-ring kits, modeling clay, grade-school-level mood worksheets, puerile journaling assignments. *Goo-goo gaa-gaa: What time are my meds?* Emily has an IV in, pumping high-test antibiotics to fight off a nasty leg infection, the IV stand her constant companion, humming and clicking and pushing liquids through a snarl of tubing. She has recurrent dreams about a long bridge under the Texas sun, she tells me. Emily runs toward the center where her daughter cries out. Her husband runs from the opposite side. In the middle, they fight over the girl; they rend the child in two. And then Emily wakes up. She always wakes up at that point. She misses her daughter, she tells me, terribly. Emily talks quickly, flitting from topic to topic, her speech pressured. She tells me the doctors think that she's manic, and I say allegedly so am I. "Really, you, manic?" she says. "I don't think so. You're too depressed to be manic. They just tell everyone they're 'bipolar' these days. It's the big, new thing. Bipolar, bipolar, bipolar. Bipolar this, and bipolar that." It's just us for two days, then a few other sad sacks trickle in.

I'm allowed without fanfare to leave after three days. On my final morning, I spot a flyer on the wall, a tear-off sheet with a number for a benzo-withdrawal support group. I rip off a stub, put it in my wallet, and forget that it's there. Or maybe I don't forget; maybe it's that I'm too scared to call, that I don't want to hear how bad off I am. I come to the hospital's afternoon outpatient program for the next two weeks, another stop on the list of daily appointments. I'm tired of expending so much energy fruitlessly trying to "get well"; going from here to there and back again. My life has become so empty now, however, the blank hours so imbued with nameless horror, that it's good to have somewhere to go. The only person who seems to get what I'm going through is the yoga teacher Steven, whose sister faced a similar struggle. When I tell him that I've been diagnosed as bipolar and that I have a new medicine for that, his face falls and he says, "Matt, I worry that they're undoing everything you and I are trying to work on here."

I am not yet ready to admit that Steven is correct. I continue to seek external fixes: I cut out gluten after reading somewhere that it heightens anxiety. I put full-spectrum light bulbs throughout the house, having read that they help with depression. I try the seasonal affective disorder lightbox my mother gave me, but it makes me feel speedy. And I take a magnesium-calcium supplement for muscle spasms, which the psychiatrist has said will help with myoclonic jerks.

I only get sicker.

I have no optimism left—zero. The updose of Klonopin has made sure of that. I now fear, and for good reason, that I will never get off benzodiazepines. I visit a general practitioner associated with Mapleton, who runs bloodwork and diagnoses vitamin B deficiency and hypothyroidism. I dutifully take vitamins and Synthroid. I only get sicker. My mother, as eager as I am for a tangible, treatable malady, is excited that we finally have a working diagnosis: bipolar disorder plus hypothyroidism. Me, I'm not so sure. Needing to resume her work as a pet sitter, she returns to New Mexico. I ask Dr. Porridge to switch me from Klonopin to Ativan, as Ativan was my original benzo and thus might be easier to quit. I immediately begin tapering but it scarcely matters. I only get sicker. Every step now is the wrong one. Too many wrong turns have been taken.

I only get sicker.

I attend group at Mapleton each afternoon with the other outpatients. There I encounter a middle-aged woman, a benzo lifer who was taken off seven milligrams of Klonopin at detox back East—in three weeks. She sits beside me with her straw hair and her black, unblinking, stuffed-animal eyes, takes my hand, and says, "You can do it, honey. If I did it—and lord knows, five times in thirty years now—then you can too." Her skin is cool, papery; she drops my hand. She's not all there. I ask how she is doing after benzos, and she says, "The truth is, honey, that I'm in hell. I'm burning all over, itching and burning everywhere on my skin. And I don't get to sleep for the burning. But you're young, honey—you can do it. Don't you let them keep you on those pills all your life. Don't be like me. You should do this for yourself."

It is mid-October now, a time of darkening. I tote my climbing pack to group and try to boulder on Sanitas afterward, squeezing in an hour on the rock before dusk. It was my promise to myself on the ward that no matter how poorly I felt, I'd return to the rocks. So I go, but when I get more than five feet up a coppery taste floods my mouth and I start to tremble, even on huge holds off which it should be impossible to slip. I can't trust my feet—they're at the end of a stumblebum's legs—and I picture my hands rocketing off apropos of nothing or the holds spontaneously exploding. Throngs stream past on the trail, their voices tinny and reverberant, conversations incomprehensible and polyglot as if I have aphasia. I'm splintered, shattered, refracted into shards; the center cannot hold because there is no longer a center.

One day during session with a hospital therapist I tell her that my goal is to quit benzos. After we finish she leads me over to meet Mapleton's addiction specialist.

I stand before this latest expert's desk, asking if she has any insight, extending little hope that she will.

"Benzos are terrible," this woman says. "Really addictive, really terrible, really hard to quit. I'm surprised that a doctor had you on them for so long."

"I know," I manage. "Me, too."

"But you took them, right? You *knew* what you were getting into." She frowns at me, another humorless devotee of the addiction and recovery school of tough love. Jaded, I'm sure, by years of having to hear out prevaricating parolees, years of crappy, linoleum-floored barracks offices, rickety desks, missing pens, continual relapsers with crocodile tears, methadone stragglers, DT veterans, the whole drab, shabby addict parade.

"Yes . . . and no. I guess so. It's a long story. . . ."

"We need to get you off of these drugs," she says. "Right away."

"Okay, but how?" I ask. "That is the thing that keeps happening—no one can tell me how. Or how quickly to go. Or where to go to do it. Or where to even begin. Or what to expect . . ."

"Well, that's going to have to be up to the doctors," she says. "I'd suggest you check yourself in as an inpatient. They're very smart and can help sort it out for you."

"I see," I say. "Thank you."

The woman then suggests NA and hands me some addiction pamphlets. Hospitals are full of pamphlets, kiosks of them in every corner, bouquets of booklets, leaflets, and free magazines on whatever condition: bipolar, ADD, ADHD, schizophrenia, substance abuse, depression. Most of the literature tout the benefits of pharmaceuticals and most, if you stop to look at who produces them, have been paid for by Big Pharma, the American Psychiatric Association, patient-advocacy groups, and other vested interests. I'll take her pamphlets home and drop them atop the free bipolar "news" magazine in which a famous cartoonist *rah-rah-rah's* the curative effects of ECT. Later, I will dump this propaganda in the recycling bin where it belongs.

I shuffle two blocks home through dry, drifting leaves, beneath streetlamps humming white pools into a blue-black gloom. Two cyclists breeze past, half-shouting at each other in conversation, while a runner with a headlamp trots fleetly along the sidewalk opposite, heading for a night lap up Sanitas. The air is clear and cool, devoid of substance. The Boulder überathlete mill grinds on, but it's alien to me. I'm now an outsider in my own town. I now realize, perhaps for the first time, that if I don't research and solve this nightmare myself, no one will. These so-called mental-health professionals are not equipped to help someone like me, nor do they seem particularly willing. All they can do is get you *on* drugs—not off. It's not in their financial interest to wean you from the pharmaceutical teat, and hence they have not studied the issues. They'd phase themselves right out of a job.

It is in their interest to keep you eternally sick. To diagnose you. To re-diagnose you. To superimpose new diagnoses atop these. To hospitalize you. To remove the power of decision from your hands. To infantilize you. To lobotomize you with chemicals and shock treatments. To cram your individual story and personality into a diagnostic box. To poison you pill by pill until that box is all that remains—Schrodinger's cat both dead and alive, crated up and observed unto its own quantum demise.

Either I solve this *now*, or no one will.

I go home and hop on the Web, staying up all night feverishly researching on Kasey's laptop in our spare bedroom. Finally it's two simple keywords—"benzo" and "withdrawal"—which will reveal that I'm not an aberration and that the symptoms I'm feeling are in fact my nervous system's natural response to withdrawal from the tranquilizers. Thank God for the Internet: Before it, benzo people had hardly anywhere to turn. One of the first sites I visit is benzo.org.uk, which is exactly where anyone interested should start. This online clearinghouse, with twelve-hundred-plus pages of articles and information, including survivor stories, was founded in 2000 by Ray Nimmo of the United Kingdom. Nimmo was on Valium for fourteen years. Only two years into taking the drugs, he had to quit his job as director of a successful company due to escalating anxiety, agoraphobia, paranoia, and depression. (Nimmo was originally prescribed benzos as a muscle relaxant, for abdominal pain. In an interview, he said, "I was . . . told I needed to take this medication for the rest of my life because I developed symptoms of anxiety and later depression."[21]) Nimmo successfully sued the doctor who'd strung him out, winning £40,000 in 2002.[22] To this day he maintains and continues to add new content to his invaluable online resource.

The crucial document at benzo.org.uk is *The Ashton Manual*, or more precisely, Dr. Heather Ashton's three-chapter protocol, "Benzodiazepines: How They Work and How to Withdraw." For benzoheads looking to quit, it's the Holy Bible. In it, Ashton promotes a gradual taper via Valium, as she writes, ". . . usually over a period of some months." She recommends Valium because it has a much longer half-life (twenty to one hundred hours, and up to two hundred hours before the active metabolites leave the body) than the fast-acting benzos like Ativan, Klonopin, and Xanax. If you're on the fast-acting drugs, she recommends that you first switch over before you taper; as Ashton points out, this is because they "are eliminated fairly rapidly with the result that concentrations fluctuate with peaks and troughs between each dose." You therefore need to take the fast-acting forms several times a day, with many people experiencing, as I have, interdose withdrawal, i.e., "a 'mini-withdrawal,' sometimes a craving, between each dose," as she writes. However, tapering via Valium facilitates a more gradual drop in blood level ("the blood level for each dose falls by only half in about 8.3 days," writes Ashton) with which the body can more readily keep pace, letting your GABA receptors slowly come back online to minimize symptoms. As Ashton codifies it in her manual, with Valium you "obtain a smooth, steady and slow decline in blood and tissue concentrations of benzodiazepines so that the natural systems in the brain can recover their normal state." Valium also comes in handy ten-, five-, and two-milligram pills, letting you customize doses.

I'm reading this at 1:00 A.M., eyes bright for the first time in months but my spirits also falling because I know that, having abused Valium in the past, I'll be hard-pressed to find anyone to prescribe it. (And anyway, precisely because of this abuse it might not work for me.) Then I find it: Schedule 7 in Ashton's high-dose timetables—"Withdrawal from alprazolam (Xanax) 4mg daily with diazepam (Valium) substitution." According to this table, from my high point of four milligrams of Xanax/Klonopin, going at Ashton's suggested pace with a Valium switchover, I should have tapered over 62 to 115 weeks: one to two years, not the seven-odd months that brought me precipitously to this point. No wonder I feel so rotten. Confirmation of my misstep is found in chapter two: "Abrupt or over-rapid withdrawal, especially from high dosage, can give rise to severe symptoms (convulsions, psychotic reactions, acute anxiety states) and may increase the risk of protracted withdrawal symptoms." I lived this firsthand back in 1996—I should have known!—though it seems odd that I should feel even sicker this time around. As I'll discover later on a Yahoo support group, likely because of that cold-turkey jolt and the subsequent years of on-again/off-again use, I've yo-yo'ed my nervous system around and set the stage for a most grueling final withdrawal, perhaps even a protracted one.

I Google "protracted benzo withdrawal" and end up at a now-defunct site called benzoliberty.com. "Benzos Aren't Us" is their motto, and the site incorporates a header graphic with the stars and stripes, an upbeat, spiritual tone, and links to tips and graphic creations by survivors. One section in particular catches my eye: "Old Timer Stories," a list of thirty-one names hyperlinked to their respective tales. It is all there, my story as reflected by others: years on the drugs, a host of baffling, creeping, worsening problems like insomnia, agoraphobia, emotional blunting, bowel distress, depression, tinnitus, muscle weakness or spasms, and anxiety. Various attempts to quit, many of them cold turkey or close enough, often upon physicians' advice or at hospitals or detox centers. All hell breaking loose. A denial by the professionals that benzos have anything to do with the insanity, perhaps with more psychiatric drugs added to treat various red-herring diagnoses. And then months and sometimes years of illness before a gradual return to health. One story in particular stands out: that of "Rik." Rik was placed on a low dose of Xanax, a drug to which he became "severely paradoxical" within twelve weeks. In his quest to get off, he writes, "I was in and out of four treatment centers, two mental hospitals and more doctors than I can count and at one year [off benzos] was so sick on the drugs I had to hire a live-in caretaker." Rik rented an apartment one block from a hospital during his eight-month titration, preparing for what lay ahead. His first two years off benzos were the worst: He maxed out at only two hours of sleep per night and passed his days walking constantly, sometimes up to eight hours. Rik's nights "were passed screaming into a pillow or curled up in a fetal position rocking myself." He bought police handcuffs to chain himself to the bed, so as not to commit suicide on the worst days. Rik describes this dark night of his soul: "I prayed to see the next sunrise and the tiny bit of reality the daylight brought." He became immuno-compromised—cold and flu viruses persisted for months, and his liver felt poisoned "from all the drugs I took to stop the symptoms." Rik experienced "hundreds of physical breakdowns due to the stress and lack of sleep, and was on a first-name basis with the local ER staff for years."

This is way hard core.

I cannot tell you how much Rik's story frightens me, because it so resembles my own. I'm not paradoxical like Rik, but like him I am weak in a way I never imagined possible. Even during my most fearful moments in the mountains, those ill-advised free solos or sprinting from a raging lightning storm above treeline, I've never felt so close to death. Right now, a falling leaf could fell me. On bad days, I wish one would. I'm so low that I *want* to die. My brain is winding down like an old pocket watch; I've passed that threshold at which life itself becomes worse than dying, at which the urge to suicide becomes the only clear and logical choice. More than once I've begged my father to "let me go" so I can wander off quietly to end it. But another part of me, the small, impenetrable kernel that represents my will to live, slogs along on autopilot. So I keep peeling away the drugs in hopes of someday returning to my true self.

Within two weeks I'm off Paxil and have halved my Ativan. Paxil is a terrible antidepressant to withdraw from, leaving you with tremors, hot flashes, nightmares, rebound depression, and strange, electric "brain zaps." I pass my days on the duplex floor while Kasey is at work, kicking, sobbing, howling, and clutching Clyde. He's a lively Plott hound puppy, but manifests in this burgeoning psychosis as loose skin draped over greening bones. All is corruption; all is death. To break up the hours, Clyde and I take short walks under pig-iron skies. We shamble through late-autumn sleet and sheets of grauple blown by a stern north wind, the tarmac oily-wet beneath our feet, the corn-flake smell of decaying leaves rising from the gutters. The days dawn bleak and drear and lightless, each worse than the last. One day I end up at Dr. Porridge's office, and I tell him about the "Ashton Manual." His response? One word: "Huh." He expresses no interest in reading it, no interest in trying a switchover to Valium. Instead, he says that I'm at great risk now because I no longer have an antidepressant on board and that we must quickly find a solution. One drug he's mentioned in the past is Remeron (mirtazapine), and I've found a forum post somewhere in which a man mentioned successfully using Remeron to get off Klonopin. I bring it up, and we agree to try yet another pill.

Another good benzo site, bcnc.org.uk, didn't exist in 2005, but if it had I might have found this tidbit from one author about adding in antidepressants during withdrawal: "From a personal point of view the only antidepressant that I would advise against is mirtazapine . . . I have noticed many people having horrendous symptoms, which seem to last an extremely long time after discontinuation of this drug." For me, Remeron is the last straw: I lose what few moorings remain. I call my parents daily, hourly, but can only groan, sob, and plead into the phone in subverbal snippets. More floor time, more clutching at Clyde. "Desperate" does not even begin to describe the situation. I return after two days to the psychiatrist's office, where he diagnoses more "mixed states" and urges me not to give up on this new drug, adding that perhaps we need to increase the Depakote. I am unable to form an opinion one way or the other. I simply can't think. I can't stand to be around anybody; I can't stand to be alone. Kasey gives up: I've worn her out. She will break up with me over the phone two weeks later, and I can't say I blame her. Finally my father flies out to collect me and bring me back to Johns Hopkins for my third and final hospitalization since September.

CHAPTER 10

Mountain men aren't supposed to dwell on adornments, on minutiae: the cartoon tablecloth pilgrims, the grinning tom turkeys on Dixie plates, the orange fork-and-spoon sets, the chocolate-brown napkins. But mountain men do not spend Thanksgiving locked in psychiatric wards either. They should be in the Utah desert climbing red sandstone spires or parallel-sided fissures up blank panes of rock. They should be down at Hueco Tanks, auguring in on razor crimps, heel-hooking above their heads, hucking dynos for distant potholes. They should be in Las Vegas, climbing two-thousand-foot flying buttresses of Aztec sandstone. But not here at Johns Hopkins, not in some airless big-city hospital with nary a rock in sight, unless it's been quarried for flagstone cladding.

I look down at tablecloth pilgrims, push mashed potatoes around the plate, weep openly before the other patients. No one notices. No one says anything. No one cares. This is par for the course on a ward. Tears, bags under the eyes, screaming fits, aimless shuffling, manic bromides, panic attacks, muteness—business as usual on the fourth-floor "Affective Disorders" unit in Meyer Building at Hopkins. It is sundown, when my symptoms are strongest. My father and his girlfriend came by during visiting hours but then had a proper Thanksgiving dinner elsewhere to attend. They came; they saw; they went. I eat with my fellow mentals. I'm thirty-four, a mountain man given to long days solo above treeline, on granite aiguilles raked by wind and grauple. To ascending ropeless up thousand-foot inclines of sandstone, racing my stopwatch as sweat pours into my eyes with each ragged pant. To clinging to the overhanging underbellies of limestone caves, swarming toward daylight. I'm a "tough guy" with twenty-two years in the mountains, bawling over cartoon turkeys. The fake turkey on the plate is a not-alive turkey; he wears a pilgrim hat and smiles even as he holds the musket that will be used to kill him. He's so cute, so happy and carefree, but he will soon be dead within his own cartoon universe. The turkey in my mouth is a dead turkey. A real dead turkey. Yanked from the coop, shipped off, and beheaded at some factory. Moist and easy to chew, but dead. I have killed them both. I have killed everyone. I have destroyed everything. I feel bottomless pity for myself and for anyone who's ever known me. I am the world's biggest fuckup.

Another patient's parents brought the feast in. I wipe away my tears and come back around long enough to thank them. Their son is Mark, a thin young man with dark hair: diagnosis, major depression. Mark sits rigidly in a plastic chair, adrift in a bizarre, sparkle-eyed catatonia while his mother tries to interest him in a flake of turkey. She gets it into his mouth; he chews automatically. When he speaks, which is rare, it's in a disconnected robot voice. Anemic Maryland sleet spatters the hospital's sealed, tinted, double-paned windows, dimming bruise hued with the day's end. We're in the dining area fifty feet—one-quarter of a ropelength—above the enclosed courtyard where the patients go to smoke. There's a lot of that on wards: smokers. Nervous, aimless, idle, compulsive, yellow-toothed smokers. The fluorescents buzz overhead. Their harsh glare separates me even more from reality. It will be this way for years: Fluorescent-lit industrial spaces, grocery stores, gyms, and offices will foment going-over-the-waterfall feelings of derealization (the sense that your surroundings aren't real; the world compressing into two dimensions and receding) and depersonalization (the feeling that you yourself aren't real). When DP/DR comes on, I will have to grab a fold of skin and pinch *hard* to confirm my very existence.

I cannot picture climbing again, I'm so amped with withdrawal and scared of just . . . *being*. The fear is with me—it *is* me—but outside me too. It often feels like some inchoate astral presence hurtles toward Earth, and all I can do is sit shivering, awaiting its arrival. It's worse when I sit still, when I'm not distracted by group therapy or a nurse taking my blood pressure or conversation with other patients about our diagnoses, our meds, about what led to this point. There's not much else to talk about on a psych ward, so you find this common ground. If I stop moving for more than five seconds the fear comes crashing down again. The worst thing is that it will never arrive; it is always traveling but never arriving, suspended in the air like that moment in a horror flick when the coed poises to pull back the shower curtain, looking for the killer.

At Hopkins, we comprise a unit of twenty patients. The ward is shaped like a rectangular racetrack, the day area and nurses' station at the center, the rooms leading off the halls. My first morning there, a psychiatry intern pulled a chair up to my bed and sat before me with his pen and notepad. I slumped against the wall, retelling my history. It took three hours. He and other staff then talked to my father, phoned my mother, my stepmother (my father's ex-wife), and my girlfriend to investigate any history of mania. I will give them that—Hopkins at least sorted out that I wasn't bipolar. No one among my inner circle could recall a manic episode or even such tendencies. Soon they have a med plan: The Depakote will be replaced by lithium. Once I begin asking around, I'll learn that almost everyone on the ward has been placed on lithium; it's like the leis with which you're garlanded at the Honolulu airport. A naturally occurring salt, lithium is an old-school, first-line treatment for bipolar disorder. It flattens you, neutralizes you, neuters your moods—it's a chemical straitjacket, an agent of control to keep the inmates fat and docile, all in the same whatever-the-fuck-happens-is-fine mood. The pill makes me feel heavy-limbed and spacey, swaying to and fro with *mal de débarquement*, my hands fluttering with the shakes. I will taper it as soon as I'm back in Colorado. You can become toxic on lithium; dehydration or an increased dose can elevate your blood levels and land you in a coma, or worse. And climbers can't always carry enough water with them up the rock. Later, my father and I will have a discharge meeting with the doctors and a social worker, and I'll point out that I don't want to be on lithium—that I can't risk becoming toxic in the mountains.

They push back, these Chesapeake flatlanders with no concept of anything higher than the Alleghenies. "Okay, Matt," says the social worker. "Fair enough. You don't want to be on lithium. But I don't think you need to worry about toxicity if you can't get out of bed in the first place." I bite my tongue. I've gotten good at that. Another part of the plan is to taper me directly off Ativan, substituting the epilepsy drug Neurontin as an anxiolytic, slowly increasing the dosage as the benzo wanes. This will take about two weeks. Neurontin is the second drug I will shed back in Boulder, and its withdrawal will be horrendous. I will augur in, grit my teeth, and taper off 2,100 milligrams amidst three weeks of pain, horror, and ghastly hallucinations. Such will be my resolve. Neurontin's generic name is gabapentin and, like Zyprexa, it has been the focus of prosecution for aggressive, illegal off-label marketing, in this case by Warner-Lambert, a division of Pfizer. The molecule, a GABA analog, is structurally similar to GABA, having been formulated to mimic the neurotransmitter, though it's unclear if it works directly on GABA receptors. Neurontin will take the edge off, but also makes me dizzy and bleary, and I don't like the 100-milligram capsules that float at the back of my throat and the 600-milligram horse pills that stick going down. I've never, believe it or not, cared for swallowing pills—at least not the physical act of it.

The doctors also add the tricyclic antidepressant nortriptyline, which, they tell me, is useful in treating anxiety. "It has been very well studied," one psychiatrist barks at me when I dare to question his selection. He's younger than I am, in his late twenties, with a vaguely unctuous demeanor to match his outthrust jawline. Studies; doctors love their studies. Studies upon studies; studies that reverse earlier studies; studies in which the data is later shown to be flawed or manipulated; studies sponsored by drug companies; studies run by KOL doctors on the Big Pharma take; studies conducted with an outcome already in mind, in which the data and sampling are tailored to fit the predetermined conclusion; and studies that cite other, previous and possibly flawed studies, a mad game of research telephone. Studies: Turn on the news and there's another damnable study telling you what to do with your life, and which pill to take for it. Doctors love studies, often more than they love actual patients. At Hopkins, outside five minutes each morning during rounds, I won't speak with the doctors more than twice, and neither are there any therapists or psychologists to meet with individually. On the Affective Disorders unit, everything is treated as a chemical malfunction of the brain, the organ, and not a crisis of the mind, emotions, or soul. The doctors rush to and fro in their white coats devising chemical cocktails, but never stop to chat in the halls. Sad people, you can tell, make them uneasy. Messy, snotty, smelly, teary, gray-skinned sad people are, in corporeal form, best left to the nurses. Perhaps this brisk veneer of officialdom is necessary to lend their whole drug-and-shock circus medical legitimacy, to somehow elevate the black art of psychiatry from its ignominious roots of basement asylums, lobotomies, imprisonment, and torture. The contradiction is highlighted during morning rounds, when a half-dozen doctors, residents, and interns come to hover over my bed in a hyenas' killing circle. Some look like they're barely out of high school with their pink, newly minted skin. They ask me to rate my moods—anxiety, depression—on a scale from one to ten, as if I am telling them how badly a broken ankle hurts. I spit out numbers, lie still on my crinkly plastic mattress, and try to project a smile through my caul of pain, fear, and disorientation, undignified in my boxers and with my wan, winter torso bared to the assemblage.

Each night as darkness descends over the Meyer Building, a cloak of smoggy, river-cooled air drapes the city and I enter the blackest hours—the insensate, cave-newt doll coiled unblinking at the matryoshka core. The hospital lights paint the other patients' skin in cadaver green-whites; I shake as I push food around my dinner tray. When they glance at me, their eyes retract snail-like into bottoming sockets. Voices clamor and clash, a shambles of sound. Security guards saunter by, putting on their best swagger for the pretty nurses, blue blazer tails swaying, trailing a wake of testosterone. I'm eating starch, starch, starch, and my wastes smell like the cafeteria food. I am becoming the hospital, stale roll by stale roll, rubbery broccoli spear by rubbery broccoli spear. My dad brings in some items, gourmet crackers and chocolates. I share them with the other patients. The soap—even the shower soap—comes from wall dispensers, with a cloying odor of bleach and cotton candy. This viscous pink hand soap starts to seep into my skin, to merge with my cells and turn me into gelatin. Some nights the smog morphs into a lowering bank of halogen orange and a light snow spits, so I crack my window the prescribed half-centimeter, inhale the moisture, and recall that I was once alive in a meaningful way. That I was "a climber."

My father has lent me a digital radio and I listen to that. When it is off, I set it on the window ledge by photos of Kasey and Clyde, by my stuffed frog Smeech. I call Kasey each night but she doesn't always answer, or when she does is usually walking somewhere, huffing into the phone, distracted, out with friends or leaving work, her boot heels clicking over the pavement. On a good night, I'll get three hours of sleep. You don't really sleep in a hospital—there's always some to-do out in the hallway, nurses rushing about, cleaning people bantering, floor-waxers thrumming, lights eternally on, someone coming around to pester you about something. Because they're monitoring my progress off Ativan via pulse rate and blood pressure, the nurses awaken me twice a night for vitals. This is a "medically safe" taper: As long as I'm not having seizures, then everything is hunky-dory. Sometimes a nurse will come in and find me hugging myself in bed, saying, "I love you, Matt. I love you," because these are still words that a person needs to hear.

Night terrors begin to penetrate my sleep, like when I was a child of ten. I wake up one night in a room red-orange with reflected street light and stand wordless before the blur of metal mirror in some primordial epoch when the earth shook with the tantrums of the gods. I do not recognize the man looking back. I can register only shock and disappointment smeared across his features, veins of white threading his hair, eyes burning like embers. My final dose of Ativan comes on December 4, 2005—almost seven years ago at the time of this writing. Two nights before that an ancient fear kicked me out of bed. I ran down the hall barefoot, groaning, wringing my hands. By the time I completed a half-lap around the ward I realized who and where I was, and slowed to a halt at the nurse's station to ask for warm milk. The doctors will learn of the incident, will hold me an extra few days to "make sure you're not running down the halls screaming anymore!" as the lead doctor says in a jokey tone. As if I amuse her, as if the fear that has destroyed my life is somehow funny to this woman.

I pass the days shuffling to groups, observing, cataloguing as a distraction to take my eyes off the clock where I must mark the hours until the next crumb of Ativan. There are the major-depressives, stents lewdly adangle from their arms and resembling bovine aortas, lined up on stretchers before the elevators as they await morning electroshock. Then the eating-disorder patients, IV machines their constant companions, curled into themselves in the dayroom chairs, downy-limbed, ethereal, dozing. One girl hugs a teddy bear, and you can tell that she'd be stunning if she gained forty pounds, or sixty. I'm starting to forget the words for things—at art therapy, I can't distinguish a hammer from a saw on the pegboard. The doctors worry about me being "snowed under" by Neurontin, but I tell them to keep it coming because I'm apprehensive about how much worse I'd be without it. I feel the terror coiling in my gut like a snake. I always feel like I need to shit, whether that's the case or not. They move us around in elevators, using a key to activate the lift, ascending and descending through the throat of the colossus. We go to the first floor twice a day for art therapy and cognitive-behavioral therapy. I construct a wooden key holder from a kit for my father and present it to him during visiting hours. He and his girlfriend are moving into a new house next to Patterson Park, and I hope they appreciate my gift. I can't really tell; they do a good job of pretending. In exchange for however many thousands of dollars he's paying, I can offer my father a key holder. One day another patient, a frail, waif-like woman, erupts during cognitive therapy. She has been receiving ECT, been hospitalized and shocked before, relapsed, whispers like a mouse, and rarely makes eye contact. The poor, poor woman: Her depression radiates off her like a fierce, almost holy aura. The psychologist, up there before the blackboard confident in her white Hopkins lab coat, is trying to goad the woman into answering some pointless question when the woman starts slamming her fists down on the table screaming, "It's hopeless, *hopeless*, *HOPELESS!*" We always have cognitive therapy after lunch, at 1:00 P.M. At that time of day my hands go numb and the veins retreat into my arms, obscuring the roadmap of vasculature cultivated through years of climbing.

Two weeks in, I meet another climber. We're standing in the elevator together and slowly come to recognize each other. He is a photographer, and in a better year we collaborated on a shoot down in New Mexico: muscle ripping up limestone, the camera shutter clicking, warm June air pregnant with flowering cholla cactus and chamisa. I had just returned from six months in Europe, where I'd spent the final month in Corfu, then climbing in Provence. I was skinny, tan, psyched, had weathered that first benzo withdrawal and felt well again. The photographer resided in Santa Fe, making a good living playing. Now, however, he lives back East, consumed by rage, breaking computers, throwing things out his windows, thinking of ending it. He asks me why I'm here, and I say it's to quit benzos. "Oh, yeah, like Klonopin," he says. "I was on that and then stopped pretty quickly. What a nasty one that was . . ."

How long ago? I ask. Oh, a year, he says, maybe less. I tell him I've read about the pills on the Web, and that they can cause problems well after you stop. He nods his head, as if recognizing some truth.

It's an illuminating conversation, one I will repeat with half the patients on the ward, all having been at this time or in the recent past withdrawn from benzodiazepine tranquilizers. It's somehow fitting to have these chats at Hopkins, the hospital in part responsible for William Styron's bestselling memoir of depression, *Darkness Visible*. (It was at a Hopkins-sponsored symposium that a talk given by Styron turned into a *Vanity Fair* article, later expanded into his seminal book.[1]) I've read *Darkness Visible* three times— it's a page-turner—the first while still on benzos. I stopped on pages seventy and seventy-one in particular to reread two para- graphs. Here Styron describes telling a hospital doctor, upon ad- mission for his suicidal depression, that he had been taking 0.75 milligrams of Halcion every night. Halcion is an infamous pill, the shortest half-life benzodiazepine (two hours) and one banned in certain countries for negative effects including amnesia, depres- sion, anxiety, and psychosis. The doctor, duly appalled, tells Styron that this is triple the standard dose for someone his age and switches him to the slower-acting hypnotic Dalmane, after which the author's "suicidal notions dwindled and then disappeared." Even as he accepts responsibility for carelessly taking so much Halcion, Styron implicates it in supercharging his depression—not as the sole culprit (he also points to his abrupt withdrawal from alcohol, among other factors), but a pill without which he "might not have been brought so low." Styron also calls out benzos in gen- eral, writing that his own cavalier attitude toward them had formed a few years earlier "when I began to take Ativan at the behest of the breezy doctor who told me that I could, without harm, take as many of the pills as I wished."[2] Styron also bemoans the "promiscu- ous prescribing of these potentially dangerous tranquilizers."

Unfortunately, little has changed since the book's first printing, in 1990. They hand out these pills like candy, and then yank you off way too quickly if they bother to do so at all.

I soon learn that all my fellow patients who were on benzos have in fact stopped *abruptly*, some upon doctor's orders, some self-directed, and some on this very ward. One gentleman a year earlier had a Hopkins doctor taper his three milligrams of Klonopin in less than a week; he paced laps around the halls, not sleeping, feeling like he "was on crack." He'd been bouncing in and out of hospitals ever since, playing med roulette. Another, a young woman, very smart with bright, intense eyes and of Middle Eastern heritage, is a hospital veteran—her family hospitalizes her every time she becomes manic. She tells me she takes three or four milligrams of Klonopin out in the world, but stops cold turkey before each hospitalization because she knows that the doctors will take the pills away once she's inside. At Hopkins, she paces and paces and paces, day and night until ordered to her room. Another woman, middle-aged and divorced, tried to commit suicide a year earlier via a Klonopin overdose, after which she was no longer given the drug. Now she is lower than low, trying ECT for her depression. Another patient, a fellow in his early twenties, cold-turkeyed Klonopin but used marijuana to temper the withdrawal. He ended up holed up with a sniper rifle in a motel across the street from a park before they brought him in. Another, a retired farmer who sustained a head injury falling off a ladder, is being tapered rapidly from his "sleeping pills"—Ativan, it turns out. He lines up at the med station an hour early, pleading for his meds, saying he feels "funny." A woman whom I've remained friends with, a vibrant, talented woman who held a high-powered university job, has been yanked off two milligrams of Xanax in only a week after her admission two weeks earlier. This, I tell her, is likely too fast, and a blush of realization blooms across her face. "Oh, my God," she says. "That explains so much—I've been so angry, so mean to my husband and short with him when he visits. And I can't sleep, and all these heart palpitations and panic attacks I've been having . . ." Whenever she can, she uses her day pass to run laps around the outside of the Hopkins complex, even on days bitter with wind and snow.

You could say I'm conducting my own one-man study. When the

nurses come into my room, I grill them about what *they've* seen, as it's really them and not the doctors down in the trenches. The closest I get to an answer is one nurse saying that, as far as he knows, there have been no benzo-related "sequellae" and that I shouldn't pay attention to anything I read on the Internet. He parrots the doctors' spiel that apart from a week or two of flu-like symptoms and a slight elevation in anxiety, I will soon feel like myself again. Of course, what happens to patients once they're off the ward is anyone's guess, hence the lack of "sequellae." Psychiatric hospitals do not follow up to see if their treatment has worked. Out in the world, patients can easily go back on benzos, continue to mask withdrawal symptoms with other medications, or re-intake with issues possibly related to cessation of the pills but that go undiagnosed as such. Even "the best hospital in America" can't acknowledge the existence of a benzodiazepine withdrawal syndrome nor their potential role in causing it. To them, these pills are like baby aspirin, to be stopped or started rapidly with impunity. Even when half their patients are experiencing issues that might be linked to benzos, they do not stop to connect the dots; they do not ask questions. The paradigm seems to be: "Benzos are bad, really, really bad, so we're going to get you off them." But then, paradoxically, "Anything you feel beyond our official, drug-study-sanctioned, med-school-taught view of brief symptomology is due strictly to your own flawed biochemistry."

If you continue down this road, you'll end up a lifer. In spring 2005, just as I began to taper, I met the Ghost of Christmas Future. A onetime climber who'd come to Carbondale to visit a coworker, he used a *fishing-tackle box* as a travel kit for his psychiatric meds. I will later learn, from a friend who interned at a VA hospital, about veterans with PTSD on thirty or more medications a day, including benzos. The chemicals accrue over the years, he tells me. Even once one med stops working, the doctors are reluctant to taper a patient off and hence keep piling on pills. I'm not sure how these vets' livers function or how the men get through the day. I cannot imagine. I will also, through a support group on Yahoo, read countless tales of people like me, dependent on or trying to stop benzos but placed instead on five, eight, ten meds a day: antidepressants, mood stabilizers, antipsychotics, barbiturates. I feel for these people even as I praise the Fates that I escaped before this too became my final chapter. You see, I left the hospital and have not looked back. Within a month, I found my solution: that number for a benzo-support group I should have called months if not years earlier.

This was not going to be my life.

CHAPTER 11

The first thing to realize about acute benzo withdrawal is that it's not "anxiety" as you know it. If anxiety is a yippy little Chihuahua in a handbag, then this is a Rottweiler mauling your face off—for months. A clinician listening to you describe your symptoms might diagnose anxiety, but deep inside, in your subjective experience where it truly matters, you will feel a primal and monolithic terror that cannot, as with garden-variety anxiety, be reasoned with: Your calming GABA "light switch" is busted or even frozen in the off position, and you will not experience reality as it was until your receptors renormalize. The merest trifle—a barking dog, a near fender-bender, an angry word from a friend, an upsetting movie—will push you off the panic cliff. This much I learned by studying my own reactions to stress: If anger or fear entered my system, or if I overexerted myself physically, I'd have panic attacks and remain flooded with adrenaline for hours and sometimes days. The parasympathetic nervous system would not bring me back down reliably, as it had in the past, and sometimes it would not bring me back down at all.

I return alone on a four-hour nonstop flight home from Baltimore to Denver, raw around the edges, away from the hospital and my father's house. After a final two weeks as an outpatient at Hopkins, after countless panic attacks and night terrors at my father's, after the night he came to my bedroom and stroked my brow as he had when I was a child and woke up distressed, I need to let him resume his life. And I need to try to get on with my own. I swallow a Neurontin before boarding, take my seat, and pretend to read a potboiler novel. It's difficult, but I'm doing it, which is no small thing. Then the plane aborts its takeoff. The nose is up, the engines are firing, and then they suddenly cut to nil and the pilot is slamming on the brakes. He comes over the intercom to let us know that the tower mistakenly gave us clearance, and that we need to wait ten minutes to try again. My heart hiccups, it slams, my hands shake, I sweat. I wait for the panic to pass, as it has in the past, but it doesn't. I will stay in this heightened, hyperalert state for the next four hours, avoiding eye contact with other passengers, gripping my closed paperback like it's the Holy Bible, my gaze flitting about the cabin like a moth in a bell jar. As we descend into Denver, dropping through white, arctic-front storm clouds, the pilot comes on again to tell us that the runways are too icy to land. He eases the plane back up and we start circling, the ground invisible, the moist air turning pink with molecules of frozen sunset. The plane jostles in the mist, its engines firing intermittently to keep us at elevation while snowplows clear the runways.

Ice starts to crust on the wings, plastering over the landing lights—this is how jetliners crash. I think I might puke. I would rather open an exit door and jump out than feel this fear for one more second. When we finally land, I feel no relief being back on the ground. I should, but I don't. Kasey is waiting outside the airport. It's night. We drive home through lashing snows. The gentle prairie swells along Peña Boulevard heading south from Denver International overhead, poised to break like massive waves. I cringe in my seat, trying to disappear into the upholstery. Kasey talks about her infant nephew who's having seizures, and I can't stand to listen. This is too dark, too intense and scary, this poor, ailing baby boy. I become him, feeling that I might have a seizure myself, my gut as empty and stale as a mummy's core.

At Hopkins, they warned me that the transition back home would be hard, but this is something else entirely—this is sinister.

That night, I do not sleep. I do not even approximate sleep. The adrenaline keeps me awake, firing and firing until morning, until a thin meniscus of orange forms in the east and pale dishwater light seeps over Boulder. I thought I would feel stronger back in Colorado, but I'm weaker than ever, a textbook agoraphobe. I rarely leave the house. I pace and fret and writhe and sweat as the walls close in. I have nothing to do, but neither am I able to do anything because I'm so distracted and distractable. I was supposed to go to Hawaii with my father, his girlfriend, and her children for my dad's sixtieth birthday, but I demur. My father and I get into a shouting match on the phone—he wants me there and keeps saying, "You have to come. You have to," partially for selfish reasons but also, I'm sure, because he wants the hospital to have fixed me. Kasey heads home to Oregon, and I'm alone over Christmas. I drive her a half mile to the bus depot from where she'll leave for the airport. Tiny Boulder seems immense—downtown, with its fifty-foot buildings, looks towering and frenetic as if I've been picked up by a tornado in Nebraska and deposited in Times Square. But also distant, like the surface of a glacier glimpsed through a telescope. I begin to taper the lithium and Neurontin; I don't care what might happen. One of these meds has brought a rash over my belly, and they need to go. I have a med check-in with Dr. Porridge. He urges me not to quit the pills, but I tell him that I'm doing it anyway. He reiterates that I have anxiety and depression, which must be medicated, and that I'm undoing all the "great treatment" I received at Hopkins. *Fine, whatever.* During those first two weeks back home, I'll e-mail my friend Jim: "I'm in complete and utter hell . . . the withdrawal and panic attacks are awful, and the fucking shithead docs at Hopkins and my doctor here are trying to tell me it's my 'natural anxiety.' I feel pretty overwhelmed [and] can't leave the house much. . . ."

It's a La Niña year so great fronts back up along the Continental Divide, sending Chinook winds howling over Mount Sanitas, flexing the windows, tearing the screen doors from their hinges. I fear that our duplex might, like me, blow away into the darkness, streaming off atom by atom. Clyde has figured out a way to escape under the backyard fence and launches rogue missions down the alley, upsetting trashcans to scrounge for food scraps. He's quick—if I don't stand watch atop the stairs, if I turn away for so much as ten seconds, he's gone, and I must spend an hour, maybe two, hunting him out in frigid winds under the sterile moonlight, beneath dead leaves rattling on threadbare trees reaching skeleton hands skyward. I can hardly breathe amidst a thick, molasses-like fatigue, lurching like some creep along the alleys, calling for the hound in a high, reedy wheeze. If Clyde heads uphill, toward Fourth and Third streets, it takes even longer to find him because then I can only shuffle, pausing every few steps for breath like a Himalayan mountaineer in the Death Zone. I'm always out looking for Clyde. He thinks it's the greatest game.

Mornings are bad because I wake up spitting blood, my throat and sinuses inflamed from chronic hyperventilation. I hack up the corrupt red blossoms, spit them into the toilet, and flush them away, wiping bloody sputum from my lips. This will go on for a year. I will start to sleep with nasal strips on and duct tape over my mouth in the hopes of promoting slow, diaphragmatic breathing.

Daytime is bad because I have nothing to do, am constantly in a state of fear, and my focus is shattered, a trifecta of idleness, terror, and distraction. I can no longer read books or even long-format magazine articles. It will remain this way for months. I will start back with *Maxim*, work my way up to *Esquire*, and finally *The New Yorker* before I can engage with a novel again. Also, I can't stand to let anything end, even a simple task like washing the dishes, because I'll immediately have to face the empty minutes again. But conversely, I hate to begin anything because I'm not sure I'll be able to finish. So I flit from meaningless chore to meaningless chore, breezing in and out of Web sites, cleaning the house in stages, pacing, going out to the front patio to sit in the sun for two minutes, picking up Clyde's poop, turning on the television, turning it off, trying to do breathing exercises, repeating it all over again. It's a simple pleasure, really, to sit still and be at peace—the healthy take it for granted—but it's one that will ever elude the benzo sufferer.

Nights are bad because I cannot sleep. At best I get two hours, and often wake up screaming, seeing phantoms levitate above me to wash against the ceiling and dissolve into squidlings of ectoplasm. I ask the neighbors, sheepishly, if they can hear me bellowing, but they cannot. It will be nine months before I take my first daytime nap—a one-minute nap; an incredible victory—and two years before I get more than five hours of continuous sleep at night. Some nights, scratching noises come from inside the bedroom closet, like someone is raking his fingernails along the doors. But when I turn on the lights and slide the doors back, no one is there and the noises stop. My brain is incredibly suggestible: If I watch an upsetting movie, it seeps into me until I inhabit whatever bad event has occurred on-screen. Before she left, Kasey and I watched the Russell Crowe boxing film *Cinderella Man*, and I almost had to leave the room. When rough punches landed and heads snapped back during the fight scenes, I could feel my own gray matter sloshing around in sympathy. With horror movies, it's even worse.

Who is this scared, pathetic man?

I continue to see the therapist. To her credit, she gets me out the door when no one else can. I help at the food bank where she volunteers, go to her house with Clyde, take walks around Mapleton Hill with its brick Victorians and silent, tree-lined sidewalks. She is not an unkind person, but again, she does not understand benzo withdrawal and neither does she try to. She does not listen when I say that I don't think that this is my natural state. This woman reiterates that I have the worst anxiety of anyone she's seen, that I need to stop focusing on symptoms and feeling sorry for myself, and that I need to stop letting myself have panic attacks because it will only reinforce the neurological channel along which they travel. The therapist tells me that I have what the Buddhists call "wild mind," and that I need to harness my racing thoughts through meditation. She advises me not to stop my current meds, saying that the doctors must have had "a good reason" for prescribing.

And she diagnoses that I'm "OCD about my breathing," as the inability to draw a full breath has become my strongest symptom and hence an obsession.

My brain is so porous, so rudderless and unkempt, that I imprint her words. I start to worry that I've become permanently locked in a psychotic fear state. I fret that all my years of panic attacks, of drugging, of feathering the edge on the rocks, of too many adrenaline rushes, of harsh withdrawals from benzodiazepines, have changed my brain forever. *I will always be this frightened.* This notion makes me deeply suicidal. One day I call my mother threatening to kill myself, and she—upon the therapist's advice—says she's going to hang up and call the sheriff. The sheriff will, of course, take me back to the hospital, where they'll probably reinstate benzos. I hang up and beat the living shit out of the couch as Clyde slinks into his crate. Poor Clyde: He has to bear witness to these things. As I calm down, he approaches with concern writ in his eyes, and I knead his neck folds and tell him that I love him until he licks my tears with dog kisses that smell of cold cuts. Clyde keeps me alive, where no one else can. He was abandoned outside Taos, New Mexico, as a puppy, and I cannot revisit this same unkindness upon him. The suicide urge will continue for the next year, lessening only in fits and starts. Many mornings I will wake up, look in the mirror, and say, "I promise not to kill you today," leaving myself no choice but to continue.

The depression peaks, thick and oily like fresh tarmac over a mass grave. I shudder atop the bed awash in black waves of guilt and self-hatred, grieving the destruction of my mind and body, lamenting the freedom I've lost to climb and simply be in the world. Also, I'm remembering every bad thing I've ever done, including things I hadn't realized were bad at the time. As accompaniment, my therapist's voice pops into my head, intoning, archly as if accusing the villain in an old gangster film, "Thief . . . rapist . . . *murderer!*" I am none of these, but the voice keeps coming unbidden. Soon my mind-therapist has morphed into the "Chicken-Woman," like the character Cleopatra, limbless in her box at the end of the film *Freaks*.

The Chicken-Woman nests in an ornate gilded Santeria altar and says, "Hoffen-puffalo, *ba-gawk*." She expunges vomit, ruffles her feathers, settles in on black demon eggs, and then proclaims, "Rawtch-rawtch-rawtch." The Chicken-Woman shuts her eyes and goes to sleep, incubating her eggs until the next visitation. It would be funny if it weren't so awful. The Chicken-Woman is dense and tacky and tangible, one of a host of bizarre, intrusive, self-torturing thoughts that will plague me for months. The thoughts grow synchronously worse with other withdrawal symptoms—panic, depression, sweats, muscle rigidity, tremors—offering proof that they are external and hence not to be trusted.

The fits of self-recrimination are worse after 2:00 P.M. They crucify me to the bed as the sun hooks toward Boulder Canyon and afternoon shadows spread across the snow like inkblots. I lie corpse-flat atop the comforter, mulling over every rotten thing I've done, sounds and images resurfacing in strobe-lit snippets and endlessly looping mini-films. I'm stuck, with crystalline recall, reliving the myriad shabberies committed under the benzos' disinhibiting sway. I remember every unkind expletive during a fight with a girlfriend, every arrogant fit at the cliffs, every pill I stole from the medicine cabinets of friends and family. I remember every scathing or self-congratulatory magazine article I wrote, fueled by my own bottomless insecurity and metastasized ego. And I think of the selfish, near-sociopathic things I did that went far beyond these minor sins, like the time I deliberately free-soloed in front of a girlfriend, Haven, outside Socorro, New Mexico, despite her strong misgivings. Haven turned from the cliff and walked down to the dry, cobbled arroyo floor of Box Canyon in bright December sun, sobbing, shoulders heaving while I tightened my shoelaces and set off up a 5.11 I hadn't climbed in a decade. You should never solo with a bad head, and you should never solo if it's making someone else uncomfortable. Haven, a talented writer and editor with black hair and ice-blue eyes, wanted marriage and children, but I'd been too immature to even move in together. Climbing, drugging, and screwing around took precedence at the time. I was thirty, refusing